POETRY IN AUSTRALIA

Volume 1

From the Ballads to Brennan

Professor T. Inglis Moore, who has edited Volume I, is Professor of Australian Literature in the Australian National University, Canberra. He provides a brilliant and provocative Introduction. Volume II, *Modern Australian Verse*, covering the period from 1930 to the present day, is edited by Douglas Stewart.

Poetry in Australia

VOLUME I

FROM THE BALLADS TO BRENNAN

chosen by

T. INGLIS MOORE

UNIVERSITY OF CALIFORNIA PRESS

Berkeley and Los Angeles

1965

University of California Press
Berkeley and Los Angeles
California

Printed in Australia

ACKNOWLEDGMENTS

FOR permission to reprint poems in this anthology the publishers' special thanks are due to Lothian Book Publishing Co. and Mrs Constance Robertson for poems by Shaw Neilson from *Collected Poems*; also to Lothian Book Publishing Co. for poems by Bernard O'Dowd from *Collected Poems*; and also to the *Bulletin* in which many of the poems and bush ballads were first printed. The extract from Charles Harpur's "The Temple of Infamy" is printed from an unpublished MS in the Mitchell Library, by courtesy of the Trustees. Acknowledgment is due to the Trustees of the estate of William Baylebridge for the poems from *Life's Testament* and *Love Redeemed*.

The publishers of other copyright poems, together with the titles of the poems and of the books from which they have been selected, are listed below.

Angus & Robertson Ltd: "The Coachman's Yarn" by E. J. Brady (*Australian Bush Ballads*); "Let Us Go Down, the Long Dead Night Is Done", "I Saw My Life as Whitest Flame", "The Years That Go to Make Me Man", "My Heart Was Wandering in the Sands", "Fire in the Heavens, and Fire along the Hills", "The Anguish'd Doubt Broods over Eden", extracts from "Lilith", "Interlude: The Casement", "How Old Is My Heart", "I Cry to You as I Pass Your Windows", "Come Out, Come Out, Ye Souls That Serve", "O Desolate Eves", "The Land I Came thro' Last", and "I Said, This Misery Must End" by Christopher Brennan (*The Verse of Christopher Brennan*); "Elegy on an Australian Schoolboy" by Zora Cross (*Elegy on an Australian Schoolboy*); "He Could Have Found His Way" by Kathleen Dalziel (*Australian Poetry 1953*); "The Play" by C. J. Dennis (*The Sentimental Bloke*); "Song of the Captured Woman", "The Evening Gleam", and "Mortality" by James Devaney (*Poems*); "Red Jack" by Mary Durack (*Australian Bush Ballads*); "Cleaning Up" by Edward Dyson (*Rhymes from the Mines*); "Emus", "Lovers", "Lichen", "Lion", "Communal", "Flesh" and "Cubes" by Mary Fullerton ("E") (*Moles Do So Little With Their Privacy*), and "Inspiration" (*The Wonder and the Apple*); "Anzac Cove", "In the Trench", "These Men", and "The Jester in the Trench" by Leon Gellert (*Songs of a Campaign*); "Eve-song", "Never Admit the Pain", "Nurse No Long Grief", "The Baying Hounds", "Swans at Night", "Old Botany Bay", "The Shepherd", "The Myall in Prison", "The Waradgery Tribe", "The Song of the Woman-drawer", "The Tenancy" by Mary Gilmore (*Selected Verse*), and "The Pear-tree" and "Nationality" (*Fourteen Men*); "The Cicada" by H. M. Green (*Australian Poetry 1943*); "West of Alice" by W. E. Harney (*Australian Poetry 1954*); "Said Hanrahan" and "Tangmalangaloo" by "John O'Brien" (P. J. Hartigan) (*Around the Boree Log*); "Ballad of the Drover", "Talbragar", "The Teams", and "The Sliprails and the Spur" by Henry Lawson (*Poetical Works of Henry Lawson*); "Desert Claypan" by Frederick T. Macartney (*Selected Poems*); "Colombine", "Muse-Haunted", "I Blow My Pipes", "Ambuscade", "Mad Marjory", "The Uncouth Knight", "Joan of Arc", "June Morning", "Evening", "Song of the Rain", "Enigma", "The Mouse", and "Camden Magpie" by Hugh McCrae (*The Best Poems of Hugh McCrae*); "Fancy Dress" by Dorothea Mackellar (*Fancy Dress*); "The Crane is My Neighbour", "Beauty Imposes", "The Poor Can Feed the Birds", and "The Sundowner" by Shaw Neilson (*Beauty Imposes*), and "Strawberries in November" and "The Cool Cool Country" (*Unpublished Poems*); "From the Gulf" and "How the Fire Queen Crossed the Swamp" by Will Ogilvie (*Fair Girls and*

Gray Horses), and "The Death of Ben Hall" (*Australian Bush Ballads*); "Sea-grief" by Dowell O'Reilly (*The Prose and Verse of Dowell O'Reilly*); "The Man from Snowy River", "The Man from Ironbark", "A Bush Christening", "A Bushman's Song", "Clancy of the Overflow" and "Waltzing Matilda" by A. B. Paterson (*Collected Verse*); "The Camp Within the West" and "The Fisher" by Roderic Quinn (*Poems*); "What the Red-Haired Bo'sun Said", "After Johnson's Dance", "Irish Lords", and "Old John Bax" by Charles H. Souter (*The Mallee Fire*); "On a Shining Silver Morning", "My Love is the Voice of a Song", and "Danny's Wooing" by David McKee Wright (*An Irish Heart*).

Australasian Authors' Agency: "Lofty Lane" by Edwin Gerard (*Australian Light Horse Ballads and Rhymes*); "My Country" by Dorothea Mackellar (*The Closed Door*).

Australasian Book Co. and Allans Music (Australia) Pty Ltd: "The Bushrangers", "Morgan", and "My Old Black Billy" by Edward Harrington (*The Swagless Swaggie*).

The Bulletin Co.: "Lost and Given Over" by E. J. Brady (*The Way of Many Waters*).

Citizens of Leeton: "Whalan of Waitin' a While" by J. W. Gordon ("Jim Grahame") (*Under Wide Skies*).

J. M. Dent Ltd: "Buffalo Creek" by J. Le Gay Brereton (*Swags Up!*).

H. T. Dwight: extract from *Mamba, the Bright-Eyed* by G. G. McCrae.

Dymock's Book Arcade: "The Reaper" by L. H. Allen (*Araby and Other Poems*); "Bill the Whaler" by Will Lawson (*Bill the Whaler*).

Sydney J. Endacott: "Faithless" by Louis Lavater (*Blue Days and Grey Days*), and "Mopoke" (*This Green Mortality*); "The Farmer Remembers the Somme" by Vance Palmer (*The Camp*).

ACKNOWLEDGMENTS

Euston Press, London: "The Mother" by Nettie Palmer (*Shadowy Paths*).

Gordon & Gotch Ltd: "Where the Pelican Builds" by Mary Hannay Foott (*Where the Pelican Builds*).

Wm. Heinemann Ltd: "Faith" and extract from "On Australian Hills" by Ada Cambridge (*The Hand in the Dark*).

Frank Johnson: "Artemis" by Dulcie Deamer (*Messalina*).

T. Werner Laurie Ltd: "My Mate Bill" and "A Ballad of Queensland" ("Sam Holt") by G. H. Gibson (*Ironbark Splinters from the Australian Bush*).

Longmans, Green & Co. Ltd: "Dusk in the Domain" by Dorothea Mackellar (*Dreamharbour*).

Lothian Book Publishing Co.: "The Shearer's Wife" by Louis Esson (*Bells and Bees*); "Thredbo River" by Sydney Jephcott (*Penetralia*); "A Gallop of Fire" by Marie E. J. Pitt (*Selected Poems*).

Melbourne University Press: "Beauty and Terror", "Day's End", "Experience", "He Had Served Eighty Masters", "Revolution", and "This Way Only" by Lesbia Harford (*Poems*).

H. E. Stone, Adelaide: "The Skylark's Nest" and "Poet and Peasant" by R. H. Long (*Verses*).

Tyrrell's Pty Ltd: "Fine Clay" by Winifred Shaw (*The Aspen Tree*).

E. A. Vidler: "Sunset" and "Marlowe" by Arthur Bayldon (*The Eagles*).

Vision Press: "Budding Spring" by Jack Lindsay (*Poetry in Australia 1923*).

Whitcombe & Tombs Ltd: "The Australian" by Arthur H. Adams (*Collected Verses*).

CONTENTS

		PAGE
Introduction		xxi

I. FOLK SONGS AND BALLADS

Jim Jones	ANON.	3
Botany Bay	ANON.	4
A Convict's Lament on the Death of Captain Logan	ANON.	5
The *"Waterwitch"*	ANON.	6
The Settler's Lament	ANON.	7
The Old Bullock Dray	ANON.	9
The Old Keg of Rum	ANON.	12
The Old Bark Hut	ANON.	14
The Wild Colonial Boy	ANON.	18
Brave Donahue	JACK DONAHUE (?)	19
Look Out Below!	CHARLES THATCHER	20
The Broken-down Digger	ANON.	22
The Golden Gullies of the Palmer	ANON.	22
The Broken-down Squatter	ANON.	23
The Numerella Shore	"COCKATOO JACK"	24
Cockies of Bungaree	ANON.	26
The Overlander	ANON.	27
The Dying Stockman	ANON.	29
Bullocky Bill	ANON.	30
Click Go the Shears, Boys	ANON.	31
The Banks of the Condamine	ANON.	32
On the Road to Gundagai	ANON.	34
The Shearer's Song	ANON.	35
Flash Jack from Gundagai	ANON.	37
Australia's on the Wallaby	ANON.	38
Me and My Dog	ANON.	39

CONTENTS

		PAGE
The Ramble-eer	ANON.	40
Waltzing Matilda	A. B. ("BANJO") PATERSON	41

II. THE COLONIAL AGE

WILLIAM CHARLES WENTWORTH
From Australasia — 45

ROBERT LOWE
Songs of the Squatters No. 1 — 48

WILLIAM FORSTER
From The Devil and the Governor — 50

CHARLES HARPUR
A Midsummer Noon in the Australian Forest — 53
Words — 54
From The Creek of the Four Graves — 55
From The Tower of the Dream — 56
Love Sonnets, VIII — 57
From The Temple of Infamy — 57

GEORGE GORDON McCRAE
From Mâmba the Bright-eyed — 59

ADAM LINDSAY GORDON
The Sick Stockrider — 60
A Dedication — 64
From The Rhyme of Joyous Garde — 65

JAMES BRUNTON STEPHENS
The Dominion of Australia — 66
My Other Chinee Cook — 68

HENRY KENDALL
Orara — 71
Bell-birds — 73
September in Australia — 75

PAGE

Beyond Kerguelen 76
The Last of His Tribe 79
Jim the Splitter 80

ADA CAMBRIDGE
Faith 82
From On Australian Hills 82

MARY HANNAY FOOTT
Where the Pelican Builds 84

III. BUSH BALLADS AND POPULAR VERSE

THOMAS E. SPENCER
How McDougal Topped the Score 89

G. H. GIBSON ("IRONBARK")
My Mate Bill 93
A Ballad of Queensland (Sam Holt) 95

JAMES L. CUTHBERTSON
A Racing Eight 96

W. T. GOODGE
Daley's Dorg Wattle 97

A. B. ("BANJO") PATERSON
The Man from Snowy River 98
The Man from Ironbark 102
A Bush Christening 105
A Bushman's Song 106
Clancy of the Overflow 108

CHARLES H. SOUTER
What the Red-haired Bo'sun Said 109
After Johnson's Dance 110
Irish Lords 111
Old John Bax 112

PAGE

EDWARD DYSON
Cleaning Up   113

BARCROFT BOAKE
Where the Dead Men Lie   115

HENRY LAWSON
Ballad of the Drover   117
Andy's Gone with Cattle   119
Talbragar   120
The Teams   122
The Sliprails and the Spur   124

WILL H. OGILVIE
From the Gulf   125
How the Fire Queen Crossed the Swamp   128
The Death of Ben Hall   131

E. J. BRADY
Lost and Given Over   134
The Coachman's Yarn   137

J. W. GORDON ("JIM GRAHAME")
Whalan of Waitin' a While   140

WILL LAWSON
Bill the Whaler   142

C. J. DENNIS
The Play (*from* The Sentimental Bloke)   145

P. J. HARTIGAN ("JOHN O'BRIEN")
Said Hanrahan   149
Tangmalangaloo   152

EDWIN GERARD ("GERARDY")
Lofty Lane   153

W. E. ("BILL") HARNEY
West of Alice   156

CONTENTS

PAGE

EDWARD HARRINGTON
The Bushrangers   157
Morgan   159
My Old Black Billy   160

MARY DURACK
Red Jack   161

IV. POETS OF THE NINETIES

VICTOR J. DALEY
In a Wine Cellar   167
Dreams   169
Tamerlane   169
The Ascetic   171
Faith   171
From Night   171
Narcissus and Some Tadpoles   173

G. ESSEX EVANS
The Women of the West   175

SYDNEY JEPHCOTT
Thredbo River   177

ARTHUR BAYLDON
Sunset   178
Marlowe   178

WILLIAM GAY
The Crazy World   179

DOWELL O'REILLY
Sea-grief   180

BERNARD O'DOWD
From Young Democracy   180
The Cow   182
From The Bush   182

CONTENTS

Australia   187
From Alma Venus   187

LOUIS LAVATER
Mopoke   188
Faithless   189

RODERIC QUINN
The Camp Within the West   190
The Fisher   191

MARY FULLERTON ("E")
Emus   193
Lovers   194
Lichen   194
Lion   195
Communal   195
Flesh   196
Cubes   196
Inspiration   197

DAVID McKEE WRIGHT
From Dark Rosaleen:
    I. On a Shining Silver Morning   197
    IX. My Love Is the Voice of a Song   198
Danny's Wooing   199

MARIE E. J. PITT
A Gallop of Fire   201

CHRISTOPHER BRENNAN
From Towards the Source:
    Let Us Go Down, the Long Dead Night
      Is Done   202
    I Saw My Life as Whitest Flame   203
From The Twilight of Disquietude:
    The Years That Go to Make Me Man   203
    My Heart Was Wandering in the Sands   204

PAGE

From The Quest of Silence:
Fire in the Heavens, and Fire along the
Hills   205
From Lilith:
The Anguish'd Doubt Broods over Eden   205
Adam to Lilith   205
Lilith on the Fate of Man   206
Interlude: The Casement   208
From The Wanderer:
How Old Is My Heart   208
I Cry to You as I Pass Your Windows   209
Come Out, Come Out, Ye Souls That Serve   210
O Desolate Eves   211
The Land I Came thro' Last   211
From Pauca Mea:
I Said, This Misery Must End   212

V. THE EARLY TWENTIETH CENTURY

J. LE GAY BRERETON
Buffalo Creek   217

SHAW NEILSON
Song Be Delicate   218
Love's Coming   218
Beauty Imposes   219
Break of Day   220
Strawberries in November   220
The Orange Tree   221
To a School-girl   222
May   223
'Tis the White Plum Tree   223
The Poor Can Feed the Birds   224
To a Blue Flower   225

	PAGE
The Crane is My Neighbour	226
The Sundowner	227
The Cool, Cool Country	228

ARTHUR H. ADAMS

The Australian	230

R. H. LONG

The Skylark's Nest	232
Poet and Peasant	233

HUGH McCRAE

Colombine	233
Muse-haunted	234
I Blow My Pipes	234
Ambuscade	235
Mad Marjory	236
The Uncouth Knight	236
Joan of Arc	237
June Morning	241
Evening	241
Song of the Rain	241
Enigma	242
The Mouse	242
Camden Magpie	243

LOUIS ESSON

The Shearer's Wife	244

L. H. ALLEN

The Reaper	243

H. M. GREEN

The Cicada	245

WILLIAM BAYLEBRIDGE (WILLIAM BLOCKSIDGE)
From Life's Testament:

II. The Brain, The Blood, The Busy Thews	246

PAGE

VI. I Worshipped, When My Veins
Were Fresh   246
VIII. This Miracle in Me I Scan   247
XI. All That I Am to Earth Belongs   247
XIII. God, to Get the Clay That Stayed
Me   248
XVII. A Choir of Spirits on a Cloud   249
From Love Redeemed:
XXXII. Love Feeds, Like Intellect, His
Lamp with Truth   249
LXXXII. Who Questions If the Punctual
Sun Unbars   250
LXXXVIII. As Fire, Unfound Ere Pole
Approaches Pole   250

DOROTHEA MACKELLAR
My Country   251
Fancy Dress   252
Dusk in the Domain   253

NETTIE PALMER
The Mother   254

VANCE PALMER
The Farmer Remembers the Somme   255

FREDERICK T. MACARTNEY
Desert Claypan   255

ZORA CROSS
From Elegy on an Australian Schoolboy   256

JAMES DEVANEY
Song of the Captured Woman   258
The Evening Gleam   259
Mortality   259

B

CONTENTS

PAGE

DULCIE DEAMER
Artemis 260

LESBIA HARFORD
Beauty and Terror 262
Revolution 262
Day's End 263
Experience 264
He Had Served Eighty Masters 264
This Way Only 265

KATHLEEN DALZIEL
He Could Have Found His Way 265

LEON GELLERT
Anzac Cove 266
In the Trench 266
These Men 267
The Jester in the Trench 267

JACK LINDSAY
Budding Spring 268

WINIFRED SHAW
Fine Clay 268

MARY GILMORE
Eve-song 269
Never Admit the Pain 270
Nurse No Long Grief 270
The Baying Hounds 271
From Swans at Night 271
Old Botany Bay 272
The Shepherd 273
The Myall in Prison 274
The Waradgery Tribe 275

CONTENTS

	PAGE
The Song of the Woman-drawer	275
From The Disinherited	276
The Pear-tree	277
The Tenancy	278
Nationality	278
Index of Authors	279
With Biographical and Bibliographical Notes	
Index of Titles	299
Index of First Lines	306

INTRODUCTION

AUSTRALIAN literature stands today, like American and Canadian literatures, as a national body of writing in English with its own distinctive character, traditions, and idiom. It is no longer merely an antipodean twig of the great tree of English literature, but a lusty sapling firmly rooted in its own soil. In the short space of less than two centuries it has produced a limited but creditable achievement, especially in poetry, since out of the astonishing quantity of verse written here emerged a few poets of high quality and many of individual merit. This poetry has, moreover, the distinction of producing not only a collection of rough yet racy folk songs and ballads but also a considerable school of popular bush balladists for which there is no exact parallel in English, American or Canadian literatures.

The general aim of the two volumes of this anthology is to present a comprehensive picture of Australian poetry from its beginnings to the present day. To fulfil this aim it introduces novel features that make it differ sharply from previous anthologies.

Firstly, it goes beyond the usual single book to its two volumes. Such expansion provides a wider sweep of representation and, more particularly, a fuller treatment of the more important poets. This first volume covers broadly both the traditional and the popular poetry of the nineteenth century and the early twentieth century. The second volume covers the modern and contemporary poetry which began in the 1930s with the work of Kenneth Slessor.

In this first volume, which deals with the past, the poets have been chosen for their merits in their own genres, not merely for any historical interest, although the selection indicates the development of our poetry as well as its quality, scope, and variety. Since this field has been worked over frequently before, fresh material was sought, but it was found on careful scrutiny of each poet's work that the consensus of past critical opinion was sound in most cases, so that the most suitable poems for inclusion here proved often to be those already tried by time. To have preferred less suitable pieces merely for the sake of being different—an occupational hazard for any anthologist—would have been unfair to the poets concerned. On the other hand, time has changed poetic values and caused some reputations to fade, so that a number of poets included in earlier anthologies have been dropped as outmoded, especially in the sentimentality that pervaded so much verse of this period. A considerable body of new work has been introduced. The personal preferences of the editor have determined, of course, the choice of selection and the balances established between the major and minor poets.

Secondly, to bring the picture of our poetry into clearer focus, the poets in this volume are grouped into five sections. These comprise: I. Folk Songs and Ballads; II. The Colonial Age, taken as the period running from the First Settlement in 1788 to the death of Kendall in 1882; III. Bush Ballads and Popular Verse, which began in the 1880s and flourished in the nineties and the first decades of the twentieth century; IV. Poets of the Nineties, a term now accepted as covering the period from 1880, the founding year of the *Sydney Bulletin*, the weekly that led and inspired a nationalist outburst of popular, indigenous writing, to 1914, the beginning of the first world war, which produced a new outlook and temper in Australian affairs and literature; V. The Early Twentieth Century, especially after 1914, since the 1920s saw the fading of the nationalist sentiment, the replacement of the unity of the centripetal Nineties under the *Bulletin's* leadership by centrifugal forces, and the development of individual poets following disparate paths.

These sectional groupings, therefore, have both a formal and a broad historical validity. They are valuable aids in gaining some perspective on the poetry, providing also that their limitations are kept in mind. For poetry, of course, is a living and growing organism. It cannot be cut easily, like a cake, into neat chronological chunks. The first three sections are reasonably clean-cut, for the popular verse allies itself naturally with the bush ballads, but there is inevitable overlapping in the last two sections, just as it has been difficult to decide sometimes whether poets whose work spans the decades from the 1920s to the 1940s should be placed in this volume or its successor. Here the choice was made by the editors on various factors, partly on the character of the poetry concerned, partly on the year in which the poet was born or the years in which his poetry made its original impact.

Some poets raised special difficulties. Where, for example should one place the outstanding figure of Brennan? In his central themes of inward conflict he is undoubtedly "modern" in character, so that a case could be argued for placing him in the second, or "contemporary" volume. Or he could fit into the final section of this volume. On the other hand, he was born in 1870, the literary influences to which he was indebted belonged to the nineteenth century, much of his thought and certainly his style, with its rhetoric and traditional usages, belonged to that century's romanticism. Most of his poetry, finally, was written in the 1890s. On the whole therefore, he seemed to fall most suitably as a climax to the section devoted to Poets of the Nineties. Then there was the special problem of that remarkable personality Dame Mary Gilmore. Where should one place a poet who was born as early as 1865 and died as late as December, 1962? Whose first book of poetry was published in 1910 and her last in 1954? She flouts chronology completely. She was so exceptional in these respects, as she was in many others, that in her case I have made a special exception to the general rule of placing all poets in chronological order of their births. Since her last poems, appearing as late as the 1950s, bridge the earlier poetic styles in this volume and the more recent developments in its successor, it seemed most fitting to let her have the last word here.

The third step taken to make the poetic picture more truly comprehensive is a revolutionary one. This book throws overboard the conventional restriction of our anthologies to lyric verse in accordance with the Victorian romantic concept of poetry. It adopts instead the wider concept traditional to English literature by the inclusion here of folk ballads, narrative verse (in the bush ballads), satire and humour. The breadth of English poetry contains not only "The Ode to a Nightingale" and "Tintern Abbey", but also "Sir Patrick Spens" and "Chevy Chase", "The Ancient Mariner" and "Marmion", "Absalom and Achitophel" and "Don Juan", "The Canterbury Tales" and "Tam O'Shanter". So too, Australian poetry contains "The Wild Colonial Boy", "The Man from Snowy River", Victor Daley's witty, incisive satire on A. G. Stephens in "Narcissus and Some Tadpoles", and "The Sentimental Bloke". All these form an integral part of our poetic tradition. Here, then, for the first time in any general verse anthology, appear sections representing both the folk songs and ballads and the bush balladists. So, too, for the first time appear the satires of Lowe and Forster, Harpur and Daley, with Kendall's satiric side illustrated by his realistic "Jim the Splitter".

For the first time, too, the popular element of humour in our verse is given its due recognition. Brunton Stephens, after all, wrote better in "My Other Chinee Cook" than in

the inflated artificialities of his ambitious "Convict Once".
Even H. M. Green, who criticises C. J. Dennis sharply, con-
cludes that he was "one of the most humorous and by far
the wittiest and most ingenious writer of verse that Australia
has produced". With its recent success on reprinting and as
a musical it seems that "The Sentimental Bloke" has become
established more firmly than ever as a popular classic.
Humour is predominant, of course, in both the folk songs
and the bush ballads, with the ever-popular Paterson leading
the field. This humour is usually simple and direct, with
little subtlety but much vigour. It corresponds to American
"frontier" humour.

Within its obvious limits, however, it has a considerable
range, from the rollicking gusto of Spencer's cricket match,
the "tall stories" of Brady and Goodge, and the trickster
tales of Paterson to the sophisticated touch of Souter and
Dennis or the gentle irony of "Said Hanrahan". There are
frequent instances of that dry, sardonic realism, engendered
naturally in a country of droughts and floods, that is dis-
tinctively Australian. If this reaches its most artistic expression in Henry Lawson's short stories, it also flavours such
folk songs as "The Numerella Shore".

The inclusion here of the popular poetry found in the folk
songs, the bush ballads, satires and humorous verse presents
our poetry as a far livelier and much more vital creation,
closer in touch with life, more native in character, and
stronger in its general appeal than the narrower representation of it in orthodox collections. In giving it a fresh and
wider composition that corresponds more closely to its historical reality, this volume demands a revision, if not a re-
versal, of past critical interpretations of the poetry written
here in the nineteenth century. Hitherto, for instance, emphasis has been laid on its serious "literary" expression of
English romanticism. Its popular, indigenous realism has

been largely ignored except in a few special cases like Gordon, Paterson, and Lawson. Yet years of studying and teaching Australian literature at university level have convinced me strongly that during the nineteenth century it was as realistic as romantic. Thus I have tried here to restore the correct balance between the two elements within a broad historical perspective.

Confirmation of my view has recently come from Canada, where an Australian, Professor J. P. Matthews, has published a stimulating comparison between Australian and Canadian poetry of the nineteenth century in his *Tradition in Exile*. He finds that in each case "two parallel streams in literature developed", which he calls the "academic" and the "popular". "Academic poetry", he considers, "received the greatest attention in Canada, virtually driving Popular poetry beneath the literary surface. Popular poetry, on the other hand, came to dominate the Australian literary scene, obscuring the Academic." This was strictly true only of the Nineties period when the bush ballad was prominent. Professor Matthews is right, however, in stressing the special importance here of our folk and bush balladry, and in making a distinction between the two parallel traditions of Academic and Popular poetry, or, as I should put it, of literary romanticism and popular realism.

If the line of realism ran most strongly in the folk songs and bush ballads, it took many forms and continued throughout the century. It started as early as the convict songs and the very first "poem" in our first newspaper, when the *Sydney Gazette*, as early as 1803, published a punning quatrain on the drink habit entitled "A Rum Effect". It is our earliest instance of that sardonic humour already noted. In 1805 the *Gazette* published our first bush ballad, "Colonial Hunt", complete with "rich gums" sweeping the sky, "the fleet-footed WALLABA (wallaby), and the colonial hunter

Exclaiming, transported the course to review,
"Hoick! Hoick my bold Lurcher! Well led KANGUROO!"
Following these rudimentary essays in popular verse, completely native in theme and idiom, came innumerable lampoons, pipes, and full-blown satires, whilst the romantic poets such as Harpur and Kendall, Brunton Stephens, Daley and Quinn, all wrote popular, realistic satires and ballads. Right through the nineteenth century, therefore, the two streams of literary romanticism according to the English tradition and a popular Australian realism ran side by side, so that the frequent view that the verse of the century was only a pale, ineffectual "imitation" of English poetry is seen as quite untenable.

Equally false is its fanciful corollary that the poetry of the first half of the nineteenth century was a melancholy mourning of "nostalgic exiles" for England. The truth is the exact reverse. Nostalgic verse by homesick British immigrants was small in amount and negligible in quality. On the other hand, the exiled versifiers were engaged, from the very start, in exploring the utopian possibilities of the new land and singing its praises. Even the earliest of recognized versifiers, the convict laureate Michael Massey Robinson, used his royal odes to hymn the coming glories of Australia. Even Judge Barron Field, who produced the first published book of verse, sang the beauties of the local flora and the quaintness of its fauna. A strong patriotism for their adopted land pervades the verses of such emigrants as William Forster and Henry Parkes, both Premiers of New South Wales, and the versatile J. D. Lang. Adam Lindsay Gordon's melancholy was temperamental, not nostalgic, and he also exulted in the open air life, riding when " 'Twas merry in the glowing morn", and singing of the wattle gold and "each dew-laden air draught" that resembled "a long draught of wine". He identified himself with the country so effectively that he pioneered the bush ballad as an acceptable literary form with "The Sick Stock-rider" and was acclaimed as our "National Poet" both here and on the bust of him placed in Westminster Abbey. As for the native-born poets, Harpur and Kendall, they were fervent patriots who dedicated themselves to rendering the land of their birth in poetry. In short, exile was an historical fact in some cases, but the myth of nostalgia is nonsense. This volume offers an ironic comment on it in that the only two nostalgic poems were written in England, one by an Australian, Wentworth, and the other by an Englishwoman, Ada Cambridge, who had returned home after living here for thirty years. Both turn the tables on the myth by expressing nostalgia for a beloved Australia.

What this collection does reveal is the fundamental fact that Australian literature began as a colonial one and that in its literary poetry, as distinguished from its indigenous popular realism, it continued as such through most of the nineteenth century. This was not "a poetry of exiles" as it has been called, but it was, in truth, a poetry in exile in that it was the English poetic tradition transplanted into an alien, exotic land. It can only be understood fully and properly assessed when we recognize that it had to face, first and foremost, the dilemma of colonialism. It had to reconcile the clash of two conflicting cultures, the imperial and the indigenous, by adapting the poetic tradition of the mother country to assimilate creatively a totally different physical and social environment. It has had to battle with the difficulties common to the literatures of other former British colonies—the American, Canadian, New Zealand, and South African. Like them, it too passed through similar stages of colonial dependence and imitation, nationalist revolt, and eventual maturity of poetic independence.

In all cases the growth of a native poetry was protracted and painful. In America Poe might declare in the first half of the nineteenth century that "in letters as in government we require a Declaration of Independence," but truly independent writing only appeared with Walt Whitman and Mark Twain, and one American critic declared that the dominance of the English tradition "forced American literature to remain a colonial literature until practically the beginning of the twentieth century". In both Australian and Canadian literature an outburst of national sentiment produced literary independence in the Nineties. Lacking such an upsurge, New Zealand poetry evolved more slowly, assuming an authentic voice in the 1930s.

Colonialism meant that the basic need of our poets during the nineteenth century colonial period was to develop from being English to being Australian. The poetry had to become Australian before it could become genuine poetry. This was not, of course, a matter of nationalism as such, which is irrelevant to poetic values. It was simply that in being colonial our poetry remained derivative, imitative and self-conscious and it had to fight its way to become independent, original, and natural. Before the advent of the bush balladists most of the verse written in the English romantic tradition, with the exception of that of Harpur and Kendall, was weak and derivative. How badly it suffered from colonial anaemia can be seen in the appalling collections of it published by Douglas Sladen in 1888. The independent folk and bush balladry, on the other hand, was fresh and vital.

Colonialism placed great obstacles to independence in the path of the colonial poets. First, they had to battle, as Harpur did, against the inferiority complex that held that no cultural good could come out of the colonial Nazareth. Then, as early as Kendall and well before the patriotism of the Nineties, came the nationalist sentiment insisting on "local colour". This proved a two-edged weapon. It was valuable in stimulating a poetry closer to the realities of its life and scene.

On the other hand, its revolt was still part of the colonial complex, and it worsened the poets' self-consciousness, as it often did with Kendall. It was also bad in that it substituted a false localist touchstone of poetry for a true poetic one. This nationalism formed an indispensable and natural stage in the development of our writing, but it was, after all, only an adolescent stage leading to eventual maturity. This came on the popular level with the bush balladists, who were completely at home with their country. None of our poets has written more naturally than Paterson. Then our poetry at a higher level grew fully adult with Brennan, Neilson, and McCrae. Our poets have now long outgrown the colonial and nationalist stages. It is only in some literary criticism that these have lingered on belatedly to bedevil poetic judgment and to produce some academic flogging of the dead nationalist horse. Indeed, the criticism has lagged so far behind the actual poetry itself that it has produced such extremes as the Jindyworobak throwback to nationalism or the anachronistic revival of the colonial inferiority complex in the praise of a poet's work on the quaint ground that it was nobly wanting in wallabies.

For colonial poetry the central English tradition, with all the weight of its great riches, was at once a fertile source of inspiration and an almost overwhelming handicap. The earliest inheritance was that of the English eighteenth century poetry, but the Augustan rhetoric and the polished, urbane couplets of Pope only grew painfully incongruous when applied to the raw realities of the colonial scene. Then belatedly—since distance always imposed a substantial time-lag between English and Australian cultural developments—came the influence of the English Romantic Movement. This dominated most of our nineteenth century verse. It was beneficial in offering an approach and a form of sensibility that could be applied to a native rendering of the new world. Its emphasis on nature came happily to poets who felt that their first task was to assimilate their landscape just as, later in the century, the approach and technique of the French Impressionists, with their emphasis on light and colour, enabled painters like Roberts and Streeton to capture the light values of our sunlit country.

On the other hand, how could one translate the Australian scene in its wildness and what D. H. Lawrence called "the age-unbroken silence of the Australian bush" by the language of Wordsworth and Tennyson, redolent with connotions of an English society and a countryside humanized for centuries? There were traditional terms to describe oaks and deer, but none to grapple with the gum-tree or cope with the kangaroo. How could one possibly make romantic poetry out of such outlandish words as *billabong, paddock,* and *kookaburra*? Or make poetically acceptable in a Keatsian sonnet such local place-names as Woolloomooloo and Cuppacumbalong, Dingo Flat and Dead Horse Gully? Or, hardest of all perhaps, how transmute into romantic figures such realistic characters as Bill the Bullocky or One-eyed Bogan?

Thus the primary problem for the colonial poets in the English romantic tradition was the creation of a suitable diction to reveal their antipodean world. They had to find a new poetic language for the new land. They had to reverse the seasonal associations of English poetry to fit a country where Christmas came in with midsummer bushfires instead of winter snows. They had to struggle towards a native diction slowly, since they had no genius like Walt Whitman original enough to create a fresh language and an individual verse form. Indeed, Australian poets as a whole, with a few exceptions, have shown little pioneering enterprise in experimenting with new verse techniques. Nor could the poets of the nineteenth century profit by a Poe stressing supremacy of form. Their work, from Gordon and Kendall to O'Dowd and

Brennan, remained extremely uneven, with unequal crafts-
manship. All of them, even Brennan, often wrote badly. It is
significant that they usually wrote best when they wrote most
simply. By simplicity they sidestepped the artificial effect of
the English romantic diction, with its alien associations, and
came closer to a universal poetic language. Like Kendall in
"Orara" or Brennan in "The Wanderer", they were then
most natural, and most themselves.

As well as the nationalist stimulus, two other forces contributed to the liberation of our poetry from its colonial
bonds: the pioneering work of Harpur and Kendall and the
popular realism of the bush balladists. Both the early poets
were deeply dedicated to their common twin causes: poetry
and their native land. Fervent patriots, they tried to serve
their country by expressing it in the only terms available to
them, the English poetic tradition. To slight them for this
betrays a complete lack of historical perspective, just as it is
false to dub them "imitative" poets. Harpur was influenced
by Milton, Wordsworth, and Shelley; Kendall by Wordsworth, Tennyson, and Swinburne. But these influences of
their times were no stronger on them than his varied poetic
influences were on Brennan. Writers of today such as Slessor,
Judith Wright, and Hope also at times owe a debt to different English poets. The important thing is that the early poets,
like the later ones, worked through their echoes to authentic
voices of their own. The modern ones mentioned happen, of
course, to be far stronger poets in themselves, but then again,
it was much easier for them to be so, because time and their
predecessors in Australian writing, both in prose and verse,
had made them feel more at home in their environment.
Without these foundations such modern poets as Slessor and
FitzGerald could not have built their work so assuredly.

As the earliest, the first of our genuine poets, Harpur had
the hardest job to do in breaking the virgin ground. In both

his life and his work he struggled manfully against odds that were often too heavy for him. He had to encounter the unabated force of the primary difficulties of diction I have mentioned. His was the first unaided attempt to translate the Australian scene into poetry in the English tradition. The latter was often too powerful for him, so that his verse became bookish, abstract in its idealism, lacking intimacy with his theme. The marks of his labour were left upon his style. But he had character and imagination. His natural vigour asserted itself in a few poems and many isolated passages. He captured effectively, for instance, the heat and stillness of summer noon in the bush. At times he saw the world about him clearly and imaginatively—the mountains in a storm, the "upward tapering feathery swamp-oaks", and the woods "whitened over by the jolly cockatoo". Usually at his best in description, he could also phrase ideas epigrammatically, even memorably, as in "Words".

Kendall was forced, like Harpur, to struggle desperately against poverty, lack of recognition, and the problem of diction, but enjoyed the advantages of Harpur's example and a more favourable cultural climate. He was extremely uneven and had limitations that prevented him from becoming a major poet. Yet our literary historian H. M. Green came close to the mark when he concluded that "Kendall is much more than merely a landmark in Australian poetry; Harpur was that, and a little more as well, but Kendall is one of Australia's leading poets, and a landmark besides . . . his work, in its own kind, has not been surpassed here." Kendall was the first of our poets to receive recognition overseas. His work found a place in standard English and American anthologies. Oscar Wilde praised it highly, especially "Beyond Kerguelen" for its "marvellous music" and "real richness of utterance". Longfellow selected six poems from it for his *Poems of Places*. The South African poet, Roy Campbell, singling

Kendall out of British colonial poets for praise, acknowledged also: "He influenced me very much indeed." Kendall was a natural singer whose best lyrics have melody, grace, and feeling. In many poems, uneven as a whole, felicities flash out in stray lines. His poems on classical subjects, too long to reproduce here, contain passages of true beauty or dignity. Historically, he was a landmark since he achieved the intimacy with his landscape that Harpur missed, so that his contemporaries felt that "It is not so much he that speaks as Australia in him." Even that sharp critic A. G. Stephens, looking back on his work from the vantage point of the nationalist Nineties, declared "There has been no writer more generically Australian than Kendall." The poet had triumphed sufficiently over his English romantic diction to become an authentic native voice, and to help pave the way for further development.

The second liberating force, the bush balladists, followed the native tradition of popular realism begun with the folk ballads, and themselves created a folk poetry. It is significant that the leading balladist, "Banjo" Paterson, made the first substantial collection of the folk ballads in his *Old Bush Songs* and his poem "Waltzing Matilda" grew over time into a folk song, whilst his minor epic, "The Man from Snowy River", became an integral part of our national traditions. The bush balladists wrote of the people for the people—and the people responded wholeheartedly. Where Kendall had sold his volumes by the hundred, Paterson and Lawson sold theirs by the thousands. Their verses were known throughout the continent, recited by camp fires and in shearing sheds, and quoted in the pubs. The bush balladists, furthermore, made several important contributions to the evolution of our poetry. They developed narrative verse, humour and a colloquial language. They humanized the environment, filling it with traditional figures, since theirs was a poetry of People as that of the romantic poets had been one of Places. Kendall had partially succeeded but finally failed when he attempted to assimilate Bill the Bullock Driver into poetry, because of his literary self-consciousness in dealing with his unorthodox theme. Lawson, coming later, was able to picture the same figure easily and naturally in "The Teams", whilst Judith Wright in turn could go further in her poem "Bullocky" to make him an imaginative symbol, an epitome of our history, since she could start from the stage of familiarity created by the balladists. For the bush balladists, above all, went beyond Kendall, the transitional poet, to a completely natural acceptance of the Australian life and scene, an expression of it that was mature in its indigenous character and language. The dominance of English romanticism had been broken, even if it lingered on in sentimental minor verse of the twentieth century in a debased and deliquescent form. After Paterson and Lawson, however, our poetry was at home with its land. Poets could be themselves without self-consciousness and take the next step forward from ballad verse to imaginative creation that combined realistic with romantic elements. Thus Neilson took the daily objects around him, simply and unquestioningly, to transform an orange-tree into a mystery or strawberries into human symbols.

Such was the development of our poetry, with the picture unfolding itself in this volume. Thus it seemed most fitting to begin, not conventionally with Robinson, Wentworth or Harpur, but with the folk songs and ballads as our earliest expression in verse, the poetry of the people. These are usually rough and ready, crude in form, realistic in temper, colloquial in style. They lack the felicity, dramatic passion, and imagination of their English and Scottish prototypes—such qualities were only to come later with the poetic ballads of Mary Gilmore and David Campbell, Stewart and Manifold. Only rarely do they touch poetry, although it is possible that, as suggested by one folklore authority, a poetic aura may come with an increasing patina of age as they grow romantic when "over the hills and far away" in time. Some poetic touch already comes with the intensity of feeling voiced in a few ballads, such as "Jim Jones", "John Donahue and His Gang", and "The Wild Colonial Boy". There are phrases of haunting music in "The Dying Stockman" and "Look Out Below!". There is a Chaucerian flavour in the realism of "The Ramble-eer". But the chief merits of the folk songs and ballads are their directness, raciness, and vitality. They have an earthy vigour drawn from life itself. They will continue to live when much contemporary poetry is dead and buried. As Nancy Keesing has said, "They are an important part of our literary heritage . . . the first authentic voice of this new continent."

From them I have selected what I consider are the best songs and ballads representing the main occupational types—convicts, whalers, early settlers, bushrangers, gold-diggers, squatters and selectors, stockmen and bullockies, shearers, and swaggies. The versions used are mainly those given in the excellent collection *Old Bush Songs*, edited by Douglas Stewart and Nancy Keesing, to which I am indebted, just as I have drawn on the comprehensive *Australian Bush Ballads* of the same editors for the majority of the ballads in the third section. The whaling ballad of "The *Waterwitch*" was supplied to me by Mr Lloyd Robson, who collected it in Hobart in 1960 from an old whaler of eighty-seven named Davies.

In the Colonial Age section Wentworth has been chosen to lead off because he best illustrates the English eighteenth century tradition with which our literary poetry began. He was not a poet, but the rhetoric of his Cambridge prize poem is animated by that force of personality and eloquence which made him later the greatest statesman and orator of his times. Personal feeling breaks through the conventional

Augustan couplets as he looks back to his native land with pride and declaims its glorious future, and there are graphic pictures of Sydney Harbour and of the Blue Mountains which he, with Blaxland and Lawson, was the first to conquer. Thus he rises well above such other early versifiers as Robinson, Field and Tompson who have only historical interest, although it is also entertaining to watch Field, the friend of Charles Lamb, resorting to whimsy as a baffled mode of treating the anomalous kangaroo or to note how Tompson's *Wild Notes*, like Bottom's histrionic lion, "roar you as gently as any sucking dove."

Satire was such a distinctive feature of the first half of the nineteenth century writing that it needs representation to make the picture complete. Here Lowe and Forster had the most wit and skill, just as Brunton Stephens was the most effective humorist of his period. The juxtaposition of his "My Other Chinee Cook" with his eloquent "The Dominion of Australia" may jar artistic unity, but it preserves the historic truth of how literary romanticism was paralleled by popular realism, often in the one poet, and illustrates the hitherto neglected variety of the Colonial Age. The same combination is seen again in Gordon. The legend of his gallant, Byronic figure helped to inflate his poetic reputation unduly for many decades, provoking a reaction in which he was summarily dismissed altogether. Today, with a longer perspective, we can see that, despite the weakness of most of his verse, he cannot be cut out of the poetic reckoning. He made a genuine contribution not only by making the bush ballad accepted but also by a few poems justly remembered for their vigour and graphic description. Ada Cambridge is largely forgotten, named only as a novelist, but she was also a true poet, a clergyman's wife who was yet a rebel and radical, a woman of independent thought and feeling. Another woman poet, Mary Hannay Foott, naturally links up with the next grouping of the balladists of which she was a forerunner.

The bush balladists speak for themselves. Among them Paterson established his supremacy from the first by his superior gifts as a storyteller, humorist and sketcher of characters. Of all the balladists he came closest to the spirit of the folk songs and ballads and to the easy directness of their style. Incidentally the two ballads of Gibson's given here had acquired such wide popularity that Paterson included them in his *Old Bush Songs* as anonymous items of folklore. Henry Lawson was bracketed with Paterson in the public mind, but had nothing like his range in balladry. A fine original artist in the short-story, he was second-rate in his conventional verse. In this, however, his few ballads were his best work, and occasionally he came closer to the poetry of the Border ballads than Paterson through his depth of feeling. Ogilvie, if sometimes sentimental, had outstanding vigour and fluency. Brady's forceful sea ballads are among the best in the English language. Souter was a deft craftsman equally at home with his sailors or bush characters, whilst Will Lawson has the right roll of the sea in his excellent "Bill the Whaler" series. Finally, Spencer's "How McDougal Topped the Score", for long the top favourite in bush recitations, is humorous story-telling at its liveliest. As an entertaining narrative poem it is comparable with such a minor English classic as "The Diverting History of John Gilpin", and its place in our poetry should be as assured as that of "John Gilpin" in English poetry.

The poets of the Nineties section, opening with Daley and closing with Brennan, return to the romantic tradition, but with some interesting variations. Victor Daley, for instance, has usually been regarded as a graceful poet of fantasy living in a Celtic twilight illustrated here by "Dreams". Then a totally different side of him emerged with a collection of the radical colloquial verse he wrote as "Creeve Roe". Yet Daley wrote best, I believe, not as a purely romantic dreamer or as

xxxviii

a sharp-tongued social realist, but as an individual poet of gaiety, wit, and an imagination penetrating to significances in the realities about him. He discerns an insect as a Homer "Singing his Iliad on a blade of grass," a child as an "infant Tamerlane" symbolizing the destructive force necessary to the remaking of society, and the sounds of bush life as conniving to tell the "Rich, rude, strong-striving Australian life". His epigrams strike deep. His critique of A. G. Stephens, genial, witty, and acute, remains our best literary satire in verse.

Bernard O'Dowd, patriot and prophet, radical and philosopher, has become a controversial figure, setting criticism by the ears. He set out to write a "Poetry Militant" attacking the social, political, and religious issues of his day. He became an inspiration to thoughtful contemporaries, one of whom testified to the power of "the songs of democracy that stirred us like trumpets. . . . There was a flame in him." His topical themes, however, grew outdated. Too often he wrote as philosopher rather than poet, growing aridly abstract. In his early books he overloaded his style with polysyllables and erudite allusions which he tried to cram, impossibly, into tight ballad quatrains. In his later work, however, such as his sonnets, "The Bush", and "Alma Venus", he developed a lyrical flexibility with lengthened lines in varied verse forms. Since he wrote long poems uneven in quality, he is a difficult poet to represent in an anthology, but the extracts here may indicate that O'Dowd had poetic virtues as conspicuous as his faults: a deep sincerity, the force of an original personality, the power of phrasing ideas imaginately and memorably, a subtle, far-ranging mind, and an impassioned eloquence. At his best a largeness of thought and utterance makes much other verse look trivial. He was a founder, along with Brennan, of a line of philosophic poets who have taken our poetry beyond the local descriptive lyric to some depth of universal thought.

Such thought is condensed in the brief, illuminating poems of Mary Fullerton, writing as "E" in her later years. If she owed much in style to Emily Dickinson, the greatest woman poet in the English language was a good model, and "E" preserved her own individuality.

Brennan was philosophic, perhaps, rather than a systematic philosopher in verse, like Baylebridge. He has become a personal legend owing to his rare touch of genius, his tragic career, his Johnsonian dominance amongst Sydney writers, and his remarkable scholarship. "His mind," said A.G.S., "was like a Museum, Art Gallery and Public Library rolled into one." Equally apt was the critic's description of Brennan's poetry as "his didactic, sonorous, spectacular commentary on I, Mine, Me," since it forms a spiritual autobiography at once both personal and universal. It records an inward conflict and striving for an unattained Eden of perfection, with its "Lilith" sequence picturing the dark night of the soul in symbolist terms.

Brennan tried to shape his work in the 1914 *Poems* into a symphonic whole, but only partially succeeded, since many poems were first written as individual lyrics, others written according to the plan were uninspired, and the best of the sequences, "The Wanderer", erupted as a lyrical impulse outside his scheme. Here he broke free from the European influences manifest elsewhere—Milton and Keats, Patmore and Swinburne, the Greek classics, German romanticism, and French symbolism, notably Baudelaire and Mallarmé. Much of his work is derivative, his poems on the Boer war and the first world war are inferior, and in the *Poems* some work is laboured and artificial, some obscure, and some turgid or clumsy. At its best, however, the poetry, with its impressive spaciousness, its imaginative richness, rises to genuine greatness. It can be exalted in the grand style and sweep to a majesty rare in poetry in the English tongue. In lines like

"I took the night upon my face" it has a Dantean ring. Thus Brennan is naturally accepted as the finest Australian poet, although he is surpassed in the pure lyric, I feel, by the more original Neilson.

After the turn of the century the English romantic tradition in Australia, which rose to its height in Brennan, continued its course in personal and descriptive lyrics, but profited from the natural acceptance of the environment by the bush balladists. It was a period of individualism, with the main poets, Neilson and McCrae, Baylebridge and Gilmore, all going their completely different ways. Of these Shaw Neilson stands out as the purest lyrist in all our poetry. He was little less than a miracle. He earned a bare crust as a casual bush worker, a navvy labouring heavily in quarries and sewerage trenches, and a humble office messenger. Bush-bred, he had little education or knowledge of even the standard English poets. His close eyesight was so bad that he could neither read nor even write down his "rhymes", which he had to dictate to his brother or sister or baffled working mates. Yet he was born a poet who created his own world of delicate and elusive loveliness by a vision that retained the joy and wonder of childhood and a fresh simplicity akin to that of the Blake he had never read. His simplicity and apparently narrow range, however, are both deceptive, since he goes beyond gentleness, ecstasy, and compassion to mystic intuitions of spiritual truths. Like Francis Thompson, he knows a world unknowable and clutches the intangible, seeing the simplest objects as symbols in a "cosmic metonymy". Indeed, he was more of a "symbolist" poet, in Brennan's sense, than Brennan himself. An orange-tree is strangely illuminated by intimations of enchantment, the sun comes up "as some one lost in a quaint parable", and the feeding of the birds by the poor becomes an age-old sacrament of love

Deep as forgiveness, or the tears that go
 Out somewhere to the dead.

So, too, he brings a freshness to his language, making simple words richly imaginative, full of surprising delights, such as "the summer sauntered in" and "Love cannot sabre us"—a fellow phrase to Shakespeare's "I am gored with mine own thoughts." Above all, Neilson is the natural singer whose songs move to melodies always true, often subtle, often exquisite. Although he owed much to his critic and champion, A. G. Stephens, he was himself an exacting craftsman working on his "pieces" for years until he found the right word and the perfect cadence, so that they come as if purely spontaneous.

Hugh McCrae joins Neilson as a fine artist in the lyrical forms, a painter-poet as well as singer, delighting in colour and a sculptured line. After much conventional and sentimental versifying of his time, he brought a new invigoration to poetry by his sheer joy in life and his imaginative strength, his pictorial use of the concrete image and his flexible rhythms, so that he exerted an important influence on a generation of younger poets that included Slessor, FitzGerald, and Jack Lindsay. I have tried to indicate here his breadth of range in the various worlds through which his imagination ranged: delicate fantasy, robust creations of classical myths; adventurings into the medieval world; and the later songs, serious or playful, of his home country at Camden. McCrae moved from the romantic tradition to a simpler, more realistic and personal style, but all his work had artistry and the charm of his unique, lovable personality.

Baylebridge, earnestly dedicating himself to his task as philospher-poet, combined ideas drawn from Nietzsche, Bergson, and Shaw into his own philosophy of the universe and human society. His social verse, attacking democracy and religion, remains curiously artificial, mannered, and crabbed in style. Like O'Dowd's social verse it failed as poetry, whilst it lacked O'Dowd's power of phrasing. A similar power to O'Dowd's emerges, however, in the long sonnet-sequence "Love Redeemed", in which personal feeling breaks through the Shakespearian language and the occasional echoes of Wordsworth. Baylebridge is at his best, however, in the metaphysical sequence "Life's Testament", where he speaks in his own voice and reaches the force and loftiness he desired, especially in the lyric "I worshipped, when my veins were fresh".

Finally, this volume closes aptly with Dame Mary Gilmore, whose poetry extended over forty years of this century. Its value has often been obscured by emphasis upon her remarkable character and career, and by the fact that she wrote so voluminously and on such a diversity of subjects that her finest poems were sometimes swamped by the mass of occasional verse. The condensed illuminations of her best poems, nevertheless, have a strength and disciplined economy that place her among our poets of the front rank. "Nationality", "Never Admit the Pain", "Old Botany Bay", and "The Tenancy", for instance, compress much in little with artistic assurance. They are perfect in their kind. The images are integral, and the simplicity, powered by the poet's personality, grows memorable.

T. INGLIS MOORE

I

FOLK SONGS AND BALLADS

ANON.

Jim Jones

O, listen for a moment lads, and hear me tell my tale—
How, o'er the sea from England's shore I was compelled to
  sail.
The jury says, "He's guilty, sir," and says the judge, says he—
"For life, Jim Jones, I'm sending you across the stormy sea;
And take my tip before you ship to join the iron-gang,
Don't be too gay at Botany Bay, or else you'll surely hang—
Or else you'll hang," he says, says he—"and after that, Jim
  Jones,
High up upon the gallow-tree the crows will pick your
  bones—
You'll have no chance for mischief then; remember what I
  say,
They'll flog the poaching out of you, out there at Botany
  Bay."

The winds blew high upon the sea, and the pirates came
  along,
But the soldiers on our convict ship were full five hundred
  strong,
They opened fire and somehow drove that pirate ship away.
I'd have rather joined that pirate ship than come to Botany
  Bay:
For night and day the irons clang, and like poor galley slaves
We toil, and toil, and when we die must fill dishonoured
  graves.
But by and by I'll break my chains: into the bush I'll go,
And join the brave bushrangers there—Jack Donohoo and
  Co.;
And some dark night when everything is silent in the town
I'll kill the tyrants, one and all, and shoot the floggers down:
I'll give the Law a little shock: remember what I say,
They'll yet regret they sent Jim Jones in chains to Botany Bay.

Botany Bay

Farewell to old England for ever,
Farewell to my rum culls as well,
Farewell to the well-known Old Bailey,
Where I used for to cut such a swell.

Chorus Singing, too-ral, li-ooral, li-addity,
        Singing, too-ral, li-ooral, li-ay.
        Singing, too-ral, li-ooral, li-addity,
        Singing, too-ral, li-ooral, li-ay.

There's the captain as is our commander,
There's the bo'sun and all the ship's crew,
There's the first- and the second-class passengers,
Knows what we poor convicts goes through.

'Tain't leaving old England we care about,
'Tain't cos we misspells wot we knows,
But because all we light-fingered gentry
Hops round with a log on our toes.

For fourteen long years I have ser-vi-ed,
And for fourteen long years and a day,
For meeting a bloke in the area,
And sneaking his ticker away.

Oh had I the wings of a turtle-dove,
I'd soar on my pinions so high,
Slap bang to the arms of my Polly love,
And in her sweet presence I'd die.

Now, all my young Dook-ies and Duch-ess-es,
Take warning from what I've to say—
Mind all is your own as you touch-es-es,
Or you'll meet us in Botany Bay.

A Convict's Lament on the Death of Captain Logan

I am a native of the land of Erin,
And lately banished from that lovely shore;
I left behind my aged parents
And the girl I did adore.
In transient storms as I set sailing,
Like mariner bold my course did steer;
Sydney Harbour was my destination—
That cursed place at length drew near.

I then joined banquet in congratulation
On my safe arrival from the briny sea;
But, alas, alas! I was mistaken—
Twelve years transportation to Moreton Bay.
Early one morning as I carelessly wandered,
By the Brisbane waters I chanced to stray;
I saw a prisoner sadly bewailing,
Whilst on the sunlit banks he lay.

He said, "I've been a prisoner at Port Macquarie,
At Norfolk Island, and Emu Plains;
At Castle Hill and cursed Toongabbie—
At all those places I've worked in chains,
But of all the places of condemnation,
In each penal station of New South Wales,
Moreton Bay I found no equal,
For excessive tyranny each day prevails.

Early in the morning, as the day is dawning,
To trace from heaven the morning dew,
Up we started at a moment's warning
Our daily labour to renew.

Our overseers and superintendents—
These tyrants' orders we must obey,
Or else at the triangles our flesh is mangled—
Such are our wages at Moreton Bay!

For three long years I've been beastly treated;
Heavy irons each day I wore;
My poor back from flogging has been lacerated,
And oft-times painted with crimson gore.
Like the Egyptians and ancient Hebrews,
We were sorely oppressed by Logan's yoke,
Till kind Providence came to our assistance,
And gave this tyrant his fatal stroke.

Yes, he was hurried from that place of bondage
Where he thought he would gain renown;
But a native black, who lay in ambush,
Gave this monster his fatal wound.
Fellow prisoners be exhilarated;
Your former sufferings you will not mind,
For it's when from bondage you are extricated
You'll leave such tyrants far behind!"

ANON.

The "Waterwitch"

A neat little packet from Hobart set sail,
For to cruise round the west'ard amongst the sperm whale;
Cruising the west'ard where the stormy winds blow,
Bound away in the *Waterwitch* to the west-ard we'll go.

Bound away, bound away, where the stormy winds blow,
Bound away in the *Waterwitch* to the west'ard we go.

Now at early one morning, just as the sun rose,
A man from her masthead cries out, "There she blows!"

"We're away!" cried our skipper, and springing aloft,
"Three points on the lee bow and scarce three miles off.

"Get your lines in your boats, me boys, see your box line
all clear,
And lower me down, me bully boys, and after him we'll
steer!"

Now the ship she gets full, me boys, and to Hobart we'll
steer,
Where there's plenty of pretty girls and plenty good beer.
We'll spend our money freely with the pretty girls on shore,
And when it's all gone, we'll go whaling for more.

Bound away, bound away, where the stormy winds blow,
Bound away in the *Waterwitch* to the west'ard we go.

ANON.

The Settler's Lament

All you on emigration bent
With home and England discontent,
Come listen to this my sad lament
About the bush of Australia.
Of cash I had a thousand pounds—
Thinks I how mighty grand it sounds
For a man to be farming his own grounds
In this beautiful land of Australia.
Upon the voyage the ship was lost,
In wretched plight I reached the coast,
And was very near being made a roast
By the savages in Australia.

Chorus Illawarra, Mittagong,
        Parramatta, Wollongong,

7

    If you wouldn't become an orang-outang,
    Don't go to the wilds of Australia.

Escaped from thence I lighted on
A fierce bushranger with his gun,
Who borrowed my garments every one
For himself in the bush of Australia.
Sydney town I reached at last,
Thinks I all danger now is past,
And I shall make my fortune fast
In this promised land of Australia.
So quickly went with cash in hand,
Upon the map I bought my land,
But found it nothing but barren sand
When I got to the bush of Australia.

Chorus Cabramatta, Bogolong,
       Ulladulla, Gerringong,
       If you wouldn't become an orang-outang,
       Don't go to the wilds of Australia.

Of sheep I had a precious lot
Some died of hunger, some of rot,
For a divil a drop of rain they got
In this promised land of Australia.
My servants they were always drunk,
That kept me in a constant funk,
And I said to myself, as to bed I slunk,
I wish I was out of Australia.
Of ills I've had enough, you'll own;
There's something else my woes to crown,
One night my loghouse tumbled down,
And settled me in Australia.

8

Chorus Hunter's River, Botany Bay,
       Port Macquarie, Moreton Bay,
       If you wouldn't become an orang-outang,
       Don't go to the wilds of Australia.

Of cash and homestead thus bereft,
The horrid spot I gladly left;
Making it over by deed of gift
To the savages in Australia.
Gladly I worked my passage home,
And back to England now I'm come;
Never more at large to roam,
At least to the bush of Australia.
But stones upon the road I'll break,
I'll earn my seven bob a week,
Which is surely better than the freak
Of settling in Australia.

Chorus Illawarra, Mittagong,
       Parramatta, Wollongong,
       If you wouldn't become an orang-outang,
       Don't go to the wilds of Australia.

ANON.

The Old Bullock Dray

Oh! the shearing is all over,
And the wool is coming down,
And I mean to get a wife, boys,
When I go up to town.
Everything that has two legs
Represents itself in view,
From the little paddymelon
To the bucking kangaroo.

Chorus So it's roll up your blankets,
And let's make a push,
I'll take you up the country,
And show you the bush.
I'll be bound you won't get
Such a chance another day,
So come and take possession
Of my old bullock dray.

Now, I've saved up a good cheque,
I mean to buy a team,
And when I get a wife, boys,
I'll be all-serene;
For, calling at the depot,
They say there's no delay
To get an offsider
For the old bullock dray.

Oh! we'll live like fighting cocks,
For good living, I'm your man.
We'll have leather-jacks, johnny-cakes,
And fritters in the pan;
Or if you'd like some fish
I'll catch you some soon,
For we'll bob for barramundies
Round the banks of a lagoon.

Oh! yes, of beef and damper
I take care we have enough,
And we'll boil in the bucket
Such a whopper of a duff,
And our friends will dance
To the honour of the day,
To the music of the bells
Around the old bullock dray.

Oh! we'll have plenty girls,
We must mind that.
There'll be flash little Maggie,
And buckjumping Pat.
There'll be Stringbark Joe,
And Greenhide Mike.
Yes, my colonials, just
As many as you like.

Now we'll stop all immigration,
We won't need it any more;
We'll be having young natives,
Twins by the score.
And I wonder what the devil
Jack Robertson would say
If he saw us promenading
Round the old bullock dray.

Oh! it's time I had an answer,
If there's one to be had,
I wouldn't treat that steer
In the body half as bad;
But he takes as much notice
Of me, upon my soul,
As that old blue stag
Offside in the pole.

Oh! to tell a lot of lies,
You know, it is a sin,
But I'll go up country
And marry a black gin.
Oh! "Baal gammon white feller",
This is what she'll say,
"Budgery you
And your old bullock dray."

The Old Keg of Rum

My name is old Jack Palmer,
I'm a man of olden days,
And so I wish to sing a song
To you of olden praise;
To tell of merry friends of old
When we were gay and young;
How we sat and sang together
Round the Old Keg of Rum.

Chorus Oh! the Old Keg of Rum! the Old Keg of Rum!
How we sat and sang together
Round the Old Keg of Rum.

There was I and Jack the ploughboy,
Jem Moore and old Tom Hines,
And poor old Tom the fiddler,
Who now in glory shines;
And several more of our old chums,
Who shine in Kingdom Come,
We all associated round the
Old Keg of Rum.

Chorus Oh! the Old Keg of Rum! the Old Keg of Rum!
We all associated round the
Old Keg of Rum.

And when harvest time was over,
And we'd get our harvest fee,
We'd meet, and quickly rise the keg,
And then we'd have a spree.
We'd sit and sing together
Till we got that blind and dumb

That we couldn't find the bunghole
Of the Old Keg of Rum.

Chorus Oh! the Old Keg of Rum! the Old Keg of Rum!
　　　That we couldn't find the bunghole
　　　Of the Old Keg of Rum.

It's jovially together, boys—
We'd laugh, we'd chat, we'd sing;
Sometimes we'd have a little row
Some argument would bring.
And oft-times in a scrimmage, boys,
I've corked it with my thumb,
To keep the life from leaking
From the Old Keg of Rum.

Chorus Oh! the Old Keg of Rum! the Old Keg of Rum!
　　　To keep the life from leaking
　　　From the Old Keg of Rum.

But when our spree was ended, boys,
And waking from a snooze,
For to give another drain
The old keg would refuse.
We'd rap it with our knuckles—
If it sounded like a drum,
We'd know the life and spirit
Had left the Old Keg of Rum.

Chorus Oh! the Old Keg of Rum! the Old Keg of Rum!
　　　We'd know the life and spirit
　　　Had left the Old Keg of Rum.

Those happy days have passed away,
I've seeen their pleasures fade;

13

And many of our good old friends
Have with old times decayed.
But still, when on my travels, boys,
If I meet with an old chum,
We will sigh, in conversation,
Of the Grand Old Keg of Rum.

Chorus Oh! the Old Keg of Rum! the Old Keg of Rum!
We will sigh, in conversation,
Of the Grand Old Keg of Rum.

So now, kind friends, I end my song,
I hope we'll meet again,
And, as I've tried to please you all,
I hope you won't complain.
You younger folks who learn my song,
Will perhaps in years to come,
Remember old Jack Palmer
And the Old Keg of Rum.

Chorus Oh! the Old Keg of Rum! the Old Keg of Rum!
Remember old Jack Palmer
And the Old Keg of Rum.

ANON.

The Old Bark Hut

Oh, my name is Bob the Swagman, before you all I stand,
And I've had many ups and downs while travelling through
the land.
I once was well-to-do, my boys, but now I am stumped up,
And I'm forced to go on rations in an old bark hut.

Chorus In an old bark hut, in an old bark hut.
I'm forced to go on rations in an old bark hut.

14

Ten pounds of flour, ten pounds of beef, some sugar and
    some tea,
That's all they give to a hungry man, until the Seventh Day.
If you don't be mighty sparing, you'll go with a hungry gut—
For that's one of the great misfortunes in an old bark hut.

Chorus In an old bark hut, in an old bark hut.
        For that's one of the great misfortunes in an old bark
        hut.

The bucket you boil your beef in has to carry water, too,
And they'll say you're getting mighty flash if you should ask
    for two.
I've a billy, and a pint-pot, and a broken-handled cup,
And they all adorn the table in the old bark hut.

Chorus In an old bark hut, in an old bark hut.
        And they all adorn the table in the old bark hut.

Faith, the table is not made of wood, as many you have seen—
For if I had one half so good, I'd think myself serene—
'Tis only an old sheet of bark—God knows when it was cut—
It was blown from off the rafters of the old bark hut.

Chorus In an old bark hut, in an old bark hut.
        It was blown from off the rafters of the old bark hut.

And of furniture, there's no such thing, 'twas never in the
    place,
Except the stool I sit upon—and that's an old gin-case.
It does us for a safe as well, but you must keep it shut,
Or the flies would make it canter round the old bark hut.

Chorus In an old bark hut, in an old bark hut.
        Or the flies would make it canter round the old bark
        hut.

If you should leave it open, and the flies should find your
    meat,
They'll scarcely leave a single piece that's fit for man to eat.
But you mustn't curse, nor grumble—what won't fatten will
    fill up—
For what's out of sight is out of mind in an old bark hut.

Chorus In an old bark hut, in an old bark hut.
        For what's out of sight is out of mind in an old
        bark hut.

In the summertime when the weather's warm this hut is nice
    and cool,
And you'll find the gentle breezes blowing in through every
    hole.
You can leave the old door open, or you can leave it shut,
There's no fear of suffocation in the old bark hut.

Chorus In an old bark hut, in an old bark hut.
        There's no fear of suffocation in the old bark hut.

In the winter-time—preserve us all!—to live in there's a treat,
Especially when it's raining hard, and blowing wind and
    sleet.
The rain comes down the chimney, and your meat is black
    with soot—
That's a substitute for pepper in an old bark hut.

Chorus In an old bark hut, in an old bark hut.
        That's a substitute for pepper in an old bark hut.

I've seen the rain come in this hut just like a perfect flood,
Especially through that great big hole where once the table
    stood.

There's not a blessed spot, me boys, where you could lay
    your nut,
But the rain is sure to find you in the old bark hut.

Chorus In an old bark hut, in an old bark hut.
        But the rain is sure to find you in the old bark hut.

So beside the fire I make me bed, and there I lay me down,
And think myself as happy as the king that wears a crown.
But as you'd be dozing off to sleep a flea will wake you up,
Which makes you curse the vermin in the old bark hut.

Chorus In an old bark hut, in an old bark hut.
        Which makes you curse the vermin in the old bark
        hut.

Faith, such flocks of fleas you never saw, they are so plump
    and fat,
And if you make a grab at one, he'll spit just like a cat.
Last night they got my pack of cards, and were fighting for
    the cut—
I thought the Devil had me in the old bark hut.

Chorus In an old bark hut, in an old bark hut.
        I thought the Devil had me in the old bark hut.

So now, my friends, I've sung my song, and that as well as I
    could,
And I hope the ladies present won't think my language rude,
And all ye younger people, in the days when you grow up,
Remember Bob the Swagman, and the old bark hut.

Chorus In an old bark hut, in an old bark hut.
        Remember Bob the Swagman, and the old bark hut.

The Wild Colonial Boy

'Tis of a wild Colonial boy, Jack Doolan was his name,
Of poor but honest parents he was born in Castlemaine.
He was his father's only hope, his mother's only joy,
And dearly did his parents love the wild Colonial boy.

Chorus Come, all my hearties, we'll roam the mountains
    high,
    Together we will plunder, together we will die.
    We'll wander over valleys, and gallop over plains,
    And we'll scorn to live in slavery, bound down with
    iron chains.

He was scarcely sixteen years of age when he left his father's
    home,
And through Australia's sunny clime a bushranger did roam.
He robbed those wealthy squatters, their stock he did destroy,
And a terror to Australia was the wild Colonial boy.

In sixty-one this daring youth commenced his wild career,
With a heart that knew no danger, no foeman did he fear.
He stuck up the Beechworth mail-coach, and robbed Judge
    MacEvoy,
Who trembled, and gave up his gold to the wild Colonial
    boy.

He bade the judge "Good morning", and told him to beware,
That he'd never rob a hearty chap that acted on the square,
And never to rob a mother of her son and only joy,
Or else you may turn outlaw, like the wild Colonial boy.

One day as he was riding the mountain-side along,
A-listening to the little birds, their pleasant laughing song,

Three mounted troopers rode along—Kelly, Davis, and
　　FitzRoy—
They thought that they would capture him, the wild Colonial
　　boy.

"Surrender now, Jack Doolan, you see there's three to one.
Surrender now, Jack Doolan, you daring highwayman."
He drew a pistol from his belt, and shook the little toy.
"I'll fight, but not surrender," said the wild Colonial boy.

He fired at Trooper Kelly and brought him to the ground,
And in return from Davis received a mortal wound.
All shattered through the jaws he lay still firing at FitzRoy,
And that's the way they captured him—the wild Colonial
　　boy.

JACK DONAHUE(?)

1808(?)-1830

Brave Donahue

A life that is free as the bandits' of old,
When Rome was the prey of the warriors bold
Who knew how to buy gallant soldiers with gold,
Is the life, full of danger,
Of Jack the bushranger,
Of brave Donahue!

If Ireland lies groaning, a hand at her throat,
Which foreigners have from the recreants bought,
Forget not the lessons our fathers have taught.
Though our Isle's full of danger,
And held by the stranger,
Be brave and be true!

I've left the old Island's hospitable shores,
The land of the Emmets, the Tones, and the Moores;

But Liberty o'er me her scalding tear pours,
And she points to the manger,
Where *He* was a stranger,
And perished for you.

Then hurl me to crime and brand me with shame,
But think not to baulk me, my spirit to tame,
For I'll fight to the last in old Ireland's name,
Though I be a bushranger,
You still are the stranger,
And I'm Donahue.

CHARLES R. THATCHER

1831-1882(?)

Look Out Below!

A young man left his native shores,
For trade was bad at home;
To seek his fortune in this land
He crossed the briny foam;
And when he went to Ballarat,
It put him in a glow,
To hear the sound of the windlass,
And the cry "Look out below!"

Wherever he turned his wandering eyes
Great wealth he did behold,
And peace and plenty hand in hand,
By the magic power of gold;
Quoth he, "As I am young and strong,
To the diggings I will go,
For I like the sound of the windlass
And the cry 'Look out below!'"

20

Amongst the rest he took his chance,
And his luck at first was vile;
But he still resolved to persevere,
And at length he made his pile.
So says he, "I'll take my passage,
And home again I'll go,
And I'll say farewell to the windlass
And the cry 'Look out below!' "

Arrived in London once again,
His gold he freely spent
And into every gaiety
And dissipation went.
But pleasure, if prolonged too much,
Oft causes pain, you know,
And he missed the sound of the windlass,
And the cry "Look out below!"

And thus he reasoned with himself,
"Oh, why did I return?
For the digger's independent life
I now begin to yearn.
Here purse-proud lords the poor oppress,
But *there* it is not so;
Give me the sound of the windlass,
And the cry 'Look out below!' "

So he started for this land again,
With a charming little wife;
And he finds there's nothing comes up to
A jolly digger's life.
Ask him if he'll go back again,
He'll quickly answer, "No!"
For he loves the sound of the windlass,
And the cry "Look out below."

21

E

ANON.

The Broken-down Digger

I've worked on the Nine-Mile, likewise on the River,
And out at the New-Chum, and Rocky Plains too;
At each of those places I did my endeavour,
But I've lately struck "duffers", with nothing in view;
And just now I'm longing to see the old places,
I'm longing to visit old Sydney again—
For I'm "full" of the Snowy's white hills and wild graces;
I'm a broken-down digger on Kiandra plain.

ANON.

The Golden Gullies of the Palmer

Then roll the swag and blanket up,
And let us haste away
To the Golden Palmer, boys,
Where everyone, they say,
Can get his ounce of gold, or
It may be more, a day,
In the Golden Gullies of the Palmer.

Chorus Hurrah! Hurrah! We'll sound the jubilee.
Hurrah! Hurrah! And we will merry be,
When we reach the diggings, boys,
There the nuggets see,
In the Golden Gullies of the Palmer.

Kick at troubles when they come, boys,
The motto be for all;
And if you've missed the ladder
In climbing Fortune's wall,
Depend upon it, boys,
You'll recover from the fall,
In the Golden Gullies of the Palmer.

Then sound the chorus once again
And give it with a roar,
And let its echoes ring, boys,
Upon the sea and shore,
Until it reach the mountains,
Where gold is in galore,
In the Golden Gullies of the Palmer.

ANON.

The Broken-down Squatter

Come, Stumpy, old man, we must shift while we can;
All our mates in the paddock are dead.
Let us wave our farewells to Glen Eva's sweet dells
And the hills where your lordship was bred;
Together to roam from our drought-stricken home—
It seems hard that such things have to be,
And it's hard on a "hoss" when he's nought for a boss
But a broken-down squatter like me!

Chorus For the banks are all broken, they say,
And the merchants are all up a tree.
When the bigwigs are brought to the Bankruptcy
Court,
What chance for a squatter like me?

No more shall we muster the river for fats,
Or spiel on the Fifteen-mile Plain,
Or rip through the scrub by the light of the moon,
Or see the old stockyard again.
Leave the slip-panels down, it won't matter much now,
There are none but the crows left to see,
Perching gaunt in yon pine, as though longing to dine
On a broken-down squatter like me.

23

When the country was cursed with the drought at its worst
And the cattle were dying in scores,
Though down on my luck I kept up my pluck,
Thinking justice might temper the laws.
But the farce has been played, and the Government aid
Ain't extended to squatters, old son;
When my dollars were spent they doubled the rent,
And resumed the best half of the run.

'Twas done without reason for, leaving the season,
No squatter could stand such a rub;
For it's useless to squat when the rents are so hot
That one can't save the price of one's grub;
And there's not much to choose 'twixt the banks and the Jews
Once a fellow gets put up a tree;
No odds what I feel, there's no court of appeal
For a broken-down squatter like me.

"COCKATOO JACK"

The Numerella Shore

There's a nice green little gully on the Numerella shore
Which I have ridden over many a day
Under Free Selection there I'll have acres by the score
Where I unyoke my bullocks from the dray.

Chorus To my bullocks I will say, Here for ever you may
stay;
You will never be impounded any more;
For you're running, running, running on your
owner's piece of ground,
Free-selected on the Numerella shore.

24

When the moon's behind the mountain and the stars are very
        bright
My horse and I will saddle and away;
I'll duff the squatter's cattle in the darkness of the night
And the calves I'll have all branded ere the day.

Chorus O my pretty little calf, at the squatter we will laugh,
          For he'll never be your owner any more
            While you're running, running, running on the duf-
              fer's piece of ground
            Free-selected on the Numerella shore.

And when we've got our swags we'll steal the squatter's nags
And drive them to the nearest market town;
And when we've got the cash oh won't we cut a dash
And laugh at having done the squatter brown!

Chorus And won't the bullocks bellow when to work they
          seldom go
            And they think they won't be wanted any more
            While they're running, running, running on the duf-
              fer's piece of ground
            Free-selected on the Numerella shore.

Then as to growing grain on the bleak Maneroo Plain
Where we've free-selected from our master's run
Old hands up here will say 'tis a game will never pay,
So we'll go in for no work and lots of fun.

Chorus To my bullocks I will say, Here for ever you may
          stay
            For you'll never now be wanted any more;
            Your master'll get a living more easily by thieving
            Than by farming on the Numerella shore.

Is my judgment getting blunted that I cannot see my way?
Are there no vessels loading any more?
Oh! it's no use my debating for I only have to say
Farewell now to the Numerella shore.

Chorus To Jack Robertson, I'll say, You've been leading us
            astray,
          You will never be believed any more;
          And when next you take an airing try nothing half
            so daring
          As a visit to the Numerella shore.

ANON.

Cockies of Bungaree

Come all you jolly travellers that's out of work, just mind
Take a trip to Bungaree and plenty there you'll find.
Have a trial with the cockies and just take it from me
I'm certain sure you'll rue the day you first saw Bungaree.

And how I came this weary way I mean to let you know
Being out of employment I didn't know where to go.
I called at a registry office and there I did agree
To take a job of clearing for a cocky in Bungaree.

Well on the Monday morning to work I had to go,
My Noble shouted at me, "Getting up you're rather slow;
Take this pick and shovel, set to work and grub that tree."
"Oh begob," says I, "'tis nice and light, this work in
    Bungaree."

Well on the Tuesday morning it was the usual go
He called me up to breakfast before the cocks did crow;
The stars were shining gloriously, and the moon was high,
    you see,
And I thought before the sun would rise I'd die in Bungaree.

When I went in to supper it was after half past nine
And when I had it ate sure I thought it was bed-time
But the cocky came to me saying with a merry laugh,
"I want you for an hour or two to cut a bit of chaff."

And while we are chaff-cutting, he says "It's quite a spell."
"Oh begob," says I, "it is, and it's I that knows it well."
We always were a-quarrelling, we never could agree
So at last I made up my mind to leave old Bungaree.

So now my job is over and I'm at liberty
And it's of the cocky's health and wealth I'm spending
    merrily;
I am not boasting fellow, no lies I ever told,
So if you will believe me now, it's the truth I did unfold.

ANON.

The Overlander

There's a trade you all know well—
It's bringing cattle over—
I'll tell you all about the time
When I became a drover.
I made up my mind to try the spec,
To the Clarence I did wander,
And bought a mob of duffers there
To begin as an overlander.

Chorus Pass the wine cup round, my boys;
       Don't let the bottle stand there,
       For tonight we'll drink the health
       Of every overlander.

When the cattle were all mustered,
And the outfit ready to start,
I saw the lads all mounted,
With their swags left in the cart.
All kinds of men I had
From France, Germany, and Flanders;
Lawyers, doctors, good and bad,
In the mob of overlanders.

From the road I then fed out
When the grass was green and young;
When a squatter with curse and shout
Told me to move along.
I said, "You're very hard;
Take care, don't raise my dander,
For I'm a regular knowing card,
The Queensland overlander."

'Tis true we pay no licence,
And our run is rather large;
'Tis not often they can catch us,
So they cannot make a charge.
They think we live on store beef,
But no, I'm not a gander;
When a good fat stranger joins the mob,
"He'll do," says the overlander.

One day a squatter rode up.
Says he, "You're on my run;
I've got two boys as witnesses.
Consider your stock in pound."
I tried to coax, thence bounce him,
But my tin I had to squander,
For he put threepence a head
On the mob of the overlander.

28

The pretty girls in Brisbane
Were hanging out their duds.
I wished to have a chat with them,
So steered straight for the tubs.
Some dirty urchins saw me,
And soon they raised my dander,
Crying, "Mother, quick! take in the clothes,
Here comes an overlander!"

In town we drain the wine cup,
And go to see the play,
And never think to be hard up
For how to pass the day.
Each has a sweetheart there,
Dressed out in all her grandeur—
Dark eyes and jet black flowing hair.
"She's a plum," says the overlander.

ANON.

The Dying Stockman

A strapping young stockman lay dying,
His saddle supporting his head;
His two mates around him were crying,
As he rose on his elbow and said:

Chorus "Wrap me up with my stockwhip and blanket,
And bury me deep down below,
Where the dingoes and crows can't molest me,
In the shade where the coolibahs grow.

"Oh! had I the flight of the bronzewing,
Far o'er the plains would I fly,
Straight to the land of my childhood,
And there I would lay down and die.

"Then cut down a couple of saplings,
Place one at my head and my toe,
Carve on them cross, stockwhip, and saddle,
To show there's a stockman below.

"Hark! there's the wail of a dingo,
Watchful and weird—I must go,
For it tolls the death-knell of the stockman
From the gloom of the scrub down below.

"There's tea in the battered old billy;
Place the pannikins out in a row,
And we'll drink to the next merry meeting,
In the place where all good fellows go.

"And oft in the shades of the twilight,
When the soft winds are whispering low,
And the darkening shadows are falling,
Sometimes think of the stockman below."

ANON.

Bullocky Bill

As I came down Talbingo Hill
I heard a maiden cry,
"There's goes old Bill the Bullocky—
He's bound for Gundagai."

A better poor old beggar
Never cracked an honest crust,
A tougher poor old beggar
Never drug a whip through dust.

His team got bogged on the Five-mile Creek,
Bill lashed and swore and cried,
"If Nobbie don't get me out of this
I'll tattoo his bloody hide."

But Nobbie strained and broke the yoke
And poked out the leader's eye,
Then the dog sat on the tucker-box
Five miles from Gundagai.

ANON.

Click Go the Shears, Boys

Out on the board the old shearer stands,
Grasping his shears in his long, bony hands,
Fixed is his gaze on a bare-bellied "joe",
Glory if he gets her, won't he make the ringer go.

Chorus Click go the shears boys, click, click, click,
      Wide is his blow and his hands move quick,
      The ringer looks around and is beaten by a blow,
      And curses the old snagger with the blue-bellied
        "joe".

In the middle of the floor in his cane-bottomed chair
Is the boss of the board, with eyes everywhere;
Notes well each fleece as it comes to the screen,
Paying strict attention if it's taken off clean.

The colonial-experience man, he is there, of course,
With his shiny leggin's, just got off his horse,
Casting round his eye like a real connoisseur,
Whistling the old tune, "I'm the Perfect Lure".

Now Mister Newchum for to begin,
In number seven paddock bring all the sheep in;
Don't leave none behind, whatever you may do,
And then you'll be fit for a jackeroo.

The tar-boy is there, awaiting in demand,
With his blackened tar-pot, and his tarry hand;
Sees one old sheep with a cut upon his back,
Hears what he's waiting for, "Tar here, Jack!"

Shearing is all over and we've all got our cheques,
Roll up your swag for we're off on the tracks;
The first pub we come to, it's there we'll have a spree,
And everyone that comes along it's, "Come and drink with
    me!"

Down by the bar the old shearer stands,
Grasping his glass in his thin bony hands;
Fixed is his gaze on a green-painted keg,
Glory, he'll get down on it, ere he stirs a peg.

There we leave him standing, shouting for all hands,
Whilst all around him every "shouter" stands;
His eyes are on the cask, which is now lowering fast,
He works hard, he drinks hard, and goes to hell at last!

ANON.

The Banks of the Condamine

Oh, hark the dogs are barking, love,
I can no longer stay,
The men are all gone mustering
And it is nearly day.
And I must off by the morning light

Before the sun doth shine,
To meet the Sydney shearers
On the banks of the Condamine.

Oh Willie, dearest Willie,
I'll go along with you,
I'll cut off all my auburn fringe
And be a shearer, too,
I'll cook and count your tally, love,
While ringer-o you shine,
And I'll wash your greasy moleskins
On the banks of the Condamine.

Oh, Nancy, dearest Nancy,
With me you cannot go,
The squatters have given orders, love,
No woman should do so;
Your delicate constitution
Is not equal unto mine,
To stand the constant tigering
On the banks of the Condamine.

Oh Willie, dearest Willie,
Then stay back home with me,
We'll take up a selection
And a farmer's wife I'll be:
I'll help you husk the corn, love,
And cook your meals so fine
You'll forget the ram-stag mutton
On the banks of the Condamine.

Oh, Nancy, dearest Nancy,
Please do not hold me back,
Down there the boys are waiting,
And I must be on the track;

So here's a good-bye kiss, love,
Back home here I'll incline
When we've shore the last of the jumbucks
On the banks of the Condamine.

ANON.

On the Road to Gundagai

Oh, we started down from Roto when the sheds had all cut
out.
We'd whips and whips of rhino as we meant to push about,
So we humped our blues serenely and made for Sydney town,
With a three-spot cheque between us, as wanted knocking
down.

Chorus But we camped at Lazy Harry's, on the road to
Gundagai.
The road to Gundagai! Not five miles from Gun-
dagai!
Yes, we camped at Lazy Harry's, on the road to
Gundagai.

Well, we struck the Murrumbidgee near the Yanco in a week,
And passed through old Narrandera and crossed the Burnett
Creek.
And we never stopped at Wagga, for we'd Sydney in our
eye.
But we camped at Lazy Harry's, on the road to Gundagai.

Oh, I've seen a lot of girls, my boys, and drunk a lot of beer,
And I've met with some of both, chaps, as has left me mighty
queer;
But for beer to knock you sideways, and for girls to make
you sigh,
You must camp at Lazy Harry's, on the road to Gundagai.

Well, we chucked our blooming swags off, and we walked
    into the bar,
And we called for rum-an'-raspb'ry and a shilling each cigar.
But the girl that served the pizen, she winked at Bill and I—
And we camped at Lazy Harry's, not five miles from Gun-
    dagai.

In a week the spree was over and the cheque was all knocked
    down,
So we shouldered our Matildas, and we turned our back on
    town,
And the girls they stood a nobbler as we sadly said good-bye,
And we tramped from Lazy Harry's, not five miles from
    Gundagai;

Last chorus And we tramped from Lazy Harry's, not five
    miles from Gundagai.

ANON.

The Shearer's Song

Hurrah for the Lachlan,
Come join in my cheer,
For that's the place to make a cheque
At the end of the year,
When you reach a shady bend
Your trouble's at an end,
Campin' for the shearin'
In a cosy little bend.

Chorus With me four little johnny-cakes
        All nicely cooked,
        A nice little codfish
        Fresh from the 'ook,

Little round flour-bag
Sittin' on a stump,
Little tea and sugar-bag
Lookin' nice and plump.

I've a nice little gunyah,
And any amount of wood,
My nap is rather thin,
But my rig is pretty good;
I stand at my door
And gaze round with pride,
At the tall and lofty trees
Down by the river-side.

I've a nice piece of beef
And some murphies that I shook,
Half a loaf of brownie
That I snavelled from the cook,
A pound in my pocket
That I borrowed from a friend,
Which comes in very handy
When you're campin' on the bend.

I've some books and some songs,
And some papers for to read,
A spare pipe and matches
And a good supply of weed,
I envy not those squatters
As by the fire I sit
With me paper in me hand
And me old pipe lit.

I stroll down the river
And take a quiet smoke,
And if I feel inclined
I saddle up me moke,

Take a canter through the brigalow
Or gallop o'er the plain,
Stick a pig or shoot a turkey,
And back to camp again.

When the shearing-time commences
I'm in me glory then,
Pick a shed and see the Boss
And then secure a pen.
And when the roll is called,
And the time is drawing nigh,
Roll me drum, rake me cheque,
And quickly bid good-bye.

ANON.

Flash Jack from Gundagai

I've shore at Burrabogie, and I've shore at Toganmain,
I've shore at big Willandra and upon the old Coleraine,
But before the shearin' was over I've wished myself back
again
Shearin' for old Tom Patterson, on the One-Tree Plain.

Chorus All among the wool, boys,
Keep your wide blades full, boys,
I can do a respectable tally myself whenever I like to
try,
But they know me round the backblocks as Flash
Jack from Gundagai.

I've shore at big Willandra and I've shore at Tilberoo,
And once I drew my blades, my boys, upon the famed Barcoo,
At Cowan Downs and Trida, as far as Moulamein,
But I always was glad to get back again to the One-Tree
Plain.

37

F

I've pinked 'em with the Wolseleys and I've rushed with
    B-bows, too,
And shaved 'em in the grease, my boys, with the grass seed
    showing through.
But I never slummed my pen, my lads, whate'er it might
    contain,
While shearin' for old Tom Patterson on the One-Tree Plain.

I've been whalin' up the Lachlan, and I've dossed on Cooper's
    Creek,
And once I rung Cudjingie shed, and blued it in a week.
But when Gabriel blows his trumpet, lads, I'll catch the
    morning train,
And I'll push for old Tom Patterson's on the One-Tree Plain.

ANON.

Australia's on the Wallaby

Our fathers came to search for gold,
The mine has proved a duffer;
From bankers, boss and syndicate
We always had to suffer.
They fought for freedom for themselves,
Themselves and mates to toil,
But Australia's sons are weary
—And the billy's on the boil.

Chorus   Australia's on the wallaby,
        Just listen to the coo-ee;
        For the kangaroo, he rolls his swag
        And the emu shoulders bluey.
        The boomerangs are whizzing round,
        The dingo scratches gravel;
        The possum, bear and bandicoot

Are all upon the travel.
The cuckoo calls the bats and now
The pigeon and the shag,
The mallee-hen and platypus
Are rolling up their swag;
For the curlew sings a sad farewell
Beside the long lagoon,
And the brolga does his last-way waltz
To the lyrebird's mocking tune.

There's tiger-snakes and damper, boys,
And what's that on the coals?
There's droughts and floods and ragged duds
And dried-up waterholes;
There's shadeless trees and sun-scorched plains,
All asking us to toil;
But Australia's sons are weary
And the billy's on the boil.

ANON.

Me and My Dog

Me and my dog
    have tramped together
    in cold weather
      and hot.

Me and my dog
    don't care whether
    we get any work
      or not.

The Ramble-eer

The earth rolls on through empty space, its journey's never
    done,
It's entered for a starry race throughout the Kingdom Come.
And, as I am a bit of earth, I follow it because—
And I prove I am a rolling stone and never gather moss.

Chorus For I am a ramble-eer, a rollicking ramble-eer.
        I'm a roving rake of poverty and son of a gun for
        beer.

I've done a bit of fossicking for tucker and for gold;
I've been a menial rouseabout and a rollicking shearer bold,
I've "shanked" across the Old Man Plain, after busting up a
    cheque,
And "whipped the cat" once more again, though I haven't
    met it yet.

I've done a bit of droving of cattle and of sheep,
And I've done a bit of moving with "Matilda" for a mate;
Of fencing I have done my share, wool-scouring on the green;
Axemen, navvy—Old Nick can bear me out in what I haven't
    been.

I've worked the treadmill thresher, the scythe and reaping-
    hook,
Been wood-and-water fetcher for Mary Jane the cook;
I've done a few "cronk" things too, when I have struck a
    town,
There's few things I wouldn't do—but I never did lambing-
    down.

A. B. ("BANJO") PATERSON

1864-1941

Waltzing Matilda

Once a jolly swagman camped by a billabong
Under the shade of a coolibah tree;
And he sang, as he watched and waited while his billy boiled:
"Who'll come a-waltzing Matilda with me?"

Chorus Waltzing Matilda, Waltzing Matilda,
Who'll come a-waltzing Matilda with me?
And he sang as he watched and waited while his billy
  boiled:
"Who'll come a-waltzing Matilda with me?"

Down came a jumbuck to drink at that billabong,
Up jumped the swagman and grabbed him with glee;
And he sang as he shoved that jumbuck in his tucker-bag,
"You'll come a-waltzing Matilda with me!"

Chorus Waltzing Matilda, Waltzing Matilda,
You'll come a-waltzing Matilda with me;
And he sang as he shoved that jumbuck in his tucker-
  bag:
"You'll come a-waltzing Matilda with me!"

Up came the squatter, mounted on his thoroughbred,
Up came the troopers—one—two—three!
"Whose that jolly jumbuck you've got in your tucker-bag?
You'll come a-waltzing Matilda with me!"

Chorus Waltzing Matilda, Waltzing Matilda,
You'll come a-waltzing Matilda with me:
"Whose that jolly jumbuck you've got in your tucker-
  bag?
You'll come a-waltzing Matilda with me!"

41

Up jumped the swagman and sprang into the billabong,
"You'll never catch me alive!" said he,
And his ghost may be heard as you pass by that billabong,
"You'll come a-waltzing Matilda with me!"

Chorus Waltzing Matilda, Waltzing Matilda,
   You'll come a-waltzing Matilda with me!
   And his ghost may be heard as you pass by that
    billabong,
   "You'll come a-waltzing Matilda with me!"

II
THE COLONIAL AGE

WILLIAM CHARLES WENTWORTH

1790-1872

From *Australasia*

Land of my birth! though now, alas! no more
Musing I wonder on thy sea-girt shore,
Or climb with eager haste thy barrier cliff
To catch a glimmer of the distant skiff
That ever and anon breaks into light
And then again eludes the aching sight
Till nearer seen she bends her foaming way
Majestic onward to yon placid bay
Where Sydney's infant turrets proudly rise,
The new-born glory of the southern skies—
Dear Australasia, can I e'er forget
Thee, Mother Earth? Ah no, my heart e'en yet
With filial fondness loves to call to view
Scenes which, though oft remember'd, still are new.

. . . . . .

And shall I now, by Cam's old classic stream,
Forbear to sing, and thou proposed the theme?
The native bard, though on a foreign strand,
Shall I be mute, and see a stranger's hand
Attune the lyre, and prescient of thy fame
Foretell the glories that shall grace thy name?
Forbid it, all ye Nine! 'twere shame to thee,
My Austral parent—greater shame to me.

. . . . . .

Hail mighty ridge! that from thy azure brow
Survey'st these fertile plains, that stretch below,
And look'st with careless, unobservant eye
As round thy waist the forkèd lightnings ply
And the loud thunders spring with hoarse rebound
From peak to peak, and fill the welkin round
With deaf'ning voice, till with their boist'rous play
Fatigued in mutt'ring peals they stalk away;

45

Parent of this deep stream, this awful flood,
That at thy feet its tributary mud,
Like the famed Indian or Egyptian tide,
Doth pay, but direful scatters woe beside;
Vast Austral Giant of these rugged steeps,
Within those secret cells rich glitt'ring heaps
Thick piled are doom'd to sleep, till some one spy
The hidden key that opes the treasury:
How mute, how desolate thy stunted woods,
How dread thy chasms, where many an eagle broods,
How dark thy caves, how lone thy torrents' roar,
As down thy cliffs precipitous they pour,
Broke on our hearts, when first with vent'rous tread
We dared to rouse thee from thy mountain bed!
Till gain'd with toilsome step thy topmost heath,
We spied the cheering smokes ascend beneath,
And, as a meteor shoots athwart the night,
The boundless champaign burst upon our sight,
Till nearer seen the beauteous landscape grew,
Op'ning like Canaan on rapt Israel's view.

.   .   .   .   .   .

Ah! no 'tis slav'ry's badge, the felon's shame
That stills thy voice and clouds thy op'ning fame;
'Tis this that makes thy sorrowing Judah weep,
Restrains her song, and hangs her harp to sleep.
Land of my hope! soon may this early blot,
Amid thy growing honours, be forgot;
Soon may a freeman's soul, a freeman's blade,
Nerve ev'ry arm, and gleam thro' ev'ry glade;
Nor more the outcast convicts' clanking chains
Deform thy wilds, and stigmatize thy plains.
And tho' the fathers—these—of thy new race,
From whom each glorious feat, each deathless grace,
Must yet proceed, by whom each radiant gem

Be won—to deck thy future diadem—
Did not of old th' Imperial Eagle rise,
Unfurl his pinions, and astound the skies?
Hatch'd in an aerie fouler far than thine,
Did he not dart from Tiber to the Rhine?

. . . . . .

Celestial poesy! whose genial sway
Earth's furthest habitable shores obey;
Whose inspirations shed their sacred light
Far as the regions of the arctic night,
And to the Laplander his Boreal gleam
Endear not less than Phœbus' brighter beam—
Descend thou also on my native land
And on some mountain summit take thy stand;
Thence issuing soon a purer fount be seen,
Than charm'd Castalia or famed Hippocrene;
And there a richer, nobler fane arise
Than on Parnassus met th' adoring eyes.
And though, bright goddess, on those far blue hills
That pour their thousand swift pellucid rills
Where Warragumba's rage has rent in twain
Opposing mountains, thund'ring to the plain,
No child of song has yet invoked thy aid
'Neath their primeval solitary shade—
Still, gracious pow'r, some kindling soul inspire,
To wake to life my country's unknown lyre,
That from creation's date has slumb'ring lain,
Or only breathed some savage uncouth strain;
And grant that yet an Austral Milton's song
Pactolus-like flow deep and rich along;
An Austral Shakspere rise, whose living page
To Nature true may charm in ev'ry age;
And that an Austral Pindar daring soar
Where not the Theban Eagle reach'd before.

47

And, O Britannia! shouldst thou cease to ride
Despotic Empress of old Ocean's tide;
Should thy tamed Lion—spent his former might—
No longer roar the terror of the fight;
Should e'er arrive that dark disastrous hour
When bow'd by luxury, thou yield'st to pow'r;
When thou, no longer freest of the free,
To some proud victor bend'st the vanquish'd knee—
May all thy glories in another sphere
Relume, and shine more brightly still than here;
May this, thy last-born infant, then arise,
To glad thy heart and greet thy parent eyes;
And Australasia float, with flag unfurl'd,
A new Britannia in another world.

ROBERT LOWE

1811-1892

Songs of the Squatters
No. I

The Commissioner bet me a pony—I won;
So he cut off exactly two-thirds of my run;
For he said I was making a fortune too fast,
And profit gained slower the longer would last.

He remarked, as devouring my mutton he sat,
That I suffered my sheep to grow sadly too fat;
That they wasted waste land, did prerogative brown,
And rebelliously nibbled the droits of the Crown;

That the creek that divided my station in two
Showed that Nature designed that two fees should be due.
Mr Riddle assured me 'twas paid but for show;
But he kept it and spent it; that's all that I know.

The Commissioner fined me because I forgot
To return an old ewe that was ill of the rot
And a poor wry-necked lamb that we kept for a pet;
And he said it was treason such things to forget.

The Commissioner pounded my cattle because
They had mumbled the scrub with their famishing jaws
On the part of the run he had taken away;
And he sold them by auction the costs to defray.

The Border Police they were out all the day
To look for some thieves who had ransacked my dray;
But the thieves they continued in quiet and peace,
For they'd robbed it themselves—had the Border Police!

When the white thieves had left me the black thieves
        appeared,
My shepherds they waddied, my cattle they speared;
But for fear of my licence I said not a word,
For I knew it was gone if the Government heard.

The Commissioner's bosom with anger was filled
Against me because my poor shepherd was killed;
So he straight took away the last third of my run,
And got it transferred in the name of his son.

The son had from Cambridge been lately expelled,
And his licence for preaching most justly withheld.
But this is no cause, the Commissioner says,
Why he should not be fit for a licence to graze.

The cattle that had not been sold at the pound
He took with the run at five shillings all round;
And the sheep the blacks left me at sixpence a head—
"A very good price," the Commissioner said.

The Governor told me I justly was served,
That Commissioners never from duty had swerved;
But that if I'd a fancy for any more land
For one pound an acre he'd plenty on hand.

I'm not very proud! I can dig in a bog,
Feed pigs, or for firewood can split up a log,
Clean shoes, riddle cinders, or help to boil down—
Or whatever you please, but graze lands of the Crown.

WILLIAM FORSTER

1818-1882

From *The Devil and the Governor*

DEVIL.   In New South Wales, as I plainly see,
You're carving out plentiful jobs for me.
But forgive me for hinting your zeal is such
That I'm only afraid you'll do too much.
I know this well—To subject mankind
You must tickle before you attempt to bind!
Nor lay on his shoulder the yoke until
Through his habits you've first enslaved his will.
You're too violent far—you rush too madly
At your favourite ends and spoil them sadly.
Already, I warn you, your system totters,
They're a nest of hornets these rascally Squatters,
Especially when you would grasp their cash—
Excuse me, George, but I think you're rash.

GOVERNOR.   Rash! d—n it, rash!

DEVIL.   . . . . Don't fly in a passion,
In the higher circles 'tis not the fashion;
And swearing, besides, you must allow,
Is neither polite nor useful now.

50

GOVERNOR. Would you have me forego the rights of the
        Crown,
        To be laughed at all over this factious town?
        I'll teach these Squatters to pay their rent,
        And don't care one rush for their discontent;
        They've abused me in print, they've made orations,
        They've their papers and pastoral associations;
        To England they've sent their vile petitions—
        They've their Agents in swarms like heathen mis-
        sions;
        They've gone to the length of caricaturing—
        But I'll show them the evil's past their curing.

DEVIL. Come, come, be cool or your aim you'll miss,
        Your temper's too hot for work like this;
        This people I say will submit the more readily
        If you've only the wit to grind them steadily.
        You've a snug little tyranny under your thumb—
        But manage it well, or down 'twill come.
        'Twere a pity to peril this rich possession
        By a foolish rashness or indiscretion;
        Wentworth and Windeyer are troublesome chaps,
        And the Council's a thorn in your side, perhaps;
        But let them grumble and growl their fill,
        You know very well their power is nil. . . .
        Then calmly proceed, and with prudence act;
        "In the middle lies safety"—that's a fact—
        Subdue by degrees, and slowly oppress,
        Or, I tell you, you'll get yourself into a mess.
        While people petition, they'll find it "a sell"
        But don't push them too hard, they might rebel.

GOVERNOR. Rebel! ha! ha! you're surely in joke;
        Rebellion here—a mere puff of smoke.
        What would the people of England say
        A rebellion! how queer! in Botany Bay!

Pick-pockets, swindlers, thieves, and jobbers,
Cut-throats, and burglars, and highway robbers—
A mob that escaped the gallows at home
'Tis worse than "the servile wars at Rome"!
A handful of troops would put them down,
And the higher classes would join the Crown.

DEVIL. It might be so, but just mark, my friend—
Who come to be losers in the end?
No doubt there'd be fun well worth enjoying—
Burning, and plundering, and destroying;
Fighting for towns not worth disputing—
Skirmishing, robbing, and rifle-shooting
From bushes and trees, and rocks for barriers—
Murdering of post boys and plundering of car-
    riers,
Storming of camp by midnight entries
Driving off horses, and popping off sentries—
Seizing of stock for purposes royal,
Pressing of men to make them loyal;
Some heroes might fall in that petty strife,
Whom bondage had taught a contempt of life,
Some patriots leading in civil storms,
Might dangle on gibbets their martyr forms
Or exiled afar, to return no more,
Might bury their bones on a foreign shore,
Proscribed by the tyrants they dared to brave
And mocked by the people they fought to save;
But not in vain would they bear or bleed,
This land would have gained what most they
    need.
John Bull from his drowsy indifference waking,
Would give some of you despots a terrible shak-
    ing;
You'd be robbed of your berth and your repu-
    tation,

52

For causing your masters so much vexation—
And the people your chains so closely bind,
A tardy justice would seek and find.
Take my advice, I offer it cheap—
Why, as I live, the man's asleep!
George, George, your manners much want re-
        forming,
But I'll give your nose a bit of a warming.
[*Tweaks his nose and vanishes.*]

CHARLES HARPUR

1813-1868

A Midsummer Noon in the Australian Forest

Not a sound disturbs the air,
There is quiet everywhere;
Over plains and over woods
What a mighty stillness broods!

All the birds and insects keep
Where the coolest shadows sleep;
Even the busy ants are found
Resting in their pebbled mound;
Even the locust clingeth now
Silent to the barky bough:
Over hills and over plains
Quiet, vast and slumbrous, reigns.

Only there's a drowsy humming
From yon warm lagoon slow coming:
'Tis the dragon-hornet—see!
All bedaubed resplendently,
Yellow on a tawny ground—
Each rich spot nor square nor round,
Rudely heart-shaped, as it were

53

The blurred and hasty impress there
Of a vermeil-crusted seal
Dusted o'er with golden meal.
Only there's a droning where
Yon bright beetle shines in air,
Tracks it in its gleaming flight
With a slanting beam of light,
Rising in the sunshine higher,
Till its shards flame out like fire.

Every other thing is still,
Save the ever-wakeful rill,
Whose cool murmur only throws
Cooler comfort round repose;
Or some ripple in the sea
Of leafy boughs, where, lazily,
Tired summer, in her bower
Turning with the noontide hour,
Heaves a slumbrous breath ere she
Once more slumbers peacefully.

O 'tis easeful here to lie
Hidden from noon's scorching eye,
In this grassy cool recess
Musing thus of quietness.

Words

Words are deeds. The words we hear
May revolutionize or rear
A mighty state. The words we read
May be a spiritual deed
Excelling any fleshly one,
As much as the celestial sun

Transcends a bonfire, made to throw
A light upon some raree-show.
A simple proverb tagged with rhyme
May colour half the course of time;
The pregnant saying of a sage
May influence every coming age;
A song in its effects may be
More glorious than Thermopylae,
And many a lay that schoolboys scan
A nobler feat than Inkerman.

From *The Creek of the Four Graves*

A settler in the olden times went forth
With four of his most bold and trusted men
Into the wilderness—went forth to seek
New streams and wider pastures for his fast
Increasing flocks and herds. O'er mountain routes
And over wild wolds clouded up with brush,
And cut with marshes perilously deep,
So went they forth at dawn; at eve the sun,
That rose behind them as they journeyed out,
Was firing with his nether rim a range
Of unknown mountains that like ramparts towered
Full in their front; and his last glances fell
Into the gloomy forest's eastern glades
In golden gleams, like to the Angel's sword,
And flashed upon the windings of a creek
That noiseless ran betwixt the pioneers
And those new Apennines—ran, shaded o'er
With boughs of the wild willow, hanging mixed
From either bank, or duskily befringed
With upward tapering feathery swamp-oaks,
The sylvan eyelash always of remote

Australian waters, whether gleaming still
In lake or pool, or bickering along
Between the marges of some eager stream.

Before them, thus extended, wilder grew
The scene each moment and more beautiful;
For when the sun was all but sunk below
Those barrier mountains, in the breeze that o'er
Their rough enormous backs deep-fleeced with wood
Came whispering down, the wide up-slanting sea
Of fanning leaves in the descending rays
Danced dazzlingly, tingling as if the trees
Thrilled to the roots for very happiness.

From *The Tower of the Dream*

Yes, wonderful are dreams: and I have known
Many most wild and strange. And once, long since,
As in the death-like mystery of sleep
My body lay impalled, my soul arose
And journeyed outward in a wondrous dream.
In the mid-hour of a dark night, methought
I roamed the margin of a waveless lake,
That in the knotted forehead of the land
Deep sunken, like a huge Cyclopean eye,
Lidless and void of speculation, stared
Glassily up—for ever sleepless—up
At the wide vault of heaven; and vaguely came
Into my mind a mystic consciousness
That over against me, on the farther shore
Which yet I might not see, there stood a tower.

The darkness darkened, until overhead
Solidly black the starless heaven domed,

And earth was one wide blot; when, as I looked,
A light swung blazing from the tower (as yet
Prophesied only in my inner thought)
And brought at once its rounded structure forth
Massive and tall out of the mighty gloom.
On the broad lake that streaming radiance fell,
Through the lit fluid like a shaft of fire,
Burning its sullen depths with one red blaze.

Love Sonnets, VIII

Fair as the night, when all the astral fires
Of heaven are burning in the clear expanse,
My love is; and her eyes like star-depths glance
Lustrous with glowing thoughts and pure desires,
And that mysterious pathos which inspires
All moods divine in mortal passion's trance—
All that its earthly music doth enhance
As with the rapture of seraphic lyres!
I gaze upon her till the atmosphere
Sweetens intensely, and to my charmèd sight
All fair associated forms appear
Swimming in joy, as swim yon orbs in light. . . .
And all sweet sounds, though common, to mine ear
Chime up like silver-wingèd dreams in flight.

From *The Temple of Infamy*
[satirizing W. C. Wentworth and Robert Lowe]

But hark! What hubbub now is this that comes
Straight for the portal? Oaths and threats, like bombs
Exploding, tell that in full force and feather
March the Squattocracy, with their bell-wether!
Even thus, insane of hope, the Prince of Evil
Marshalled his luckless followers—to the Devil!

First come the Magnates—mark their Leader, he,
The would-be Tell of the Fraternity!
His state is that, so infamously sad,
When Talent hath through selfishness run mad.
In his well-masked displays of by-gone years,
With democratic wrath he tore the ears
Of Sydney's wealthy groundlings, being then
Thwarted and snubbed by Darling's party-men!
But now behold him in his native hue,
The bullying, bellowing champion of the Few!
A Patriot?—he who hath not sense nor heed
Of public ends beyond his own mere need!
Whose country's ruin, to his public fear,
Means only this—the loss of Windermere!
And by the same self-legislative rule,
Australia's growth the growth of W--tw--th's wool!
Her rights, her liberties, for number *one*,
A universal ten-pound right of Run!
A Patriot?—he from whose stastic care
All that his Country's general homes should bear
Of mind and happiness, is thrust by that
Which by some process may be turned to fat,
And, duly barrelled and exported, then
Return in *wine* for grazier *gentlemen*!

Such is yon Man! and not a whit belied!
A patriot? Let him "doff that lion's hide"!
Well may these landsharks call him their prime Gem,
For bound thus to himself, he's bound to *them*.

And who, said I, is he that pace for pace
Strains at his side with emulative face?

A rival champion, Truth replied; of shame
Equally reckless, and his ends the same.

A Scribe whose hackneyed head, and callous heart,
Can play, indifferently, a counter part.
Who through all human principles can run,
Unfixing any, and regarding none,
Save such indeed, as for the time may guide
The prurient instincts of his legal pride.
Who for his *turn*, uncaring which, would hoist
The Standard of the Bible or the Zoist!
And thus accomplished, now would sell his soul
To be the *first* name on his Faction's roll.

GEORGE GORDON McRAE

1833-1927

From *Mâmba the Bright-eyed*

The day had fled, the moon arose,
Night straight began with evening's close—
A night whose calm and silvery sheen
Befitted well the wild yapeen.
Within the circle of the camp
Blazed the clear fire, while measured tramp
Of dancing warriors shook the ground,
To song and time-sticks' throbbing sound.
There twice two hundred feet advanced,
There twice a hundred malkas glanced
Bright in the moon, that silvered o'er
The arms that all those malkas bore.
Wild the device, and strange the sign
That stared in many a snowy line
From beaming face and heaving breast,
And limbs that seldom paused to rest;
Whilst all the rib-like lines laid on
Made each man seem a skeleton.
Nodded the feathers from the red

And netted band that bound each head,
And hoarsely rustling leaves of trees
Shook round dark ankles in the breeze.
The singers with their time-sticks rang
The cadence of the song they sang;
And every face and limb below,
And tree above them, caught the glow
That spread from camp-fire's rising blaze,
Lighting the yapeen's wondrous maze
Of feet and ankles in the dance
With fitful gleam or twinkling glance.

Conspicuous 'mid the dancing crowd,
Whose ranks alternate swayed and bowed,
Shone Mâmba, tricked with wild design,
And symbol traced in waving line;
No limbs more active wore the green
At yon great Ghim-boboke yapeen;
And no two arms more graceful there
In circling motion cleft the air
Than his—and his the eagle-eye
Inspiring all the minstrelsy.
The young and old in groups around,
Drank in the sight, the joy, the sound.
And Mâmba's form throughout the dance
Attracted every wondering glance.

ADAM LINDSAY GORDON

1833-1870

The Sick Stockrider

Hold hard, Ned! Lift me down once more, and lay me in
the shade.
Old man, you've had your work cut out to guide
Both horses, and to hold me in the saddle when I swayed,
All through the hot, slow, sleepy, silent ride.

The dawn at Moorabinda was a mist-wrack dull and dense;
The sunrise was a sullen, sluggish lamp;
I was dozing in the gateway at Arbuthnot's boundary fence;
I was dreaming on the Limestone cattle camp.

We crossed the creek at Carricksford and, sharply through
    the haze,
And suddenly, the sun shot flaming forth:
To southward lay Katâwa, with the sand-peaks all ablaze,
And the flushed fields of Glen Lomond lay to north.

Now westward winds the bridle-path that leads to Lindis-
    farm,
And yonder looms the double-headed Bluff:
From the far side of the first hill, when the skies are clear
    and calm,
You can see Sylvester's woolshed fair enough.

Five miles we used to call it from our homestead to the place
Where the big tree spans the roadway like an arch;
'Twas here we ran the dingo down that gave us such a chase
Eight years ago—or was it nine?—last March.

'Twas merry in the glowing morn, among the gleaming grass,
To wander as we've wandered many a mile,
And blow the cool tobacco cloud and watch the white wreaths
    pass,
Sitting loosely in the saddle all the while.

'Twas merry 'mid the backwoods, when we spied the station
    roofs,
To wheel the wild scrub cattle at the yard,
With a running fire of stockwhips and a fiery run of hoofs
—Oh, the hardest day was never then too hard!

Ay, we had a glorious gallop after Starlight and his gang
When they bolted from Sylvester's on the flat!
How the sun-dried reed-beds crackled, how the flint-strewn
    ranges rang
To the strokes of Mountaineer and Acrobat!

Hard behind them in the timber—harder still across the
    heath—
Close beside them through the tea-tree scrub we dashed;
And the golden-tinted fern leaves, how they rustled under-
    neath,
And the honeysuckle osiers, how they crashed!

We led the hunt throughout, Ned, on the chestnut and the
    grey,
And the troopers were three hundred yards behind
While we emptied our six-shooters on the bushrangers at bay
In the creek, with stunted box-tree for a blind.

There you grappled with the leader, man to man and horse
    to horse,
And you rolled together when the chestnut reared:
He blazed away and missed you in that shallow water-
    course—
A narrow shave!—his powder singed your beard.

In these hours when life is ebbing, how those days when life
    was young
Come back to us! how clearly I recall
Even the yarns Jack Hall invented, and the songs Jem Roper
    sung
—And where are now Jem Roper and Jack Hall?

Ay, nearly all our comrades of the old colonial school,
Our ancient boon companions, Ned, are gone:

Hard livers for the most part! somewhat reckless as a rule!—
It seems that you and I are left alone.

There was Hughes, who got in trouble through that business
    with the cards—
It matters little what became of him;
But a steer ripped up MacPherson in the Cooraminta yards
And Sullivan was drowned at Sink-or-Swim.

And Mostyn—poor Frank Mostyn!—died at last a fearful
    wreck,
In the horrors at the Upper Wandinong;
And Carisbrooke, the rider, at the Horsefall broke his neck—
Faith, the wonder was he saved his neck so long!

Ah, those days and nights we squandered at the Logans'
    in the glen!
The Logans, man and wife, have long been dead:
Elsie's tallest girl seems taller than your "little Elsie" then
And Ethel is a woman grown and wed.

I've had my share of pastime, and I've done my share of toil,
And life is short—the longest life a span:
I care not now to tarry for the corn or for the oil,
Or for the wine that maketh glad the heart of man.

For good undone, and gifts misspent, and resolutions vain
'Tis somewhat late to trouble: this I know—
I should live the same life over, if I had to live again;
And the chances are I go where most men go.

The deep blue skies wax dusky, and the tall green trees grow
    dim,
The sward beneath me seems to heave and fall;
And sickly, smoky shadows through the sleepy sunlight swim
And on the very sun's face weave their pall.

Let me slumber in the hollow where the wattle blossoms
    wave,
With never stone or rail to fence my bed:
Should the sturdy station children pull the bush flowers on
    my grave
I may chance to hear them romping overhead.

A Dedication

They are rhymes rudely strung with intent less
    Of sound than of words,
In lands where bright blossoms are scentless,
    And songless bright birds;
Where, with fire and fierce drought on her tresses,
Insatiable Summer oppresses
Sere woodlands and sad wildernesses
    And faint flocks and herds.

Where in dreariest days, when all dews end,
    And all winds are warm,
Wild Winter's large flood-gates are loosened,
    And floods, freed by storm,
From broken-up fountain-heads, dash on
Dry deserts with long pent-up passion—
Here rhyme was first framed without fashion,
    Song shaped without form.

Whence gathered?—The locust's glad chirrup
    May furnish a stave;
The ring of a rowel and stirrup,
    The wash of a wave;
The chant of the marsh-frog in rushes,
That chimes through the pauses and hushes
Of nightfall, the torrent that gushes,
    The tempests that rave.

In the deepening of dawn, when it dapples
   The dusk of the sky,
With streaks like the reddening of apples,
   The ripening of rye,
To eastward, when cluster by cluster,
Dim stars and dull planets that muster,
Wax wan in a world of white lustre
   That spreads far and high;

In the gathering of night-gloom o'erhead, in
   The still silent change,
All fire-flushed when forest trees redden
   On slopes of the range;
When the gnarled, knotted trunks Eucalyptian
Seem carved like weird columns Egyptian,
With curious device, quaint inscription,
   And hieroglyph strange;

In the Spring, when the wattle-gold trembles
   'Twixt shadow and shine,
When each dew-laden air-draught resembles
   A long draught of wine;
When the sky-line's blue burnished resistance
Makes deeper the dreamiest distance
Some song in all hearts hath existence—
   Such songs have been mine.

From *The Rhyme of Joyous Garde*

We were glad together in gladsome meads,
When they shook to the strokes of our snorting steeds;
   We were joyful in joyous lustre
When it flush'd the coppice or fill'd the glade,
Where the horn of the Dane or the Saxon bray'd,

65

And we saw the heathen banner display'd
    And the heathen lances cluster.

Then a steel-shod rush and a steel-clad ring,
And a crash of the spear staves splintering,
    And the billowy battle blended,
Riot of charges, revel of blows,
And fierce flush'd faces of fighting foes,
From croup to bridle, that reel'd and rose,
    In a sparkle of sword-play splendid.

And the long, lithe sword in the hand became
As a leaping light, as a falling flame,
    As a fire through the flax that hasted;
Slender, and shining, and beautiful,
How it shore through shivering casque and skull,
And never a stroke was void and null,
    And never a thrust was wasted.

I have done for ever with all these things—
Deeds that were joyous to knights and kings,
    In days that with songs were cherish'd.
The songs are ended, the deeds are done,
There shall none of them gladden me now, not one;
There is nothing good for me under the sun,
    But to perish as these things perish'd.

BRUNTON STEPHENS

1835-1902

The Dominion of Australia
(A FORECAST, 1877)

She is not yet; but he whose ear
Thrills to that finer atmosphere
Where footfalls of appointed things,
Reverberant of days to be,

Are heard in forecast echoings,
Like wave-beats from a viewless sea,
Hears in the voiceful tremors of the sky
Auroral heralds whispering, "She is nigh."

She is not yet; but he whose sight
Foreknows the advent of the light,
Whose soul to morning radiance turns
Ere night her curtain hath withdrawn,
And in its quivering folds discerns
The mute monitions of the dawn,
With urgent sense strained onward to descry
Her distant tokens, starts to find Her nigh.

Not yet her day. How long "not yet"? . . .
There comes the flush of violet!
And heavenward faces, all aflame
With sanguine imminence of morn,
Wait but the sunkiss to proclaim
The Day of The Dominion born.
Prelusive baptism!—ere the natal hour
Named with the name and prophecy of power.

Already here to hearts intense,
A spirit-force, transcending sense,
In heights unscaled, in deeps unstirred,
Beneath the calm, above the storm,
She waits the incorporating word
To bid her tremble into form.
Already, like divining-rods, men's souls
Bend down to where the unseen river rolls;

For even as, from sight concealed,
By never flush of dawn revealed,

67

Nor e'er illumed by golden noon,
Nor sunset-streaked with crimson bar,
Nor silver-spanned by wake of moon,
Nor visited of any star,
Beneath these lands a river waits to bless
(So men divine) our utmost wilderness—

Rolls dark, but yet shall know our skies,
Soon as the wisdom of the wise
Conspires with nature to disclose
The blessing prisoned and unseen,
Till round our lessening wastes there glows
A perfect zone of broadening green,
Till all our land, Australia Felix called,
Become one Continent-Isle of Emerald;

So flows beneath our good and ill
A viewless stream of Common Will,
A gathering force, a present might,
That from its silent depths of gloom
At Wisdom's voice shall leap to light
And hide our barren feuds in bloom,
Till, all our sundering lines with love o'ergrown,
Our bounds shall be the girdling seas alone.

My Other Chinee Cook

Yes, I got another Johnny; but he was to Number One
As a Satyr to Hyperion, as a rushlight to the sun;
He was lazy, he was cheeky, he was dirty, he was sly,
But he had a single virtue, and its name was rabbit pie.

Now those who say the bush is dull are not so far astray,
For the neutral tints of station life are anything but gay;
But with all its uneventfulness, I solemnly deny
That the bush is unendurable along with rabbit pie.

68

We had fixed one day to sack him, and agreed to moot the
    point
When my lad should bring our usual regale of cindered joint,
But instead of cindered joint we saw and smelt, my wife and
    I,
Such a lovely, such a beautiful, oh! such a rabbit pie!

There was quite a new expression on his lemon-coloured face,
And the unexpected odour won him temporary grace,
For we tacitly postponed the sacking-point till by-and-by,
And we tacitly said nothing save the one word, "rabbit pie!"

I had learned that pleasant mystery should simply be endured,
And forebore to ask of Johnny where the rabbits were pro-
    cured!
I had learnt from Number One to stand aloof from how
    and why,
And I threw myself upon the simple fact of rabbit pie.

And when the pie was opened, what a picture did we see!
They lay in beauty side by side, they filled our home with
    glee!
How excellent, how succulent, back, neck, and leg, and thigh!
What a noble gift is manhood! What a trust is rabbit pie!

For a week this thing continued, rabbit pie from day to day;
Though where he got the rabbits John would ne'er vouchsafe
    to say;
But we never seemed to tire of them, and daily could descry
Subtle shades of new delight in each successive rabbit pie.

Sunday came; by rabbit reckoning, the seventh day of the
    week;
We had dined, we sat in silence, both our hearts(?) too full
    to speak,

H

When in walks Cousin George, and, with a sniff, says he, "Oh my!
What a savoury suggestion! What a smell of rabbit pie!"

"Oh, why so late, George?" says my wife, "the rabbit pie is gone;
But you *must* have one for tea, though. Ring the bell, my dear, for John."
So I rang the bell for John, to whom my wife did signify,
"Let us have an early tea, John, and another rabbit pie."

But John seemed taken quite aback, and shook his funny head,
And uttered words I comprehended no more than the dead;
"Go, do as you are bid," I cried, "we wait for no reply;
Go! let us have tea early, and another rabbit pie!"

Oh, that I had stopped his answer! But it came out with a run:
"Last-a week-a plenty puppy; this-a week-a puppy done!"
Just then my wife, my love, my life, the apple of mine eye,
Was seized with what seemed mal-de-mer—"sick transit" rabbit pie!

And George! By George, he laughed, and then he howled like any bear!
The while my wife contorted like a mad "convulsionnaire";
And I—I rushed on Johnny, and I smote him hip and thigh,
And I never saw him more, nor tasted more of rabbit pie.

And the childless mothers met me, as I kicked him from the door,
With loud maternal wailings and anathemas galore;
I must part with pretty Tiny, I must part with little Fly,
For I'm sure they know the story of the so-called "rabbit pie".

Orara

The strong sob of the chafing stream
  That seaward fights its way
Down crags of glitter, dells of gleam,
  Is in the hills to-day.

But, far and faint, a grey-winged form
  Hangs where the wild lights wane—
The phantom of a bygone storm,
  A ghost of wind and rain.

The soft white feet of afternoon
  Are on the shining meads,
The breeze is as a pleasant tune
  Amongst the happy reeds.

The fierce, disastrous, flying fire,
  That made the great caves ring,
And scarred the slope, and broke the spire,
  Is a forgotten thing.

The air is full of mellow sounds,
  The wet hill-heads are bright,
And down the fall of fragrant grounds
  The deep ways flame with light.

A rose-red space of stream I see,
  Past banks of tender fern;
A radiant brook, unknown to me
  Beyond its upper turn.

The singing silver life I hear,
  Whose home is in the green
Far-folded woods of fountains clear,
  Where I have never been.

Ah, brook above the upper bend,
　I often long to stand
Where you in soft, cool shades descend
　From the untrodden land!

Ah, folded woods, that hide the grace
　Of moss and torrents strong,
I often wish to know the face
　Of that which sings your song!

But I may linger, long, and look
　Till night is over all:
My eyes will never see the brook,
　Or sweet, strange waterfall.

The world is round me with its heat,
　And toil, and cares that tire;
I cannot with my feeble feet
　Climb after my desire.

But, on the lap of lands unseen,
　Within a secret zone,
There shine diviner gold and green
　Than man has ever known.

And where the silver waters sing
　Down hushed and holy dells,
The flower of a celestial Spring,
　A tenfold splendour, dwells.

Yea, in my dream of fall and brook
　By far sweet forests furled,
I see that light for which I look
　In vain through all the world—

The glory of a larger sky
   On slopes of hills sublime,
That speak with God and morning, high
   Above the ways of Time!

Ah! haply, in this sphere of change
   Where shadows spoil the beam,
It would not do to climb that range
   And test my radiant Dream.

The slightest glimpse of yonder place,
   Untrodden and alone,
Might wholly kill that nameless grace,
   The charm of the unknown.

And therefore, though I look and long,
   Perhaps the lot is bright
Which keeps the river of the song
   A beauty out of sight.

Bell-birds

By channels of coolness the echoes are calling,
And down the dim gorges I hear the creek falling;
It lives in the mountain, where moss and the sedges
Touch with their beauty the banks and the ledges;
Through brakes of the cedar and sycamore bowers
Struggles the light that is love to the flowers.
And, softer than slumber, and sweeter than singing,
The notes of the bell-birds are running and ringing.

The silver-voiced bell-birds, the darlings of day-time,
They sing in September their songs of the May-time.
When shadows wax strong, and the thunder-bolts hurtle,
They hide with their fear in the leaves of the myrtle;

When rain and the sunbeams shine mingled together
They start up like fairies that follow fair weather,
And straightway the hues of their feathers unfolden
Are the green and the purple, the blue and the golden.

October, the maiden of bright yellow tresses,
Loiters for love in these cool wildernesses;
Loiters knee-deep in the grasses to listen,
Where dripping rocks gleam and the leafy pools glisten.
Then is the time when the water-moons splendid
Break with their gold, and are scattered or blended
Over the creeks, till the woodlands have warning
Of songs of the bell-bird and wings of the morning.

Welcome as waters unkissed by the summers
Are the voices of bell-birds to thirsty far-comers.
When fiery December sets foot in the forest,
And the need of the wayfarer presses the sorest,
Pent in the ridges for ever and ever,
The bell-birds direct him to spring and to river,
With ring and with ripple, like runnels whose torrents
Are toned by the pebbles and leaves in the currents.

Often I sit, looking back to a childhood
Mixt with the sights and the sounds of the wildwood,
Longing for power and the sweetness to fashion
Lyrics with beats like the heart-beats of passion—
Songs interwoven of lights and of laughters
Borrowed from bell-birds in far forest rafters;
So I might keep in the city and alleys
The beauty and strength of the deep mountain valleys,
Charming to slumber the pain of my losses
With glimpses of creeks and a vision of mosses.

74

September in Australia

Grey winter hath gone, like a wearisome guest,
  And, behold, for repayment,
September comes in with the wind of the West
  And the Spring in her raiment!
The ways of the frost have been filled of the flowers,
  While the forest discovers
Wild wings, with a halo of hyaline hours,
  And the music of lovers.

September, the maid with the swift, silver feet!
  She glides, and she graces
The valleys of coolness, the slopes of the heat,
  With her blossomy traces;
Sweet month, with a mouth that is made of a rose,
  She lightens and lingers
In spots where the harp of the evening glows,
  Attuned by her fingers.

. . . . .

High places that knew of the gold and the white
  On the forehead of Morning
Now darken and quake, and the steps of the Night
  Are heavy with warning.
Her voice in the distance is lofty and loud
  Through the echoing gorges;
She hath hidden her eyes in a mantle of cloud,
  And her feet in the surges.
On the tops of the hills, on the turreted cones—
  Chief temples of thunder—
The gale, like a ghost, in the middle watch moans,
  Gliding over and under.

The sea, flying white through the rack and the rain,
 Leapeth wild at the forelands;
And the plover, whose cry is like passion with pain,
 Complains in the moorlands.

Oh, season of changes—of shadow and shine—
 September the splendid!
My song hath no music to mingle with thine,
 And its burden is ended;
But thou, being born of the winds and the sun,
 By mountain, by river,
Mayst lighten and listen, and loiter and run,
 With thy voices for ever!

Beyond Kerguelen

Down in the South, by the waste without sail on it,
Far from the zone of the blossom and tree,
Lieth, with winter and whirlwind and wail on it,
Ghost of a land by the ghost of a sea.
Weird is the mist from the summit to base of it;
Sun of its heaven is wizened and grey;
Phantom of life is the light on the face of it,
Never is night on it, never is day!
Here is the shore without flower or bird on it;
Here is no litany sweet of the springs,
Only the haughty, harsh thunder is heard on it,
Only the storm, with the roar in its wings!

Shadow of moon is the moon in the sky of it,
Wan as the face of a wizard, and far!
Never there shines from the firmament high of it
Grace of the planet or glory of star.
All the year round, in the place of white days on it,
All the year round where there never is night,

Lies a great sinister, bitter, blind haze on it:
Growth that is neither of darkness nor light!
Wild is the cry of the sea in the caves by it,
Sea that is smitten by spears of the snow;
Desolate songs are the songs of the waves by it,
Down in the South, where the ships never go.

Storm from the Pole is the singer that sings to it
Hymns of the land at the planet's grey verge.
Thunder discloses dark, wonderful things to it,
Thunder and rain, and the dolorous surge.
Hills with no hope of a wing or a leaf on them,
Scarred with the chronicles written by flame,
Stare, through the gloom of inscrutable grief on them,
Down on the horns of the gulfs without name.
Cliffs, with the records of fierce flying fires on them
Loom over perilous pits of eclipse;
Alps, with anathema stamped in the spires on them—
Out by the wave with a curse on its lips.

Never is sign of soft, beautiful green on it,
Never the colour, the glory of rose;
Neither the fountain nor river is seen on it,
Naked its crags are, and barren its snows!
Blue as the face of the drowned is the shore of it—
Shore, with the capes of indefinite cave.
Strange is the voice of its wind, and the roar of it
Startles the mountain and hushes the wave.
Out to the South and away to the north of it,
Spectral and sad are the spaces untold!
All the year round a great cry goeth forth of it,
Sob of this leper of lands in the cold.

No man hath stood, all its bleak, bitter years on it,
Fall of a foot on its wastes is unknown:
Only the sound of the hurricane's spears on it

77

Breaks with the shout from the uttermost zone.
Blind are its bays with the shadow of bale on them;
Storms of the nadir their rocks have uphurled;
Earthquake hath registered deeply its tale on them,
Tale of distress from the dawn of the world!
There are the gaps, with the surges that seeth in them—
Gaps in whose jaws is a menace that glares;
There the wan reefs, with the merciless teeth in them,
Gleam on a chaos that startles and scares.

Back in the dawn of this beautiful sphere, on it—
Land of the dolorous, desolate face—
Beamed the blue day; and the bountiful year on it
Fostered the leaf and the blossom of grace.
Grand were the lights of its midsummer noon on it,
Mornings of majesty shone on its seas;
Glitter of star and the glory of moon on it
Fell, in the march of the musical breeze.
Valleys and hills, with the whisper of wing in them,
Dells of the daffodil—spaces impearled—
Flowered and flashed with the splendour of Spring in them
Back in the morn of this wonderful world.

Soft were the words that the thunder then said to it,
Said to this lustre of emerald plain;
Sun brought the yellow, the green, and the red to it—
Sweet were the songs of its silvery rain.
Voices of water and wind in the bays of it
Lingered, and lulled like the psalm of a dream.
Fair were the nights and effulgent the days of it,
Moon was in shadow and shade in the beam.
Summer's chief throne was the marvellous coast of it,
Home of the Spring was its luminous lea:
Garden of glitter! but only the ghost of it
Moans in the South by the ghost of a sea.

The Last of His Tribe

He crouches, and buries his face on his knees,
And hides in the dark of his hair;
For he cannot look up to the storm-smitten trees,
Or think of the loneliness there—
Of the loss and the loneliness there.

The wallaroos grope through the tufts of the grass,
And turn to their coverts for fear;
But he sits in the ashes and lets them pass
Where the boomerangs sleep with the spear—
With the nullah, the sling, and the spear.

Uloola, behold him! The thunder that breaks
On the tops of the rocks with the rain,
And the wind which drives up with the salt of the lakes,
Have made him a hunter again—
A hunter and fisher again.

For his eyes have been full with a smouldering thought;
But he dreams of the hunts of yore,
And of foes that he sought, and of fights that he fought
With those who will battle no more—
Who will go to the battle no more.

It is well that the water which tumbles and fills
Goes moaning and moaning along;
For an echo rolls out from the sides of the hills,
And he starts at a wonderful song—
At the sound of a wonderful song.

And he sees through the rents of the scattering fogs
The corroboree warlike and grim,
And the lubra who sat by the fire on the logs,

79

To watch, like a mourner, for him—
Like a mother and mourner for him.

Will he go in his sleep from these desolate lands,
Like a chief, to the rest of his race,
With the honey-voiced woman who beckons and stands,
And gleams like a dream in his face—
Like a marvellous dream in his face?

Jim the Splitter

The bard who is singing of Wollombi Jim
Is hardly just now in the requisite trim
    To sit on his Pegasus fairly;
Besides, he is bluntly informed by the Muse
That Jim is a subject no singer should choose;
    For Jim is poetical rarely. . . .

You mustn't, however, adjudge him in haste,
Because a red robber is more to his taste
    Than Ruskin, Rossetti, or Dante!
You see he was bred in a bangalow wood
And bangalow pith was the principal food
    His mother served out in her shanty.

His knowledge is this—he can tell in the dark
What timber will split, by the feel of the bark;
    And, rough as his manner of speech is,
His wits to the fore he can readily bring
In passing off ash as the genuine thing,
    When scarce in the forest the beech is.

In girthing a tree that he sells in the round,
He assumes as a rule that its body is sound,
    And measures—*forgetting to bark it!*

He may be a ninny; but still the old dog
Can plug to perfection the pipe of a log
    And palm it away on the market.

He splits a fair shingle; but holds to the rule
Of his father's, and haply his grandfather's, school—
    Which means that he never has blundered,
When tying his shingles, by slinging in more
Than the recognized number of ninety and four,
    To the bundle he sells for a hundred!

When asked by the market for ironbark red,
It always occurs to the Wollombi head
    To do a "mahogany" swindle.
In forests where never the ironbark grew,
When Jim is at work, it would flabbergast you
    To see how the "ironbarks" dwindle!

He can stick to the saddle can Wollombi Jim;
And when a buckjumper dispenses with him
    The leather goes off with the rider.
And, as to a team, over gully and hill
He can travel with twelve on the breadth of a quill,
    And boss the unlucky offsider.

He shines at his best at the tiller of saw,
On the top of the pit, where his whisper is law
    To the gentlemen working below him.
When the pair of them pause in a circle of dust,
Like a monarch he poses exalted, august—
    There's nothing this planet can show him!

1844-1926

Faith

And is the great cause lost beyond recall?
Have all the hopes of ages come to naught?
Is life no more with noble meaning fraught?
Is life but death, and love its funeral pall?
Maybe. And still on bended knees I fall,
Filled with a faith no preacher ever taught.
O God—*my* God—by no false prophet wrought—
I believe still, in despite of it all!

Let go the myths and creeds of groping men.
This clay knows nought—the Potter understands.
I own that Power divine beyond my ken,
And still can leave me in His shaping hands.
But, O my God, that madest me to feel,
Forgive the anguish of the turning wheel!

From *On Australian Hills*

Oh, to be there to-night!
To see that rose of sunset flame and fade
On ghostly mountain height,
The soft dusk gathering each leaf and blade
From the departing light,
Each tree-fern feather of the wildwood glade.

From arid streets to pass
Down those green aisles where golden wattles bloom,
Over the fragrant grass,
And smell the eucalyptus in a gloom
That is as clear as glass,
The dew-fresh scents of bracken and of broom. . . .

These city glamours mute,
To hear the woodland necromancers play
    Each his enchanted lute;
That dear bird-laugh, so exquisitely gay,
    The magpie's silver flute
In vesper carol to the dying day.

    To hear the live wind blow,
The delicate stir and whisper of the trees
    As light breaths come and go,
The brooklet murmuring to the vagrant breeze,
    The bull-frog twanging low
His deep-toned mandolin to chime with these.

    And then the whispering rills,
The hushed lone wheel, or hoof, or axeman's tool;
    The brooding dark that stills
The sweet Pan-piping of the grove and pool;
    The dimly glimmering hills;
The sleeping night, so heavenly clean and cool.

    Oh, for that mother-breast
That takes the broken spirit for repair,
    The worn-out brain for rest—
That healing silence, that untainted air,
    That Peace of God . . . Blest, blest
The very memory that I once was there.

    The thought that someday yet,
In flesh, not dreams, I may return again,
    And at those altars, set
In the pure skies, above the smoky plain,
    Remember and forget
The joy of living and its price of pain . . .

That sullied earth reserves
Such spacious refuge virgin and apart,
That wasting life preserves
Such sweet retreat for the distracted heart,
Such fount of strength for nerves
Torn in the ruthless struggle of the mart . . .

That Government divine
O'er all this reek of blunders and of woes
Keeps an unravaged shrine
Not here, not there, but in the souls of those
Who neither weep nor whine,
But trust the guidance of the One Who Knows.

MARY HANNAY FOOTT

1846-1918

Where the Pelican Builds

The horses were ready, the rails were down,
But the riders lingered still—
One had a parting word to say,
And one had his pipe to fill.
Then they mounted, one with a granted prayer,
And one with a grief unguessed.
"We are going," they said as they rode away,
"Where the pelican builds her nest!"

They had told us of pastures wide and green,
To be sought past the sunset's glow;
Of rifts in the ranges by opal lit;
And gold 'neath the river's flow.
And thirst and hunger were banished words
When they spoke of that unknown West;
No drought they dreaded, no flood they feared,
Where the pelican builds her nest!

84

The creek at the ford was but fetlock deep
When we watched them crossing there;
The rains have replenished it thrice since then,
And thrice has the rock lain bare.
But the waters of Hope have flowed and fled,
And never from blue hill's breast
Come back—by the sun and the sands devoured—
Where the pelican builds her nest.

III

BUSH BALLADS AND POPULAR VERSE

THOMAS E. SPENCER

1845-1910

How McDougal Topped the Score

A peaceful spot is Piper's Flat. The folk that live around—
They keep themselves by keeping sheep and turning up the
    ground;
But the climate is erratic, and the consequences are
The struggle with the elements is everlasting war.
We plough, and sow, and harrow—then sit down and pray
    for rain;
And then we all get flooded out and have to start again.
But the folk are now rejoicing as they ne'er rejoiced before,
For we've played Molongo cricket, and McDougal topped
    the score!

Molongo had a head on it, and challenged us to play
A single-innings match for lunch—the losing team to pay.
We were not great guns at cricket, but we couldn't well say
    no,
So we all began to practise, and we let the reaping go.
We scoured the Flat for ten miles round to muster up our
    men,
But when the list was totalled we could only number ten.
Then up spoke big Tim Brady: he was always slow to speak,
And he said—"What price McDougal, who lives down at
    Cooper's Creek?"

So we sent for old McDougal, and he stated in reply
That he'd never played at cricket, but he'd half a mind to try.
He couldn't come to practise—he was getting in his hay,
But he guessed he'd show the beggars from Molongo how to
    play.
Now, McDougal was a Scotchman, and a canny one at that,
So he started in to practise with a paling for a bat.

89

He got Mrs Mac to bowl to him, but she couldn't run at all,
So he trained his sheep-dog, Pincher, how to scout and fetch
the ball.

Now, Pincher was no puppy; he was old, and worn, and
grey;
But he understood McDougal, and—accustomed to obey—
When McDougal cried out "Fetch it!" he would fetch it in
a trice,
But, until the word was "Drop it!" he would grip it like a
vice.
And each succeeding night they played until the light grew
dim:
Sometimes McDougal struck the ball—sometimes the ball
struck him.
Each time he struck, the ball would plough a furrow in the
ground;
And when he missed, the impetus would turn him three
times round.

The fatal day at length arrived—the day that was to see
Molongo bite the dust, or Piper's Flat knocked up a tree!
Molongo's captain won the toss, and sent his men to bat,
And they gave some leather-hunting to the men of Piper's
Flat.
When the ball sped where McDougal stood, firm planted in
his track,
He shut his eyes, and turned him round, and stopped it—
with his back!
The highest score was twenty-two, the total sixty-six,
When Brady sent a yorker down that scattered Johnson's
sticks.

Then Piper's Flat went in to bat, for glory and renown,
But, like the grass before the scythe, our wickets tumbled
down.

"Nine wickets down for seventeen, with fifty more to win!"
Our captain heaved a heavy sigh, and sent McDougal in.
"Ten pounds to one you'll lose it!" cried a barracker from
    town;
But McDougal said, "I'll tak' it, mon!" and planked the
    money down.
Then he girded up his moleskins in a self-reliant style,
Threw off his hat and boots and faced the bowler with a
    smile.

He held the bat the wrong side out, and Johnson with a
    grin
Stepped lightly to the bowling crease, and sent a "wobbler"
    in;
McDougal spooned it softly back, and Johnson waited there,
But McDougal, crying *"Fetch it!"* started running like a hare.
Molongo shouted "Victory! He's out as sure as eggs,"
When Pincher started through the crowd, and ran through
    Johnson's legs.
He seized the ball like lightning; then he ran behind a log,
And McDougal kept on running, while Molongo chased the
    dog!

They chased him up, they chased him down, they chased him
    round, and then
He darted through the slip-rail as the scorer shouted "Ten!"
McDougal puffed; Molongo swore; excitement was intense;
As the scorer marked down twenty, Pincher cleared a barbed-
    wire fence.
"Let us head him!" shrieked Molongo. "Brain the mongrel
    with a bat!"
"Run it out! Good old McDougal!" yelled the men of Piper's
    Flat.

And McDougal kept on jogging, and then Pincher doubled
  back,
And the scorer counted *"Forty"* as they raced across the track.

McDougal's legs were going fast, Molongo's breath was
  gone—
But still Molongo chased the dog—McDougal struggled on.
When the scorer shouted *"Fifty"* then they knew the chase
  could cease;
And McDougal gasped out *"Drop it!"* as he dropped within
  his crease.
Then Pincher dropped the ball, and as instinctively he knew
Discretion was the wiser plan, he disappeared from view;
And as Molongo's beaten men exhausted lay around
We raised McDougal shoulder-high, and bore him from the
  ground.

We bore him to McGinniss's, where lunch was ready laid,
And filled him up with whisky-punch, for which Molongo
  paid.
We drank his health in bumpers and we cheered him three
  times three,
And when Molongo got its breath Molongo joined the spree.
And the critics say they never saw a cricket match like that,
When McDougal broke the record in the game at Piper's
  Flat;
And the folk are jubilating as they never did before;
For we played Molongo cricket—and McDougal topped the
  score!

G. H. GIBSON ("IRONBARK")

1846-1921

My Mate Bill

Jimmy the Hut-keeper speaks:

That's his saddle across the tie-beam, an' them's his spurs up
    there
On the wall-plate over yonder: you kin see's they ain't a pair.
The daddy of all the stockmen as ever come musterin' here—
Killed in the flamin' mallee, yardin' a scrub-bred steer!

They say as he's gone to heaven, an' shook off his worldly
    cares,
But I can't sight Bill in a halo set up on three blinded hairs.
In heaven! What next, I wonder, for, strike me pink an' blue
If I savvy what in thunder they'll find for Bill to do!

He'd never make one o' them angels with faces as white as
    chalk,
All wool to the toes, like hoggets, an' wings like a eagle'awk:
He couldn't 'arp for apples—his voice 'ad tones as jarred,
An' he'd no more ear than a bald-faced bull, or calves in a
    brandin'-yard.

He could sit on a buckin' brumby like a nob in an easy chair
An' chop his name with a green-hide fall on the flank of a
    flyin' steer;
He could show the saints in glory the way that a fall should
    drop,
But, sit on a throne!—not William—unless they could make
    it prop.

If the heavenly hosts get boxed now, as mobs most always
    will,
Why, who'd cut 'em out like William, or draft on the camp
    like Bill?

93

An 'orseman 'd find it awkward, at first, with a push that
    flew;
But blame my cats if I knows what else they'll find for Bill
    to do!

He mightn't freeze to the seraphs, or chum with the
    cherubim,
But if ever them seraph-johnnies get pokin' it, like, at him—
Well, if there's hide in heaven, an' silk for to make a lash,
He'll yard the lot in the Jasper Lake in a blinded lightnin'-
    flash!

It's hard if there ain't no cattle, but perhaps they'll let him
    sleep,
An' wake him up at the Judgment for to draft them goats an'
    sheep:
It's playin' it low on William, but perhaps he'll buckle-to,
Just to show them high-toned seraphs what a mallee-man can
    do.

If they saddles a big-boned angel, with a turn o' speed, of
    course,
As can spiel like a four-year brumby an' prop like an old
    camp-horse—
If they puts Bill up with a snaffle, an' a four or five-inch spur,
An' eighteen foot o' green-hide for to chop the blinded fur,
He'll draft them blamed Angoras in a way, it's safe to swear,
As'll make them toney seraphs sit back on their thrones an'
    stare!

94

A Ballad of Queensland (Sam Holt)

"Over-landing" Jim apostrophizeth his quondam mate, who hath made his pile, and gone home:

Oh! don't you remember black Alice, Sam Holt,
Black Alice so dusky and dark—
That Warrego gin with the straw through her nose,
And teeth like a Moreton Bay shark?
The villainous sheep-wash tobacco she smoked
In the gunyah down there by the lake;
The grubs that she gathered, the lizards she stewed,
And the damper you taught her to bake?

Oh! don't you remember the moon's silver sheen
On the Warrego sand-ridges white?
And don't you remember the scorpions and things
We found in our blankets at night?
The wild trailing creepers, the bush buds, Sam Holt,
That scattered their fragrance around;
And, don't you remember that chest-foundered colt
You sold me and swore he was sound?

They say you've ten thousand per annum, Sam Holt,
In England, a park, and a drag,
And perhaps you've forgot you were six months ago
In Queensland a-humping your swag.
Who'd think, now, to see you a-dinin' in state
With lords, and the devil knows who,
You were "flashin' your dover" six short months ago
In a lambin' camp on the Paroo?

Say, don't you remember that fiver, Sam Holt,
You borrowed so frank and so free,
When the publicans landed your fifty-pound cheque
In Tambo, your very last spree?

Luck changes some natures, and yours, Sammy Holt,
'Ain't a grand one as ever I see,
And I guess I may whistle a good many tunes
'Fore you'll think of that fiver, or me.

Oh! don't you remember the cattle you duffed,
And yer luck at the Sandy Creek rush,
The poker you played, and the bluffs that you bluffed
And yer habit of holdin' a flush?
Perhaps you've forgotten the pasting you got
From the Micks down at Callaghan's store,
When Pat Flanagan found a fifth ace in his hand,
And you'd raised him his pile upon four!

You weren't quite the cleanly potato, Sam Holt,
And you hadn't the cleanest of fins;
But you lifted your pile at the Towers, Sam Holt,
And that covers most of your sins.
When's my turn a-comin'? Well, never, perhaps,
And it's likely enough yer old mate
'll be humping his drum on the Warrego banks
To the end of the chapter of Fate.

JAMES L. CUTHBERTSON

1851-1910

A Racing Eight

Who knows it not, who loves it not,
The long and steady swing,
The instant dip, the iron grip,
The rowlocks' linkèd ring,
The arrowy sway of hands away,
The slider oiling aft,
The forward sweep, the backward leap
That speed the flying craft?

A racing eight of perfect mould,
True to the builder's law,
That takes the water's gleaming gold
Without a single flaw.
A ship deep, resonant within,
Harmonious to the core,
That vibrates to her polished skin
The tune of wave and oar.

A racing eight and no man late,
And all hearts in the boat;
The men who work and never shirk,
Who long to be afloat.
The crew who burn from stem to stern
To win the foremost place,
The crew to row, the boat to go,
The eight to win the race.

W. T. GOODGE

1862-1909

Daley's Dorg Wattle

"You can talk about yer sheep dorgs," said the man from
    Allan's Creek,
"But I know a dorg that simply knocked 'em bandy!—
Do whatever you would show him, and you'd hardly need to
    speak;
Owned by Daley, drover cove in Jackandandy.

"We was talkin' in the parlour, me and Daley, quiet like,
When a blow-fly starts a-buzzin' round the ceilin',
Up gets Daley, and he says to me, 'You wait a minute, Mike,
And I'll show you what a dorg he is at heelin'.'

97

"And an empty pickle-bottle was a-standin' on the shelf,
Daley takes it down and puts it on the table,
And he bets me drinks that blinded dorg would do it by
    himself—
And I didn't think as how he was able!

"Well, he shows the dorg the bottle, and he points up to the
    fly,
And he shuts the door, and says to him—'Now Wattle!'
And in less than fifteen seconds, spare me days, it ain't a lie,
That there dorg had got that inseck in the bottle."

A. B. ("BANJO") PATERSON

1864-1941

The Man from Snowy River

There was movement at the station, for the word had passed
    around
That the colt from old Regret had got away,
And had joined the wild bush horses—he was worth a thous-
    and pound,
So all the cracks had gathered to the fray.
All the tried and noted riders from the stations near and far
Had mustered at the homestead overnight,
For the bushmen love hard riding where the wild bush
    horses are,
And the stock-horse snuffs the battle with delight.

There was Harrison, who made his pile when Pardon won
    the cup,
The old man with his hair as white as snow;
But few could ride beside him when his blood was fairly up—
He would go wherever horse and man could go.

And Clancy of the Overflow came down to lend a hand,
No better horseman ever held the reins;
For never horse could throw him while the saddle-girths
    would stand—
He learnt to ride while droving on the plains.

And one was there, a stripling on a small and weedy beast;
He was something like a racehorse undersized,
With a touch of Timor pony—three parts thoroughbred at
    least—
And such as are by mountain horsemen prized.
He was hard and tough and wiry—just the sort that won't
    say die—
There was courage in his quick impatient tread;
And he bore the badge of gameness in his bright and fiery
    eye,
And the proud and lofty carriage of his head.

But still so slight and weedy, one would doubt his power to
    stay,
And the old man said, "That horse will never do
For a long and tiring gallop—lad, you'd better stop away,
Those hills are far too rough for such as you."
So he waited, sad and wistful—only Clancy stood his friend—
"I think we ought to let him come," he said;
"I warrant he'll be with us when he's wanted at the end,
For both his horse and he are mountain bred.

"He hails from Snowy River, up by Kosciusko's side,
Where the hills are twice as steep and twice as rough;
Where a horse's hoofs strike firelight from the flint-stones
    every stride,
The man that holds his own is good enough.

And the Snowy River riders on the mountains make their
    home,
Where the river runs those giant hills between;
I have seen full many a horseman since I first commenced to
    roam,
But nowhere yet such horsemen have I seen."

So he went; they found the horses by the big mimosa clump,
They raced away towards the mountain's brow,
And the old man gave his orders, "Boys, go at them from
    the jump,
No use to try for fancy riding now.
And, Clancy, you must wheel them, try and wheel them to
    the right.
Ride boldly, lad, and never fear the spills,
For never yet was rider that could keep the mob in sight,
If once they gain the shelter of those hills."

So Clancy rode to wheel them—he was racing on the wing
Where the best and boldest riders take their place,
And he raced his stock-horse past them, and he made the
    ranges ring
With the stockwhip, as he met them face to face.
Then they halted for a moment, while he swung the dreaded
    lash,
But they saw their well-loved mountain full in view,
And they charged beneath the stockwhip with a sharp and
    sudden dash,
And off into the mountain scrub they flew.

Then fast the horsemen followed, where the gorges deep and
    black
Resounded to the thunder of their tread,
And the stockwhips woke the echoes, and they fiercely
    answered back

From cliffs and crags that beetled overhead.
And upward, ever upward, the wild horses held their way,
Where mountain ash and kurrajong grew wide;
And the old man muttered fiercely, "We may bid the mob
good-day,
No man can hold them down the other side."

When they reached the mountain's summit, even Clancy
took a pull—
It well might make the boldest hold their breath;
The wild hop scrub grew thickly, and the hidden ground was
full
Of wombat holes, and any slip was death.
But the man from Snowy River let the pony have his head,
And he swung his stockwhip round and gave a cheer,
And he raced him down the mountain like a torrent down its
bed
While the others stood and watched in very fear.

He sent the flint-stones flying, but the pony kept his feet,
He cleared the fallen timber in his stride,
And the man from Snowy River never shifted in his seat—
It was grand to see that mountain horseman ride.
Through the stringybarks and saplings, on the rough and
broken ground,
Down the hillside at a racing pace he went;
And he never drew the bridle till he landed safe and sound
At the bottom of that terrible descent.

He was right among the horses as they climbed the farther
hill,
And the watchers on the mountain, standing mute,
Saw him ply the stockwhip fiercely; he was right among
them still,
As he raced across the clearing in pursuit.

K

Then they lost him for a moment, where two mountain
    gullies met
In the ranges—but a final glimpse reveals
On a dim and distant hillside the wild horses racing yet,
With the man from Snowy River at their heels.

And he ran them single-handed till their sides were white
    with foam;
He followed like a bloodhound on their track,
Till they halted, cowed and beaten; then he turned their
    heads for home,
And alone and unassisted brought them back.
But his hardy mountain pony he could scarcely raise a trot,
He was blood from hip to shoulder from the spur;
But his pluck was still undaunted, and his courage fiery hot,
For never yet was mountain horse a cur.

And down by Kosciusko, where the pine-clad ridges raise
Their torn and rugged battlements on high,
Where the air is clear as crystal, and the white stars fairly
    blaze
At midnight in the cold and frosty sky,
And where around the Overflow the reed-beds sweep and
    sway
To the breezes, and the rolling plains are wide,
The Man from Snowy River is a household word today,
And the stockmen tell the story of his ride.

The Man from Ironbark

It was the man from Ironbark who struck the Sydney town,
He wandered over street and park, he wandered up and
    down,
He loitered here, he loitered there, till he was like to drop,
Until at last in sheer despair he sought a barber's shop.

" 'Ere! shave my beard and whiskers off, I'll be a man of
mark,
I'll go and do the Sydney toff up home in Ironbark."

The barber man was small and flash, as barbers mostly are,
He wore a strike-your-fancy sash, he smoked a huge cigar:
He was a humorist of note and keen at repartee,
He laid the odds and kept a "tote", whatever that may be,
And when he saw our friend arrive, he whispered "Here's a
lark!
Just watch me catch him all alive, this man from Ironbark."

There were some gilded youths that sat along the barber's
wall.
Their eyes were dull, their heads were flat, they had no brains
at all;
To them the barber passed the wink, his dexter eyelid shut,
"I'll make this bloomin' yokel think his bloomin' throat is
cut."
And as he soaped and rubbed it in he made a rude remark:
"I s'pose the flats is pretty green up there in Ironbark."

A grunt was all reply he got; he shaved the bushman's chin,
Then made the water boiling hot and dipped the razor in.
He raised his hand, his brow grew black, he paused awhile to
gloat,
Then slashed the red-hot razor-back across his victim's throat;
Upon the newly-shaven skin it made a livid mark—
No doubt it fairly took him in—the man from Ironbark.

He fetched a wild up-country yell might wake the dead to
hear,
And though his throat, he knew full well, was cut from ear
to ear,

He struggled gamely to his feet, and faced the murderous
    foe:
"You've done for me! you dog, I'm beat! one hit before I go
I only wish I had a knife, you blessed murderous shark!
But you'll remember all your life the man from Ironbark."

He lifted up his hairy paw, with one tremendous clout
He landed on the barber's jaw, and knocked the barber out.
He set to work with tooth and nail, he made the place a
    wreck;
He grabbed the nearest gilded youth, and tried to break his
    neck.
And all the while his throat he held to save his vital spark,
And "Murder! Bloody murder!" yelled the man from Iron-
    bark.

A peeler man who heard the din came in to see the show;
He tried to run the bushman in, but he refused to go.
And when at last the barber spoke, and said, " 'Twas all in
    fun—
'Twas just a little harmless joke, a trifle overdone."
"A joke!" he cried. "By George, that's fine; a lively sort of
    lark;
I'd like to catch that murdering swine some night in Iron-
    bark."

And now while round the shearing floor the listening shearers
    gape,
He tells the story o'er and o'er, and brags of his escape.
"Them barber chaps what keeps a tote, by George, I've had
    enough,
One tried to cut my bloomin' throat, but thank the Lord it's
    tough."
And whether he's believed or not, there's one thing to remark,
That flowing beards are all the go way up in Ironbark.

A Bush Christening

On the outer Barcoo where the churches are few,
And men of religion are scanty,
On a road never cross'd 'cept by folk that are lost
One Michael Magee had a shanty.

Now this Mike was the dad of a ten-year-old lad,
Plump, healthy, and stoutly conditioned;
He was strong as the best, but poor Mike had no rest
For the youngster had never been christened.

And his wife used to cry, "If the darlin' should die
Saint Peter would not recognize him."
But by luck he survived till a preacher arrived,
Who agreed straightaway to baptize him.

Now the artful young rogue, while they held their collogue,
With his ear to the keyhole was listenin';
And he muttered in fright, while his features turned white,
"What the divil and all is this christenin'?"

He was none of your dolts—he had seen them brand colts,
And it seemed to his small understanding,
If the man in the frock made him one of the flock,
It must mean something very like branding.

So away with a rush he set off for the bush,
While the tears in his eyelids they glistened—
" 'Tis outrageous," says he, "to brand youngsters like me;
I'll be dashed if I'll stop to be christened!"

Like a young native dog he ran into a log,
And his father with language uncivil,
Never heeding the "praste", cried aloud in his haste
"Come out and be christened, you divil!"

But he lay there as snug as a bug in a rug,
And his parents in vain might reprove him,
Till His Reverence spoke (he was fond of a joke)
"I've a notion," says he, "that'll move him.

"Poke a stick up the log, give the spalpeen a prog;
Poke him aisy—don't hurt him or maim him;
'Tis not long that he'll stand, I've the water at hand,
As he rushes out this end I'll name him.

"Here he comes, and for shame! ye've forgotten the name—
Is it Patsy or Michael or Dinnis?"
Here the youngster ran out, and the priest gave a shout—
"Take your chance, anyhow, wid 'Maginnis'!"

As the howling young cub ran away to the scrub
Where he knew that pursuit would be risky,
The priest, as he fled, flung a flask at his head
That was labelled "Maginnis's Whisky!"

And Maginnis Magee has been made a J.P.,
And the one thing he hates more than sin is
To be asked by the folk, who have heard of the joke,
How he came to be christened Maginnis!

A Bushman's Song

I'm travellin' down the Castlereagh, and I'm a station-hand,
I'm handy with the ropin' pole, I'm handy with the brand,
And I can ride a rowdy colt, or swing the axe all day,
But there's no demand for a station-hand along the Castle-
    reagh.

So it's shift, boys, shift, for there isn't the slightest doubt
That we've got to make a shift to the stations further out,
With the packhorse runnin' after, for he follows like a dog,
We must strike across the country at the old jig-jog.

This old black horse I'm riding—if you'll notice what's his
    brand,
He wears the crooked R, you see—none better in the land.
He takes a lot of beatin', and the other day we tried,
For a bit of a joke, with a racing bloke, for twenty pounds a
    side.

It was shift, boys, shift, for there wasn't the slightest doubt
That I had to make him shift, for the money was further out;
But he cantered home a winner, with the other one at the
    flog—
He's a red-hot sort to pick up with his old jig-jog.

I asked a cove for shearin' once along the Marthaguy:
"We shear non-union here," says he. "I call it scab," says I.
I looked along the shearin' floor before I turned to go—
There were eight or ten dashed Chinamen a-shearin' in a row.

It was shift, boys, shift, for there wasn't the slightest doubt
It was time to make a shift with the leprosy about.
So I saddled up my horses, and I whistled to my dog,
And I left his scabby station at the old jig-jog.

I went to Illawarra, where my brother's got a farm;
He has to ask his landlord's leave before he lifts his arm;
The landlord owns the countryside—man, woman, dog, and
    cat,
They haven't the cheek to dare to speak without they touch
    their hat.

It was shift, boys, shift, for there wasn't the slightest doubt
Their little landlord god and I would soon have fallen out;
Was I to touch my hat to him?—was I his bloomin' dog?
So I makes for up the country at the old jig-jog.

Clancy of the Overflow

I had written him a letter which I had, for want of better
Knowledge, sent to where I met him down the Lachlan,
    years ago;
He was shearing when I knew him, so I sent the letter to
    him,
Just on spec, addressed as follows, "Clancy, of The Overflow."

And an answer came directed in a writing unexpected
(And I think the same was written with a thumbnail dipped
    in tar);
'Twas his shearing mate who wrote it, and *verbatim* I will
    quote it:
"Clancy's gone to Queensland droving, and we don't know
    where he are."

.   .   .   .

In my wild erratic fancy visions come to me of Clancy
Gone a-drovin "down the Cooper" where the Western drovers
    go;
As the stock are slowly stringing, Clancy rides behind them
    singing,
For the drover's life has pleasures that the townsfolk never
    know.

And the bush has friends to meet him, and their kindly
    voices greet him
In the murmur of the breezes and the river on its bars,
And he sees the vision splendid of the sunlit plains extended,
And at night the wondrous glory of the everlasting stars.

.   .   .   .

I am sitting in my dingy little office, where a stingy
Ray of sunlight struggles feebly down between the houses
    tall,

And the foetid air and gritty of the dusty, dirty city,
Through the open window floating, spreads its foulness over
  all.

And in place of lowing cattle, I can hear the fiendish rattle
Of the tramways and the 'buses making hurry down the
  street;
And the language uninviting of the gutter children fighting
Comes fitfully and faintly through the ceaseless tramp of feet.

And the hurrying people daunt me, and their pallid faces
  haunt me
As they shoulder one another in their rush and nervous haste,
With their eager eyes and greedy, and their stunted forms
  and weedy,
For townsfolk have no time to grow, they have no time to
  waste.

And I somehow rather fancy that I'd like to change with
  Clancy,
Like to take a turn at droving where the seasons come and
  go,
While he faced the round eternal of the cash-book and the
  journal—
But I doubt he'd suit the office, Clancy, of The Overflow.

CHARLES H. SOUTER

1864-1944

What the Red-haired Bo'sun Said

"Give me the salt spray in my face
And the sea wind in my hair;
A piping gale from the sou'-sou'-west,
And a ship bound anywhere!
With the phosphor-bells in the churning wake,
And the dancing clouds o'erhead,

And I wouldn't call the Queen my aunt!"
As the red-haired bo'sun said.

"Give me the smell of the Stockholm tar
From the serving on the shrouds,
And the rolling swell of the southern sea,
'Neath the madly racing clouds,
With a pint of rum, and a Gouda cheese,
And a pipe of negrohead,
And I wouldn't call the King my dad!"
As the red-haired bo'sun said.

"Give me a bunk in the fo'c'sle head
On the lee side as we go,
And the bilge-wash for a lullaby,
When it comes my watch below!
Give me a hammock and a good round shot,
When my span of life is sped,
And fifty fathoms of clean blue sea!"
As the red-haired bo'sun said.

After Johnson's Dance

After Johnson's dance—
Don't you recollect?
I says, "Goin' 'ome?"
You says, "I expect!"
I says, "So am I!"
You says, "Not with me!"
I says, "An' for w'y?"
Blowed if I could see!
You says, "Go to France!"
After Johnson's dance.

After Johnson's dance—
I says, "Em, you *might*!"
"*Might* I though?" says you,
"G'arn, you silly fright!"
Then I kissed you, fair—
(How you *did* object!)
Tousled all your hair;
Don't you recollect?
Took my bloomin' chance
After Johnson's dance!

After Johnson's dance—
Smacked my face, you did!
Then I caught you—so!—
Like you was a kid.
"Just do that again—
Just you *do*," you says.
You says, "Do it!" plain:
An' of course, I *does*!
Who made *that* advance—
After Johnson's dance?

Irish Lords

The clover-burr was two feet high, and the billabongs were
full,
The brolgas danced a minuet, and the world seemed made
of wool!
The nights were never wearisome, and the days were never
slow,
When first we came to Irish Lords, on the road to Ivanhoe.

The rime was on the barley-grass as we passed the homestead rails,
A Darling jackass piped us in, with his trills and turns and
scales,

And youth and health and carelessness sat on the saddlebow,
And—Mary lived at Irish Lords, on the road to Ivanhoe.

On every hand was loveliness, and the Fates were fair and
    kind;
We drank the very wine of life, and we never looked behind;
And Mary! Mary everywhere went flitting to and fro
When first we came to Irish Lords, on the road to Ivanhoe.

. . . .

The window of her dainty bower, where the golden banksia
    grew,
Stared like a dead man's glazing eye, and the roof had fallen
    through.
No violets in her garden bed, and her voice—hushed, long
    ago!
When last we camped at Irish Lords, on the road to Ivanhoe.

Old John Bax

When Old John Bax drove the mail to Coonabarabran,
His reins were made of raw-hide, his lash of kangaroo;
He'd four grey walers in his old brown shandrydan,
And we all set our watches when the coach-horn blew!

Chorus "Tan-tan-ta-ra, boys! Here comes the mail,
            Rolling down the cleared line, sun, rain, or hail!
            Rocking up the main street, as hard as she can go!"
            When Old John Bax drove the coach for Cobb and
            Co.

When Old John Bax brought his horses to a standstill
(Chuck the ribbons over, and the whip along the roof!)
His team was all a-lathery, but fit and well and grand still,
With ne'er a gall or whip-mark, and ne'er a tender hoof!

. . . . . .

It's long, long years now since Johnnie Bax was drivin',
Long years ago, before most of you were born:
But *them* were the days it was good to be alive in,
When the sun kept time to the sound of Johnnie's horn!

Chorus "Tan-tan-ta-ra, boys! Here comes the mail,
        Rolling down the cleared line, all full sail!
        Rocking up the main street with letters from below"—
        When Old John Bax drove the coach for Cobb and
        Co.

EDWARD DYSON

1865-1931

Cleaning Up

When the horse has been unharnessed and we've flushed the
    old machine,
And the water o'er the sluice is running evenly and clean;
When there's thirty load before us, and the sun is high and
        bright,
And we've worked from early morning and shall have to
        work till night,
Not a man of us is weary, though the graft is pretty rough,
If we see the proper colour showing freely through the stuff.

With a dandy head of water and a youngster at the rear
To hand along the billy, boys, and keep the tail race clear,
We lift the wash and flash the fork and make the gravel fly.
The shovelling is heavy and we're soaked from heel to thigh;
But it makes a fellow tireless and his thews and sinews tough
If the colour's showing freely as he gaily shifts the stuff.

When Geordie Best is pumping to a rollicking refrain,
And Sandy wipes his streaming brow and shakes the fork
  again,
The pebbles dance and rattle and the water seems to laugh—
Good luck is half the battle and good will's the other half;
And no day's too long and trying and no toil is hard enough,
When we see the colour showing in each shovelful of stuff.

Can the mining speculator with a pile of golden scrip,
Or the plunger who has laid his all upon a winning tip,
Or the city man who's hit upon a profitable deal,
Know the wonderful elation that the lucky diggers feel
When Fortune's smiled but grimly and the storeman's look-
  ing gruff,
And at last they see the colour showing freely in the stuff?

Never, mates! It is a feeling that no other winner knows—
Not the soldier marching homeward from the conquest of
  his foes,
Nor the scholar who's successful in his searching of the skies,
Nor the squalid miser grovelling where his secret treasure
  lies.
'Tis a keener, wilder rapture in the digger bold and bluff
Who feeds the sluice and sees the colour shining in the stuff.

Then lift the wash, and flash the fork, and make the gravel
  fly!
We can laugh at all the pleasures on which other men rely,
When the water o'er the sluice is running evenly and clean,
And the loaded ripples glitter with a lively golden sheen.
No day's too long and trying, and no toil is hard enough
When we wash her down and see the colour freely through
  the stuff.

1866-1892

Where the Dead Men Lie

Out on the wastes of the Never Never—
  That's where the dead men lie!
There where the heat-waves dance for ever—
  That's where the dead men lie!
That's where the Earth's loved sons are keeping
Endless tryst: not the west wind sweeping
Feverish pinions can wake their sleeping—
  Out where the dead men lie!

Where brown Summer and Death have mated—
  That's where the dead men lie!
Loving with fiery lust unsated—
  That's where the dead men lie!
Out where the grinning skulls bleach whitely
Under the saltbush sparkling brightly;
Out where the wild dogs chorus nightly—
  That's where the dead men lie!

Deep in the yellow, flowing river—
  That's where the dead men lie!
Under the banks where the shadows quiver—
  That's where the dead men lie!
Where the platypus twists and doubles,
Leaving a train of tiny bubbles;
Rid at last of their earthly troubles—
  That's where the dead men lie!

East and backward pale faces turning—
  That's how the dead men lie!
Gaunt arms stretched with a voiceless yearning—
  That's how the dead men lie!
Oft in the fragrant hush of nooning
Hearing again their mother's crooning,

Wrapt for aye in a dreamful swooning—
  That's how the dead men lie!

Only the hand of Night can free them—
  That's when the dead men fly!
Only the frightened cattle see them—
  See the dead men go by!
Cloven hoofs beating out one measure,
Bidding the stockmen know no leisure—
That's when the dead men take their pleasure!
  That's when the dead men fly!

Ask, too, the never-sleeping drover:
  He sees the dead pass by;
Hearing them call to their friends—the plover,
  Hearing the dead men cry;
Seeing their faces stealing, stealing,
Hearing their laughter, pealing, pealing,
Watching their grey forms wheeling, wheeling
  Round where the cattle lie!

Strangled by thirst and fierce privation—
  That's how the dead men die!
Out on Moneygrub's farthest station—
  That's how the dead men die!
Hard-faced greybeards, youngsters callow;
Some mounds cared for, some left fallow;
Some deep down, yet others shallow;
  Some having but the sky.

Moneygrub, as he sips his claret,
  Looks with complacent eye
Down at his watch-chain, eighteen carat—
  There, in his club, hard by:

Recks not that every link is stamped with
Names of the men whose limbs are cramped with
Too long lying in grave-mould, cramped with
   Death where the dead men lie.

1867-1922

Ballad of the Drover

   Across the stony ridges,
   Across the rolling plain,
   Young Harry Dale, the drover,
   Comes riding home again.
   And well his stock-horse bears him,
   And light of heart is he,
   And stoutly his old packhorse
   Is trotting by his knee.

   Up Queensland way with cattle
   He's travelled regions vast,
   And many months have vanished
   Since home-folks saw him last.
   He hums a song of someone
   He hopes to marry soon;
   And hobble-chains and camp-ware
   Keep jingling to the tune.

   Beyond the hazy dado
   Against the lower skies
   And yon blue line of ranges
   The station homestead lies.
   And thitherward the drover
   Jogs through the lazy noon,
   While hobble-chains and camp-ware
   Are jingling to a tune.

An hour has filled the heavens
With storm-clouds inky black;
At times the lightning trickles
Around the drover's track;
But Harry pushes onward,
His horses' strength he tries,
In hope to reach the river
Before the flood shall rise.

The thunder, pealing o'er him,
Goes rumbling down the plain;
And sweet on thirsty pastures
Beats fast the plashing rain;
Then every creek and gully
Sends forth its tribute flood—
The river runs a banker,
All stained with yellow mud.

Now Harry speaks to Rover,
The best dog on the plains,
And to his hardy horses,
And strokes their shaggy manes:
"We've breasted bigger rivers
When floods were at their height,
Nor shall this gutter stop us
From getting home tonight!"

The thunder growls a warning,
The blue, forked lightnings gleam;
The drover turns his horses
To swim the fatal stream.
But, oh! the flood runs stronger
Than e'er it ran before;
The saddle-horse is failing,
And only half-way o'er!

When flashes next the lightning
The flood's grey breast is blank;
A cattle-dog and packhorse
Are struggling up the bank.
But in the lonely homestead
The girl shall wait in vain—
He'll never pass the stations
In charge of stock again.

The faithful dog a moment
Lies panting on the bank,
Then plunges through the current
To where his master sank.
And round and round in circles
He fights with failing strength,
Till, gripped by wilder waters,
He fails and sinks at length.

Across the flooded lowlands
And slopes of sodden loam
The packhorse struggles bravely
To take dumb tidings home;
And mud-stained, wet, and weary,
He goes by rock and tree,
With clanging chains and tinware
All sounding eerily.

Andy's Gone with Cattle

Our Andy's gone with cattle now—
Our hearts are out of order—
With drought he's gone to battle now
Across the Queensland border.

He's left us in dejection now,
Our thoughts with him are roving;
It's dull on this selection now,
Since Andy went a-droving.

Who now shall wear the cheerful face
In times when things are slackest?
And who shall whistle round the place
When Fortune frowns her blackest?

Oh, who shall cheek the squatter now
When he comes round us snarling?
His tongue is growing hotter now
Since Andy crossed the Darling.

Oh, may the showers in torrents fall.
And all the tanks run over;
And may the grass grow green and tall
In pathways of the drover;

And may good angels send the rain
On desert stretches sandy;
And when the summer comes again
God grant 'twill bring us Andy.

Talbragar

Jack Denver died on Talbragar when Christmas Eve began,
And there was sorrow round the place, for Denver was a
man;
Jack Denver's wife bowed down her head—her daughter's
grief was wild,
And big Ben Duggan by the bed stood sobbing like a child.
But Big Ben Duggan saddled up, and galloped fast and far,
To raise the biggest funeral yet seen on Talbragar.

> By station home
> And shearing-shed
> Ben Duggan cried, "Jack Denver's dead!
> Roll up at Talbragar!"

He borrowed horses here and there, and rode all Christmas
 Eve,
And scarcely paused a moment's time the mournful news to
 leave;
He rode by lonely huts and farms until the day was done,
And then he turned his horse's head and made for Ross's Run.
No bushman in a single day had ridden half so far
Since Johnson brought the doctor to his wife at Talbragar.

> By diggers' camps
> Ben Duggan sped—
> At each he cried, "Jack Denver's dead!
> Roll up at Talbragar!"

That night he passed the humpies of the splitters on the ridge,
And roused the bullock-drivers camped at Belinfante's Bridge;
And as he climbed the ridge again the moon shone on the
 rise—
Did moonbeams glisten in the mist of tears that filled his
 eyes?
He dashed the rebel drops away—for blinding things they
 are—
But 'twas his best and truest friend who died on Talbragar.

> At Blackman's Run
> Before the dawn
> Ben Duggan cried, "Jack Denver's gone!
> Roll up at Talbragar!"

At all the shanties round the place they heard his horse's
 tramp,
He took the track to Wilson's Luck, and told the diggers'
 camp;

But in the gorge by Deadman's Gap the mountain shades
    were black,
And there a newly fallen tree was lying on the track;
He saw too late—and then he heard the swift hoof's sudden
    jar,
And big Ben Duggan ne'er again rode home to Talbragar.
        "The wretch is drunk,
        And Denver's dead—
        A burning shame!" the people said
        Next day at Talbragar.

For thirty miles round Talbragar the boys rolled up in
    strength,
And Denver had a funeral a good long mile in length;
Round Denver's grave that Christmas Day rough bushmen's
    eyes were dim—
The western bushmen knew the way to bury dead like him;
But some returning homeward found, by light of moon and
    star,
Ben Duggan lying in the rocks, five miles from Talbragar.
        And far and wide
        When Duggan died,
        The bushmen of the western side
        Rode in to Talbragar.

The Teams

A cloud of dust on the long, white road,
    And the teams go creeping on
Inch by inch with the weary load;
And by the power of the green-hide goad
    The distant goal is won.

With eyes half-shut to the blinding dust,
    And necks to the yokes bent low,

The beasts are pulling as bullocks must;
And the shining tires might almost rust
    While the spokes are turning slow.

With face half-hid by a broad-brimmed hat,
    That shades from the heat's white waves,
And shouldered whip, with its green-hide plait,
The driver plods with a gait like that
    Of his weary, patient slaves.

He wipes his brow, for the day is hot,
    And spits to the left with spite;
He shouts at Bally, and flicks at Scot,
And raises dust from the back of Spot,
    And spits to the dusty right.

He'll sometimes pause as a thing of form
    In front of a settler's door,
And ask for a drink, and remark "It's warm,"
Or say "There's signs of a thunderstorm;"
    But he seldom utters more.

The rains are heavy on roads like these
    And, fronting his lonely home,
For days together the settler sees
The waggons bogged to the axletrees,
    Or ploughing the sodden loam.

And then, when the roads are at their worst,
    The bushman's children hear
The cruel blows of the whips reversed
While bullocks pull as their hearts would burst,
    And bellow with pain and fear.

And thus—with glimpses of home and rest—
  Are the long, long journeys done;
And thus—'tis a thankless life at the best!—
Is Distance fought in the mighty West,
  And the lonely battle won.

The Sliprails and the Spur

The colours of the setting sun
Withdrew across the Western land—
He raised the sliprails, one by one,
And shot them home with trembling hand;
Her brown hands clung—her face grew pale—
Ah! quivering chin and eyes that brim!—
One quick, fierce kiss across the rail,
And, "Good-bye, Mary!" "Good-bye, Jim!"

Oh, he rides hard to race the pain
Who rides from love, who rides from home:
But he rides slowly home again,
Whose heart has learnt to love and roam.

A hand upon the horse's mane,
And one foot in the stirrup set,
And, stooping back to kiss again,
With "Good-bye, Mary! don't you fret!
When I come back"—he laughed for her—
"We do not know how soon 'twill be;
I'll whistle as I round the spur—
You let the sliprails down for me."

She gasped for sudden loss of hope,
As, with a backward wave to her,
He cantered down the grassy slope
And swiftly round the darkening spur.

Black-pencilled panels standing high,
And darkness fading into stars,
And, blurring fast against the sky,
A faint white form beside the bars.

And often at the set of sun,
In winter bleak and summer brown,
She'd steal across the little run,
And shyly let the sliprails down,
And listen there when darkness shut
The nearer spur in silence deep,
And when they called her from the hut
Steal home and cry herself to sleep.

And he rides hard to dull the pain
Who rides from one who loves him best . . .
And he rides slowly back again,
Whose restless heart must rove for rest.

WILL H. OGILVIE

1869-1963

From the Gulf

Store cattle from Nelanjie! The mob goes feeding past,
With half a mile of sandhill 'twixt the leaders and the last;
The nags that move behind them are the good old Queens-
land stamp—
Short backs and perfect shoulders that are priceless on a
camp;
And these are *Men* that ride them, broad-chested, tanned,
and tall,
The bravest hearts amongst us and the lightest hands of all:
Oh, let them wade in Wonga grass and taste the Wonga dew,
And let them spread, those thousand head—for we've been
droving too!

Store cattle from Nelanjie! By half a hundred towns,
By Northern ranges rough and red, by rolling open downs,
By stock-routes brown and burnt and bare, by flood-wrapped
    river-bends,
They've hunted them from gate to gate—the drover has no
    friends!
But idly they may ride today beneath the scorching sun
And let the hungry bullocks try the grass on Wonga run;
No overseer will dog them here to "see the cattle through",
But they may spread their thousand head—for we've been
    droving too!

Store cattle from Nelanjie! They've a naked track to steer;
The stockyards at Wodonga are a long way down from here;
The creeks won't run till God knows when, and half the
    holes are dry;
The tanks are few and far between and water's dear to buy:
There's plenty at the Brolga bore for all his stock and mine—
We'll pass him with a brave God-speed across the Border
    line;
And if he goes a five-mile stage and loiters slowly through,
We'll only think the more of him—for we've been droving
    too!

Store cattle from Nelanjie! They're mute as milkers now;
But yonder grizzled drover, with the care-lines on his brow,
Could tell of merry musters on the big Nelanjie plains,
With blood upon the chestnut's flanks and foam upon the
    reins;
Could tell of nights upon the road when those same mild-
    eyed steers
Went ringing round the river bend and through the scrub
    like spears;

And if his words are rude and rough, we know his words
    are true,
We know what wild Nelanjies are—and we've been droving
    too!

Store cattle from Nelanjie! Around the fire at night
They've watched the pine-tree shadows lift before the dancing
    light;
They've lain awake to listen when the weird bush-voices
    speak,
And heard the lilting bells go by along the empty creek;
They've spun the yarns of hut and camp, the tales of play and
    work,
The wondrous tales that gild the road from Normanton to
    Bourke;
They've told of fortune foul and fair, of women false and
    true,
And well we know the songs they've sung—for we've been
    droving too!

Store cattle from Nelanjie! Their breath is on the breeze;
You hear them tread, a thousand head, in blue-grass to the
    knees;
The lead is on the netting-fence, the wings are spreading
    wide,
The lame and laggard scarcely move—so slow the drovers
    ride!
But let them stay and feed today for sake of Auld Lang Syne;
They'll never get a chance like this below the Border Line;
And if they tread our frontage down, what's that to me or
    you?
What's ours to fare, by God they'll share! for we've been
    droving too!

How the Fire Queen Crossed the Swamp

The flood was down in the Wilga swamps, three feet over
  the mud,
And the teamsters camped on the Wilga range and swore at
  the rising flood;
For one by one they had tried the trip, double and treble
  teams,
And one after one each desert-ship had dropped to her axle-
  beams;
So they thonged their leaders and pulled them round to the
  camp on the sandhill's crown,
And swore by the bond of a blood-red oath to wait till the
  floods went down.

There were side-rail tubs and table-tops, coaches and bullock-
  drays,
Brown with the Barcoo Wonders, and Speed with the dapple
  greys
Who pulled the front of his wagon out and left the rest in
  the mud
At the Cuttaburra crossing in the grip of the 'Ninety flood.
There was Burt with his sixteen bullocks, and never a bullock
  to shirk,
Who twice came over the Border line with twelve-ton-ten to
  Bourke;
There was Long Dick damning an agent's eyes for his ton of
  extra weight,
And Whistling Jim, for Cobb and Co., cursing that mails
  were late;
And one who blasphemed at a broken chain and howled for
  a blacksmith's blood,
And most of them cursed their crimson luck, and all of them
  cursed the flood.

The last of the baffled had struggled back and the sun was
    low in the sky,
And the first of the stars was creeping out when Dareaway
    Dan came by.
There's never a teamster draws to Bourke but has taken the
    help of Dan;
There's never a team on the Great North Road can lift as
    the big roans can:
Broad-hipped beauties that nothing can stop, leaders that
    swing to a cough;
Eight blue-roans on the near-side yoked, and eight red-roans
    on the off.

And Long Dick called from his pine-rail bunk: "Where are
    you bound so quick?"
And Dareaway Dan spoke low to the roans, and aloud, "To
    the Swagman's, Dick!"
"There's five good miles," said the giant, "lie to the front of
    you, holding mud;
If you never were stopped before, old man, you are stopped
    by the Wilga flood.
The dark will be down in an hour or so, there isn't the ghost
    of a moon;
So leave your nags in the station grass instead of the long
    lagoon!"

But Dan stood up to his leader's head and fondled the big
    brown nose:
"There's many a mile in the roan team yet before they are
    feed for the crows;
Now listen, Dick-with-the-woman's-heart, a word to you and
    the rest:
I've sixteen horses collared and chained, the pick of the whole
    wide west,

And I'll cut their throats and leave them here to rot if they
    haven't the power
To carry me through to the gates of hell—with seventy bags
    of flour!

"The light of the stars is light enough; they have nothing
    to do but *plough*!
There's never a swamp has held them yet, and a swamp won't
    stop them now.
They're waiting for flour at the Swagman's Bend; I'll steer
    for the lifting light;
There's nothing to fear with a team like mine, and—I camp
    in the bend tonight!"

So they stood aside and they watched him pass in the glow of
    the sinking sun,
With straining muscles and tightened chains—sixteen pulling
    like one;
With jingling harness and droning wheels and bare hoofs'
    rhythmic tramp,
With creaking timbers and lurching load the Fire Queen
    faced the swamp!
She dipped her red shafts low in the slush as a spoonbill dips
    her beak,
The black mud clung to the wheels and fell in the wash of
    the Wilga Creek;

And the big roans fought for footing, and the spreaders
    threshed like flails,
And the great wheels lifted the muddy spume to the bend
    of the red float-rails;
And they cheered him out to the westward with the last of
    the failing light
And the splashing hoofs and the driver's voice died softly
    away in the night;

But some of them prate of a shadowy form that guided the
    leader's reins,
And some of them speak of a shod black horse that pulled in
    the off-side chains—
How every time that he lifted his feet the wagon would groan
    and swing,
And every time that he dropped his head you could hear the
    tug-chains ring!

And Dan to the Swagman's Bend came through, mud-spat-
    tered from foot to head,
And they couldn't tell which of the roans were blue and
    which of the roans were red.
Now this is the tale as I heard it told, and many believe it
    true
When the teamsters say in their off-hand way—" 'Twas the
    Devil that pulled him through!"

The Death of Ben Hall

Ben Hall was out on the Lachlan side
With a thousand pounds on his head;
A score of troopers were scattered wide
And a hundred more were ready to ride
Wherever a rumour led.

They had followed his track from the Weddin heights
And north by the Weelong yards;
Through dazzling days and moonlit nights
They had sought him over their rifle-sights,
With their hands on their trigger-guards.

The outlaw stole like a hunted fox
Through the scrub and stunted heath,
And peered like a hawk from his eyrie rocks

Through the waving boughs of the sapling box
On the troopers riding beneath.

His clothes were rent by the clutching thorn
And his blistered feet were bare;
Ragged and torn, with his beard unshorn,
He hid in the woods like a beast forlorn,
With a padded path to his lair.

But every night when the white stars rose
He crossed by the Gunning Plain
To a stockman's hut where the Gunning flows,
And struck on the door three swift light blows,
And a hand unhooked the chain—

And the outlaw followed the lone path back
With food for another day;
And the kindly darkness covered his track
And the shadows swallowed him deep and black
Where the starlight melted away.

But his friend had read of the Big Reward,
And his soul was stirred with greed;
He fastened his door and window-board,
He saddled his horse and crossed the ford,
And spurred to the town at speed.

You may ride at a man's or a maid's behest
When honour or true love call
And steel your heart to the worst or best,
But the ride that is ta'en on a traitor's quest
Is the bitterest ride of all.

A hot wind blew from the Lachlan bank
And a curse on its shoulder came;

The pine-trees frowned at him, rank on rank,
The sun on a gathering storm-cloud sank
And flushed his cheek with shame.

He reined at the Court; and the tale began
That the rifles alone should end;
Sergeant and trooper laid their plan
To draw the net on a hunted man
At the treacherous word of a friend.

False was the hand that raised the chain
And false was the whispered word:
"The troopers have turned to the south again,
You may dare to camp on the Gunning Plain."
And the weary outlaw heard.

He walked from the hut but a quarter-mile
Where a clump of saplings stood
In a sea of grass like a lonely isle;
And the moon came up in a little while
Like silver steeped in blood.

Ben Hall lay down on the dew-wet ground
By the side of his tiny fire;
And a night-breeze woke, and he heard no sound
As the troopers drew their cordon round—
And the traitor earned his hire.

And nothing they saw in the dim grey light,
But the little glow in the trees;
And they crouched in the tall cold grass all night,
Each one ready to shoot at sight,
With his rifle cocked on his knees.

When the shadows broke and the dawn's white sword
Swung over the mountain wall,
And a little wind blew over the ford,

M

A sergeant sprang to his feet and roared:
"In the name of the Queen, Ben Hall!"

Haggard, the outlaw leapt from his bed
With his lean arms held on high.
"Fire!" And the word was scarcely said
When the mountains rang to a rain of lead—
And the dawn went drifting by.

They kept their word and they paid his pay
Where a clean man's hand would shrink;
And that was the traitor's master-day
As he stood by the bar on his homeward way
And called on the crowd to drink.

He banned no creed and he barred no class,
And he called to his friends by name;
But the worst would shake his head and pass
And none would drink from the bloodstained glass
And the goblet red with shame.

And I know when I hear the last grim call
And my mortal hour is spent,
When the light is hid and the curtains fall
I would rather sleep with the dead Ben Hall
Than go where that traitor went.

E. J. BRADY

1869-1952

Lost and Given Over

A mermaid's not a human thing,
An' courtin' sich is folly;
Of flesh an' blood I'd rather sing,
What ain't so melancholy.
Oh, Berta! Loo! Juanita! Sue

Here's good luck to me and you—
    Sing rally! ri-a-rally!
The seas is deep; the seas is wide;
But this I'll prove whate'er betide,
    I'm bully in the alley!
    I'm bull-ee in our al-lee!

The Hooghli gal 'er face is brown;
The Hilo gal is lazy;
The gal that lives by 'Obart town
She'd drive a dead man crazy;
Come, wet your lip, and let it slip!
The Gretna Green's a tidy ship—
    Sing rally!
The seas is deep; the seas is blue;
But 'ere's good 'ealth to me and you,
    Ho, rally!

The Lord may drop us off our pins
To feed 'is bloomin' fishes;
But Lord forgive us for our sins—
Our sins is most delicious!
Come, drink it up and fill yer cup!
The world it owes us bite and sup,
    And Mimi, Ju-Ju, Sally;
The seas is long; the winds is strong;
The best of men they will go wrong—
    Hi, rally! ri-a-rally!

The Bowery gal she knows 'er know;
The Frisco gal is silly;
The Hayti gal ain't white as snow—
They're whiter down in Chili.
Now what's the use to shun the booze?

They'll flop your bones among the ooze
    Sou-west-by-Sou' the galley.
The seas is green; the seas is cold;
The best of men they must grow old—
    Sing rally! ri-a-rally!

All round the world where'er I roam,
This lesson I am learnin':
If you've got sense you'll stop at home
And save the bit yer earnin'.
So hang the odds! It's little odds,
When every 'eathen 'as 'is gods,
    And neither two will tally:
When black and white drink, wimmin, fight—
In these three things they're all all right—
    Sing rally! ri-a-rally!

When double bunks, fo-castle end,
Is all the kind that's carried,
Our manners they will likely mend—
Most likely we'll be married.
But till sich time as that be done,
We'll take our fun as we've begun—
    Sing rally!
The flesh is weak; the world is wide;
The dead man 'e goes overside—
    Sing rally! rally!

We're given and lost to the girls that wait
From Trinity to Whitsund'y,
From Sunda Strait to the Golden Gate
An' back to the Bay o' Fundy;
Oh, it's Mabel, Loo, an' it's Nancy-Poo,
An' 'ere's good luck, an' I love you—
    Sing rally!

136

Oh, it's cents an' dollars an' somebody hollers—
The sun comes up an' the mornin' follers—
    Sing rally!

We're given an' lost to octoroon,
The Portugee cruiser painty,
The Chinkie gal with 'er eyes 'arf-moon,
An' the Japanee darlin' dainty.
Oh, it's Tokio-town when the sun goes down,
It's 'arf-a-pint and it's 'arf-a-crown—
    Sing rally!
'Er spars may lift an' 'er keel can shift,
When a man is done 'e 's got to drift—
    Sing rally! Ho, rally!

The Hooghli gal 'er face is brown,
The Hilo gal's a daisy,
The gal that lives by 'Obart town
She'd drive a dead man crazy.
So, pretty an' plain, it's Sarah Jane
'Uggin' an' kissin' an' "Come again!"
    Sing rally! ri-a-rally!
The seas is deep; the seas is wide;
But this I'll prove what else betide,
    I'm bully in the alley,
Ho! Bullee in the Al-lee.

The Coachman's Yarn

This a tale that the coachman told,
As he flicked the flies from Marigold
And flattered and fondled Pharaoh.
The sun swung low in the western skies;
Out on a plain, just over a rise,
  Stood Nimitybell, on Monaro;

137

E. J. BRADY

Cold as charity, cold as hell,
Bleak, bare, barren Nimitybell—
    Nimitybell on Monaro.

"Now this 'ere 'appened in 'Eighty-three,
The coldest winter *ever* we see;
Strewth, it *was* cold, as cold as could be,
    Out 'ere on Monaro;
It froze the blankets, it froze the fleas,
It froze the sap in the blinkin' trees,
It made a grindstone out of cheese,
    Right 'ere in Monaro.

"Freezin' an' snowin'—ask the old hands;
They seen, they knows, an' *they* understands.
The ploughs was froze, and the cattle brands,
    Down 'ere in Monaro;
It froze our fingers and froze our toes;
I seen a passenger's breath so froze
Icicles 'ung from 'is bloomin' nose
    Long as the tail on Pharaoh!

"I ketched a curlew down by the creek;
His feet was froze to his blessed beak;
'E stayed like that for over a week—
    That's *cold* on Monaro.
Why, even the *air* got froze that tight
You'd 'ear the awfullest sounds at night,
When things was put to a fire or light,
    Out 'ere on Monaro.

"For the *sounds* was froze. At Haydon's Bog
A cove 'e cross-cut a big back-log,
An' carted 'er 'ome ('e wants to jog—
    Stiddy, go stiddy there, Pharaoh!).

138

As soon as his log begins to thaw
They 'ears the sound of the cross-cut saw
A-thawin' out. Yes, his name was Law.
　　Old hands, them Laws, on Monaro.

"The second week of this 'ere cold snap
I'm drivin' the coach. A Sydney chap,
'E strikes this part o' the bloomin' map,
　　A new hand 'ere on Monaro;
'Is name or game I never heard tell,
But 'e gets off at Nimitybell;
Blowin' like Bluey, freezin' like 'ell
　　At Nimitybell on Monaro.

"The drinks was froze, o' course, in the bar;
They *breaks* a bottle of old Three Star,
An' the barman sez, 'Now, there y' are,
　　You can't beat *that* for Monaro!'
The stranger bloke, 'e was tall an' thin,
Sez, 'Strike me blue, but I think *you* win;
We'll 'ave another an I'll turn in—
　　It's blitherin *cold* on Monaro.'

" 'E borrowed a book an' went to bed
To read awhile, so the missus said,
By the candle-light. 'E must ha' read
　　(These nights is long on Monaro)
Past closin' time. Then 'e starts an' blows
The candle out; but the wick 'ad froze!
Leastways, that's what folks round 'ere suppose,
　　Old hands as lived on Monaro.

"So bein' tired, an' a stranger, new
To these mountain ways, they think he threw
'Is coat on the wick; an' maybe, too,
　　Any old clothes 'e'd to spare. Oh,

139

This ain't no fairy, an' don't *you* fret!
Next day came warmer, an' set in wet—
There's some out 'ere as can mind it yet,
   The real old 'ands on Monaro.

"The wick must ha' thawed. The fire began
At breakfast time. The neighbours all ran
To save the pub . . . an' forgot the man
   (Stiddy, go stiddy there, mare-oh).
The pub was burned to the blanky ground;
'Is buttons was all they ever found.
The blinkin' cow, *'e owed me a pound*—
   From Cooma his blinkin' fare, oh!

"That ain't no fairy, not what I've told;
I'm gettin' shaky an' growin' old,
An' I hope *I* never again see cold,
   Like that down 'ere on Monaro!" . . .
He drives his horses, he drives them well,
And this is the tale he loves to tell
Nearing the town of Nimitybell,
   Nimitybell on Monaro.

J. W. GORDON ("JIM GRAHAME")

1874-1949

Whalan of Waitin' a While

Long life to old Whalan of Waitin' a While;
Good luck to his children and wife;
They gain all the pleasure and gladness that come
And miss all the worries of life.
They do not complain if the season is dry.
They go into debt with a smile.
"It's no use of moaning, it might have been worse,"
Says Whalan of Waitin' a While.

The gates on the boundary fences are down
And buried in rubbish and dust;
The white ants and weevils have eaten the rungs,
The hinges are rotting with rust.
The sheep wander in, and the sheep wander out
And ramble for many a mile:
"I must take a day off and fix up those gates,"
Says Whalan of Waitin' a While.

The pigs roam at large, but they come home at night
And sleep head and tail by the door,
And sometimes a sow has a litter of pigs
That sleep with her under the floor.
They suckle and squabble around her all night,
The odours arising are vile;
"We'll sell them right out when a buyer comes up,"
Says Whalan of Waitin' a While.

The brand on the calves is as big as a plate
And looks like a slash or a wale,
And sometimes it reaches from shoulder to hip,
And sometimes it reaches the tail.
'Twas made from the side of a square iron tank,
Cut out with a chisel or file,
"It's not very neat, but it might have been worse,"
Says Whalan of Waitin' a While.

The boys and the girls all at riding excel,
They stick to a saddle like glue,
And follow a bullock through low mulga scrub
As straight as a die and as true.
They're no good at figures and can't read at all,
Nor write in an elegant style.
"We'll give them a bit of a schooling some day,"
Says Whalan of Waitin' a While.

The tanks and the dams very seldom get full,
No matter how heavy it rains;
They've a halo of bones of the sheep that have bogged,
And the dust-storms have silted the drains.
Storm-water is wasted and sweeps down the flat—
A flood that would fill up the Nile—
"We'll clean out those drains when the weather gets cool,"
Says Whalan of Waitin' a While.

The sulky and buggy stand out in the sun,
The woodwork is gaping with cracks,
The leather is wrinkled and perishing fast,
And pulling away from the tacks.
The wheels are all loose and the paint's falling off
And the cushions have long lost their pile;
"I'd put up a shed, but I cannot find time,"
Says Whalan of Waitin' a While.

Good luck to old Whalan of Waitin' a While.
He'll live just as long as the rest,
And smile at the things that make most people frown,
And his health is as good as the best.
Good luck to the mother at Waitin' a While,
Who waddles along with a smile;
She'll have a fine time when the good seasons come,
And she doesn't mind Waitin' a While.

WILL LAWSON

1876-1957

Bill the Whaler

Old Bill the Whaler said to me
One day in Hobart Town,
"You must've spent your life at sea;
I'll wager half-a-crown
You've seen the big bulls blow when Dawn

142

Was hailing Night to say
"When all your nigger troops are gone,
We'll have another day." . . .

"You must have been a whaler,
That's clear as clear can be,
For you walk like one
And you talk like one,"
Said Whaler Bill to me;
"And you think like one
And you drink like one—
You must have been to sea.

"You must have seen Solander Bill
That not a ship could take
Till young George Attwell made his kill
For the Hobart whalers' sake.
You must have been—why, damn my eyes
And may my eyes be damned—
You might have been in the *Surprise*,
The ship the *Black Bull* rammed.

"You've seen the Campbells' misty peaks—
The way you talk, you must—
And how the Campbells' whirlwind speaks,
The wind no man can trust.
You've seen the trypots' lurid glow
Light up the big, dim sails,
And seen the Flyin' Dutchman go
In them Antarctic gales.

"You know about the Spotted Bull
And old Torpedo Tom;
I'll bet you had a bellyful
Of pulling out and home

When big winds blew like blooming guns—
Just sons of guns, they were.
You know the way the big surge runs
Along the sides of her

"When you're dead-beat and grabbing at
The boat-falls, swinging wide.
You've worn the outward-bounder's hat
And waited for the tide,
And fought the cops who took you out
From pride and stubbornness—
It was a kind of final shout;
Your pay was one quid less."

Old Bill the Whaler filled his glass.
"No glass should have a lid!
I bet you've seen some summers pass
Since you were just a kid.
I know I have, and that's a fact—
Fourscore and more I am,
And every darned year has been packed
With fun and rum and jam."

Old Bill the Whaler died that day,
And though his lips were still
As I stood there they seemed to say
What they had said on many a day. . . .
O God! I missed Old Bill.

Maybe in Sundown Shanty-bars
On Resurrection Morn
We'll meet far out, where western stars
And westerlies are born.
Beyond Kerguelen—far beyond—
Where comets light the nights,

Old Bill and I will correspond
From distant, dizzy heights.

"You must have been a whaler"
—His message will be free—
" 'Cos you talk like one
And you walk like one—
You must have been to sea.
And you think like one
And you drink like one,"
Old Bill will signal me.

C. J. DENNIS

1876-1938

The Play

(*from* The Sentimental Bloke)

"Wot's in a name?" she sez . . . An' then she sighs
An' clasps 'er little 'ands, an' rolls 'er eyes.
"A rose," she sez, "be any other name
Would smell the same.
Oh, w'erefore art you Romeo, young sir?
Chuck yer old pot, an' change yer moniker!"

Doreen an' me, we bin to see a show—
The swell two-dollar touch. Bong tong, yeh know.
A chair apiece wiv velvit on the seat;
A slap-up treat.
The drarmer's writ be Shakespeare, years ago,
About a barmy goat called Romeo.

"Lady, be yonder moon I swear!" sez 'e.
An' then 'e climbs up on the balkiney;
An' there they smooge a treat, wiv pretty words
Like two love-birds.
I nudge Doreen. She whispers, "Ain't it grand!"
'Er eyes is shinin'; an' I squeeze 'er 'and.

145

"Wot's in name?" she sez. 'Struth, I dunno.
Billo is just as good as Romeo.
She may be Juli-er or Juli-et—
'E loves 'er yet.
If she's the tart 'e wants, then she's 'is queen,
Names never count . . . But ar, I like "Doreen!"

A sweeter, dearer sound I never 'eard;
Ther's music 'angs around that little word,
Doreen! . . . But wot was this I starts to say
About the play?
I'm off me beat. But when a bloke's in love
'Is thorts turn 'er way, like a 'omin' dove.

This Romeo 'e's lurkin' wiv a crew—
A dead tough crowd o' crooks—called Montague.
'Is cliner's push—wot's nicknamed Capulet—
They 'as 'em set.
Fair narks they are, jist like them back-street clicks,
Ixcep' they fights wiv skewers, 'stid o' bricks.

Wot's in a name? Wot's in a string o' words?
They scraps in ole Verona wiv the'r swords,
An' never give a bloke a stray dog's chance,
An' that's Romance.
But when they deals it out wiv bricks an' boots
In Little Lon., they're low, degraded broots.

Wot's jist plain stoush wiv us, right 'ere today,
Is "valler" if yer fur enough away.
Some time, some writer bloke will do the trick
Wiv Ginger Mick,
Of Spadger's Lane. 'E'll be a Romeo,
When 'e's bin dead five 'undred years or so.

146

Fair Juli-et, she gives 'er boy the tip.
Sez she: "Don't sling that crowd o' mine no lip;
An' if you run agin a Capulet,
Jist do a get."
'E swears 'e's done wiv lash; 'e'll chuck it clean.
(Same as I done when I first met Doreen.)

They smooge some more at that. Ar, strike me blue!
It gimme Joes to sit an' watch them two!
'E'd break away an' start to say good-bye,
An' then she'd sigh
"Ow, Ro-me-o!" an' git a strangle-holt,
An' 'ang around 'im like she feared 'e'd bolt.

Nex' day 'e words a gorspil cove about
A secrit weddin'; an' they plan it out.
'E spouts a piece about 'ow 'e's bewitched:
Then they git 'itched . . .
Now, 'ere's the place where I fair git the pip.
She's 'is for keeps, an' yet 'e lets 'er slip!

Ar, but 'e makes me sick! A fair gazob!
'E's jist the glarssy on the soulful sob,
'E'll sigh and spruik, an' 'owl a love-sick vow—
(The silly cow!)
But when 'e's got 'er, spliced an' on the straight,
'E crools the pitch, an' tries to kid it's Fate.

Aw! Fate me foot! Instid of slopin' soon
As 'e was wed, off on 'is 'oneymoon,
'Im an' 'is cobber, called Mick Curio,
They 'ave to go
An' mix it wiv that push o' Capulets.
They look fer trouble; an' it's wot they gets.

A tug named Tyball (cousin to the skirt)
Sprags 'em an' makes a start to sling off dirt.
Nex' minnit there's a reel old ding-dong go—
'Arf round or so.
Mick Curio, 'e gets it in the neck,
"Ar rats!" 'e sez, an' passes in 'is check.

Quite natchril, Romeo gits wet as 'ell.
"It's me or you!" 'e 'owls, an' wiv a yell,
Plunks Tyball through the gizzard wiv 'is sword.
'Ow I ongcored!
"Put in the boot!" I sez. "Put in the boot!"
" 'Ush!" sez Doreen . . . "Shame!" sez some silly coot.

Then Romeo, 'e dunno wot to do.
The cops gits busy, like they allwiz do,
An' nose around until 'e gits blue funk
An' does a bunk.
They wants 'is tart to wed some other guy.
"Ah, strike!" she sez. "I wish that I could die!"

Now, this 'ere gorspil bloke's a fair shrewd 'ead.
Sez 'e, "I'll dope yeh, so they'll *think* yer dead."
(I tips 'e was a cunnin' sort, wot knoo
A thing or two.)
She takes 'is knock-out drops, up in 'er room:
They think she's snuffed, an' plant 'er in 'er tomb.

Then things gits mixed a treat an' starts to whirl.
'Ere's Romeo comes back an' finds 'is girl
Tucked in 'er little coffing, cold an' stiff,
An' in a jiff,
'E swallers lysol, throws a fancy fit,
'Ead over turkey, an' 'is soul 'as flit.

Then Juli-et wakes up an' sees 'im there,
Turns on the water-works an' tears 'er 'air,
"Dear love," she sez, "I cannot live alone!"
An' wiv a moan,
She grabs 'is pockit knife, an' ends 'er cares . . .
"Peanuts or lollies!" sez a boy upstairs.

P. J. HARTIGAN ("JOHN O'BRIEN")

1879-1952

Said Hanrahan

"We'll all be rooned," said Hanrahan
In accents most forlorn
Outside the church ere Mass began
One frosty Sunday morn.

The congregation stood about,
Coat-collars to the ears,
And talked of stock and crops and drought
As it had done for years.

"It's lookin' crook," said Daniel Croke;
"Bedad, it's cruke, me lad,
For never since the banks went broke
Has seasons been so bad."

"It's dry, all right," said young O'Neil,
With which astute remark
He squatted down upon his heel
And chewed a piece of bark.

And so around the chorus ran
"It's keepin' dry, no doubt."
"We'll all be rooned," said Hanrahan,
"Before the year is out.

149

N

"The crops are done; ye'll have your work
To save one bag of grain;
From here way out to Back-o'-Bourke
They're singin' out for rain.

"They're singin' out for rain," he said,
"And all the tanks are dry."
The congregation scratched its head,
And gazed around the sky.

"There won't be grass, in any case,
Enough to feed an ass;
There's not a blade on Casey's place
As I came down to Mass."

"If rain don't come this month," said Dan,
And cleared his throat to speak—
"We'll all be rooned," said Hanrahan,
"If rain don't come this week."

A heavy silence seemed to steal
On all at this remark;
And each man squatted on his heel,
And chewed a piece of bark.

"We want an inch of rain, we do,"
O'Neil observed at last;
But Croke "maintained" we wanted two
To put the danger past.

"If we don't get three inches, man,
Or four to break this drought,
We'll all be rooned," said Hanrahan,
"Before the year is out."

In God's good time down came the rain;
And all the afternoon
On iron roof and window-pane
It drummed a homely tune.

And through the night it pattered still,
And lightsome, gladsome elves
On dripping spout and window-sill
Kept talking to themselves.

It pelted, pelted all day long,
A-singing at its work,
Till every heart took up the song
Way out to Back-o'-Bourke.

And every creek a banker ran,
And dams filled overtop;
"We'll all be rooned," said Hanrahan,
"If this rain doesn't stop."

And stop it did, in God's good time:
And spring came in to fold
A mantle o'er the hills sublime
Of green and pink and gold.

And days went by on dancing feet,
With harvest-hopes immense,
And laughing eyes beheld the wheat
Nid-nodding o'er the fence.

And, oh, the smiles on every face,
As happy lad and lass
Through grass knee-deep on Casey's place
Went riding down to Mass.

While round the church in clothes genteel
Discoursed the men of mark,
And each man squatted on his heel,
And chewed his piece of bark.

"There'll be bush-fires for sure, me man,
There will, without a doubt;
We'll all be rooned," said Hanrahan,
"Before the year is out."

Tangmalangaloo

The bishop sat in lordly state and purple cap sublime,
And galvanized the old bush church at Confirmation time;
And all the kids were mustered up from fifty miles around,
With Sunday clothes, and staring eyes, and ignorance profound.
Now was it fate, or was it grace, whereby they yarded too
An overgrown two-storey lad from Tangmalangaloo?

A hefty son of virgin soil, where nature has her fling,
And grows the trefoil three feet high and mats it in the spring;
Where mighty hills unlift their heads to pierce the welkin's rim,
And trees sprout up a hundred feet before they shoot a limb;
There everything is big and grand, and men are giants too—
But Christian Knowledge wilts, alas, at Tangmalangaloo.

The bishop summed the youngsters up, as bishops only can;
He cast a searching glance around, then fixed upon his man.
But glum and dumb and undismayed through every bout he sat;
He seemed to think that he was there, but wasn't sure of that.

The bishop gave a scornful look, as bishops sometimes do,
And glared right through the pagan in from Tangmalang-
    aloo.

"Come, tell me, boy," his lordship said in crushing tones
    severe,
"Come, tell me why is Christmas Day the greatest of the
    year?
How is it that around the world we celebrate that day
And send a name upon a card to those who're far away?
Why is it wandering ones return with smiles and greetings,
    too?"
A squall of knowledge hit the lad from Tangmalangaloo.

He gave a lurch which set a-shake the vases on the shelf,
He knocked the benches all askew, up-ending of himself.
And oh, how pleased his lordship was, and how he smiled
    to say,
"That's good, my boy. Come, tell me now; and what is
    Christmas Day?"
The ready answer bared a fact no bishop ever knew—
"It's the day before the races out at Tangmalangaloo."

EDWIN GERARD ("GERARDY")

1891-

Lofty Lane

Buckle the spur and belt again,
Saddle, and charge the magazine,
Toe the stirrup and touch the rein,
Speed where the foothills skyward lean;
Open your eyes and count the miles,
Gallop your horse through dark defiles,
And look for the body of Lofty Lane
Before you halt at the lines again.

Lofty Lane was a squadron scout,
Supple and long and loose of limb;
All spare happiness round about
Shone in the laughing eyes of him:
  Never a man in his troop could show
  Lane in the saddle the way to go.

Lane was a man who played with chance,
Times whenever the work came fast;
First man out in the swift advance,
Last man in when the day was past.
  Many a clip of Turkish lead
  Was aimed at Lane's gay heart and head.

Brazen summer began to brood,
Shrouding the hills with sombre haze;
Acres of uncut wheat that stood,
Shuddered and smoked and leapt ablaze.
  Nature hardened its heart like stone,
  When Lane rode into the hills alone.

Lane rode off from his squadron mate,
Over the fretting skyline's rim;
Laden with harm and black with hate,
Gully and hill in smoke grew dim.
  Shots rang out in the hills that day,
  And Lane was never so long away;

Never so long, that grave alarm
Before had murmured, "Lofty's dead."
Rumour announced: "The hand of harm
Let loose an ounce of well-aimed lead
  And jolted the life-light from the face
  That ever was welcome round the place."

Never had action waned his pluck,
Quelled or slackened his pleasing power,
And many assert that rotten luck
Hemmed him around in an evil hour;
  And some men vow that Lofty Lane
  Will live to greet all hands again.

Doubt hangs over the horselines still,
Yet we have searched and searched, in vain,
North and east of the furthest hill
That ever was crossed by Lofty Lane;
  And there are many who gravely say
  That Lane's alive in the east today.

Gaps are many at times, alas;
War is heavy on life and limb,
And many a weary day will pass
Before a man replaces him,
  A man with a smile upon his face
That ever is welcome round the place.

Buckle the spur and belt again,
Saddle, and charge the magazine
Toe the stirrup and touch the rein,
Speed where the foothills skyward lean;
Open your eyes and count the miles,
Gallop your horse through dark defiles,
And look for the body of Lofty Lane
Before you halt at the lines again!

W. E. ("BILL") HARNEY

1895-1963

West of Alice

We are travelling west of Alice Springs, and Sam is at the
    wheel;
Riding the diesel-grader I am watching its blade of steel
Roll back the dark-red sandy loam or grind the limestones
    grey,
And the wheels whirl in a red-dust swirl along the new
    highway.

We pass where Sturt-peas clothe the earth with a scarlet
    sweep of flowers,
And burst through green acacia-trees that send down golden
    showers;
The parakeelia's purple blooms are crushed in the dry, red
    sand
When the bright blade sweeps as the grader creeps over the
    stern, strange land.

The mulga, mallee, desert-oaks fall prostrate as we pass,
The lizards, pigeons, porcupines crouch low in stone and
    grass;
We brush the spinifex aside; tear down the bush-rat's shade,
And the desert mole in its sandhill hole digs faster from our
    blade.

The honey-ants are rooted out to roll upon the sand,
But ever the ramping, stamping fiend goes roaring through
    the land;
The tyres grind and the steel blade cuts the pads where
    camels trod
And claws at the ground of a stony mound where tribesmen
    praised their God.

We cross the desert rivers, formed when the world was new,
And churn to dust the fossil-bones of the giant kangaroo;
I wave to naked native kids upon Erldunda's plain,
And we fill our tank where the black men drank from rock-
　　holes filled by rain.

We camp in Kulgera's weathered hills, scarred core of an
　　ancient range,
Where the camp-fire flame throws out its light on a scene
　　that is ever strange
As a dingo wails by the painted wall of a sacred cave near by
And the stars shine bright as we lie at night beneath a frosty
　　sky.

We rise as mulga-parakeets go whirling through the dawn,
We see old star-man Manbuk rise from depths of midnight
　　drawn;
We hear the grader's engine roar with Sam behind the wheel,
And I sing my song as we plunge along to the chatter of
　　wheel and steel.

EDWARD HARRINGTON
1896-

The Bushrangers

Four horsemen rode out from the heart of the range,
Four horsemen with aspects forbidding and strange.
They were booted and spurred, they were armed to the teeth,
And they frowned as they looked on the valley beneath,
As forward they rode through the rocks and the fern—
Ned Kelly, Dan Kelly, Steve Hart and Joe Byrne.

Ned Kelly drew rein and he shaded his eyes—
"The town's at our mercy! See yonder it lies!

To hell with the troopers!"—he shook his clenched fist—
"We will shoot them like dogs if they dare to resist!"
And all of them nodded, grim-visaged and stern—
Ned Kelly, Dan Kelly, Steve Hart and Joe Byrne.

Through the gullies and creeks they rode silently down;
They stuck-up the station and raided the town;
They opened the safe and they looted the bank;
They laughed and were merry, they ate and they drank.
Then off to the ranges they went with their gold—
Oh! never were bandits more reckless and bold.

But time brings its punishment, time travels fast—
And the outlaws were trapped in Glenrowan at last,
Where three of them died in the smoke and the flame,
And Ned Kelly came back—to the last he was game.
But the Law shot him down (he was fated to hang),
And that was the end of the bushranging gang.

Whatever their faults and whatever their crimes,
Their deeds lend romance to those faraway times.
They have gone from the gullies they haunted of old,
And nobody knows where they buried their gold.
To the ranges they loved they will never return—
Ned Kelly, Dan Kelly, Steve Hart and Joe Byrne.

But at times when I pass through that sleepy old town
Where the far-distant peaks of Strathbogie look down
I think of the days when those grim ranges rang
To the galloping hooves of the bushranging gang.
Though the years bring oblivion, time brings a change,
The ghosts of the Kellys still ride from the range.

Morgan

When Morgan crossed the Murray to Peechelba and doom
A sombre silent shadow rode with him through the gloom.
The wild things of the forest slunk from the outlaw's track,
The boobook croaked a warning, "Go back, go back, go
　　back!"
It woke no answering echo in Morgan's blackened soul,
As onward through the darkness he rode towards his goal.

An evil man was Morgan, a price was on his head;
The simple bush-folk whispered his very name with dread;
Before the fierce Dan Morgan the bravest man might quake—
A cold and callous killer, he killed for killing's sake.
Past swamp and creek and gully, and settler's lone abode,
Towards the station homestead the grim Dan Morgan rode.

And still that hooded horseman that Morgan could not see,
Watched by the wild bush-creatures, rode close beside his
　　knee.
Before them in a clearing a drover's campfire burned:
The phantom rode with Morgan, and turned when Morgan
　　turned.
And loud the boobook's warning came on the cold night air,
"Go back, go back, Dan Morgan. Beware, beware, beware!"

He reached the station homestead; into the hall he strode,
And on his evil features the flickering lamplight glowed.
"Into one room!" he thundered. "Bring me a glass of grog!
If any disobey me I'll shoot him like a dog!"
With pistols cocked and ready, dark-eyed and beetle-browed—
Before the famous outlaw the bravest hearts were cowed.

All night with loaded pistols he dozed and muttered there,
All night the evil shadow stood close beside his chair.

The brave Scotch girl McDonald, a lass who knew no fear,
Slipped out unseen by Morgan to warn the homesteads near.
And in the hours of darkness, before the break of dawn,
Around the fierce Dan Morgan the fatal net was drawn.

Day broke upon the Murray, the morning mists were gone,
The magpies sang their matins, the river murmured on.
When Morgan left the homestead and neared the stockyard
    gate
He heard the boobook's warning, and turned but turned too
    late—
For Quinlan pressed the trigger as Morgan swung around,
And sent the grim bushranger blaspheming to the ground.

So fell the dread Dan Morgan in Eighteen sixty-five,
In death as much unpitied as hated when alive.
He lived by blood and plunder, an outlaw to the end;
In life he showed no mercy, in death he left no friend.
And all who seek to follow in Morgan's evil track
Should heed the boobook's warning: "Go back, go back, go
    back!"

My Old Black Billy

I have humped my bluey in all the States
With my old black billy, the best of mates.
For years I have camped, and toiled, and tramped
On roads that are rough and hilly,
With my plain and sensible,
Indispensable,
Old black billy.

My old black billy, my old black billy,
Whether the wind is warm or chilly
I always find when the shadows fall
My old black billy the best mate of all.

I have carried my swag on the parched Paroo
Where water is scarce and the houses few,
On many a track, in the great Out Back
Where the heat would drive you silly
I've carried my sensible,
Indispensable,
Old black billy.

When the days of tramping at last are o'er
And I drop my swag at the Golden Door,
Saint Peter will stare when he sees me there.
Then he'll say "Poor wandering Willie,
Come in with your sensible,
Indispensable,
Old black billy."

MARY DURACK

1913·

Red Jack

She rises clear to memory's eye
From mists of long ago,
Though we met but once, in '98—
In the days of Cobb and Co.

'Twas driving into Hughenden
With mail and gold for load
That I saw Red Jack, the wanderer,
Come riding down the road.

Red Jack and Mephistopheles—
They knew them far and wide,
From Camooweal to Charters Towers,
The route they used to ride.

They knew them round the Selwyns where
The Leichhardt has its source,
Along the winding cattle ways—
A woman and a horse.

And strange the tales they told of them
Who ranged the dusty track:
The great black Mephistopheles
And the red-haired witch Red Jack.

She claimed no name but that, they said,
And owned no things but these:
Her saddle, swag and riding-kit
And Mephistopheles.

And often travellers such as I
Had seen, and thought it strange,
A woman working on the line
That crossed McKinley Range.

Had seen her in the dreary wake
Of stock upon the plains,
Her brown hand quick upon the whip
And light upon the reins.

With milling cattle in the yard
Amid the dust-fouled air,
With rope and knife and branding iron—
A girl with glowing hair.

"Red Jack's as good as any man!"
The settlers used to own;
And some bold spirits sought her hand,
But Red Jack rode alone.

She rode alone, and wise men learned
To set her virtue high,
To weigh what skill she plied her whip
With the hardness of her eye.

I saw Red Jack in '98,
The first time and the last,
But her face, brown-gaunt, and her hair, red-bright,
Still haunt me from the past.

The coach drew in as she rode in sight;
We passed the time of day;
Then shuffled out the mail she sought
And watched her ride away.

And oh! her hair was living fire,
But her eyes were cold as stone:
Red Jack and Mephistopheles
Went all their ways alone.

IV
POETS OF THE NINETIES

In a Wine Cellar

See how it flashes,
This grape-blood fine!
Our beards it splashes,
O comrade mine!
Life dust and ashes
Were, wanting wine.

Amontillado
Fires heart and eyes;
Champagne the shadow
Of care defies;
An El Dorado
In Rhine-wine lies;

Port has the mintage
Of generous deeds;
Tokay scorns stintage
And richly bleeds;
But this great vintage
The Wine-March leads.

· · · · · ·

No vintage alien
For thee or me!
Our fount Castalian
Of poesy
Shall wine Australian,
None other be.

Then place your hand in
This hand of mine,
And while we stand in
Her brave sunshine
Pledge deep our land in
Our land's own wine.

It has no glamour
Of old romance,
Of war and amour
In Spain or France;
Its poets stammer
As yet, perchance;

But he may wholly
Become a seer
Who quaffs it slowly;
For he shall hear,
Though faintly, lowly,
Yet sweet and clear,

The axes ringing
On mountain sides,
The wool-boats swinging
Down Darling tides,
The drovers singing
Where Clancy rides,

The miners driving,
The stockman's strife;
All sounds conniving
To tell the rife,
Rich, rude, strong-striving
Australian life.

Once more your hand in
This hand of mine!
And while we stand in
The brave sunshine,
Pledge deep our land in
Our land's own wine!

Dreams

I have been dreaming all a summer day
Of rare and dainty poems I would write;
Love-lyrics delicate as lilac-scent,
Soft idylls woven of wind, and flower, and stream,
And songs and sonnets carven in fine gold.

The day is fading and the dusk is cold;
Out of the skies has gone the opal gleam,
Out of my heart has passed the high intent
Into the shadow of the falling night—
Must all my dreams in darkness pass away?

I have been dreaming all a summer day:
Shall I go dreaming so until Life's light
Fades in Death's dusk, and all my days are spent?
Ah, what am I the dreamer but a dream!
The day is fading and the dusk is cold.

My songs and sonnets carven in fine gold
Have faded from me with the last day-beam
That purple lustre to the sea-line lent,
And flushed the clouds with rose and chrysolite;
So days and dreams in darkness pass away.

I have been dreaming all a summer day
Of songs and sonnets carven in fine gold;
But all my dreams in darkness pass away;
The day is fading, and the dusk is cold.

Tamerlane

Lo, upon the carpet, where
Throned upon a heap of slain
Blue-eyed dolls of beauty rare

(Ah, they pleaded all in vain!)
Sits the Infant Tamerlane!

Broken toys upon the floor
Scattered lie—a ruined rout.
Thus from all things evermore
Are—the fact is past a doubt—
Hidden virtues hammered out.

Poet's page, or statesman's bust,
Nothing comes to him amiss;
Everything he clutches must—
'Tis his simple dream of bliss!—
Suffer his analysis.

O my little Tamerlane,
Infantile Iconoclast,
Is your small barbaric brain
Not o'erawed by the amassed
Wit and Wisdom of the Past?

Type are you of that which springs
Ever forth when comes the need,
Overthrowing thrones and kings,
Faithless altar, sapless creed;
Sowing fresh and living seed.

On the worn-out Roman realm,
In whose purple gnawed the moth,
Thus its pride to overwhelm,
And its state to carve like cloth,
Swept the fierce, long-sworded Goth.

Age preserves with doting care
Things from which life long has fled,

Shrieks to see Youth touch a hair
On the mouldiest mummy-head—
So Egyptians kept their dead.

Youth comes by with head high-reared,
Stares in scorn at these august
Effigies by age revered—
Gilded shapes of Greed and Lust—
Shakes them into rags and dust.

Little Vandal, smash away!
Riot while your blood is hot!
If into the world each day
Such as you are entered not,
It would perish of dry-rot.

The Ascetic

The narrow, thorny path he trod.
"Enter into My joy," said God.
The sad ascetic shook his head;
"I've lost all taste for joy," he said.

Faith

Faith shuts her eyes,
Poor self-deceiver!
The last god dies
With the last believer.

From *Night*

Suns, planets, stars, in glorious array
They march, melodious, on their unknown way.

Thought, seraph-winged and swifter than the light,
Unto the dim verge of the Infinite,

171

Pursues them, through that strange ethereal flood
In which they swim (mayhap it is the blood

Of Universal God wherein they are
But corpuscles—sun, satellite, and star—

And their great stream of glory but a dim,
Small pulse in the remotest vein of Him)

Pursues in vain, and from lone, awful glooms
Turns back to earth again with weary plumes.

. . . . . .

Through glacial gulfs of Space the soul must roam
To feel the comfort of its earthly home.

Ah, Mother dear! broad-bosomed Mother Earth,
Mother of all our Joy, Grief, Madness, Mirth,

Mother of flower and fruit, of stream and sea—
We are thy children and must cling to thee.

I lay my head upon thy breast and hear,
Small, small and faint, yet strangely sweet and clear,

The hum and clash of little worlds below,
Each on its own path moving, swift or slow.

And listening, ever with intenter ear,
Through din of wars invisible I hear

A Homer—genius is not gauged by mass—
Singing his Iliad on a blade of grass.

And nations hearken: his great song resounds
Unto the tussock's very utmost bounds.

States rise and fall, each blade of grass upon,
But still his song from blade to blade rolls on

Through all the tussock-world, and Helen still
Is Fairest Fair, and Ajax wild of will—

An Ajax whose huge size, when measured o'er,
Is full ten-thousandth of an inch or more—

Still hurls defiance at the gods whose home
Is in the distant, awful, dew-drop dome

That trembling hangs, suspended from a spray
An inch above him—worlds of space away.

Old prophecies foretell—but Time proves all—
The day will come when it, like Troy, shall fall.

Lo! through this small great wondrous song there runs
The marching melody of stars and suns.

Narcissus and Some Tadpoles

Scene I. THE RED PAGE ROOM.

[*The* RED PAGE EDITOR *discovered sitting,* en boucher, *in his shirt sleeves. Proof sheets of new Australian poems on his desk. Coils of more new Australian poems (in manuscript) hanging over back of his chair. He reads one of the latter, and mutters, shaking his head:* "Won't do. Lacks the indefinable something which is the soul of Poetry. Must define that one of these days." *Takes up another poem. Strikes out*

six verses and leaves two. Murmurs "Pith in these—all the
rest is padding," and sweeps the refuse into the W.P. Basket.
Hums softly—]

> The critic of the days of yore
> (I aptly call him Blunderbore)
> Ground bones of bards to make him bread—
> I scoop their marrow out instead.

> [*Muses a few moments, then lilts loudly*]

> I am the Blender of the pure
> Australian Brand of Literature.
> No verse, however fine, can be
> The radiant thing called Poetry
> Unless it is approved by me.
> I am the Critic set on high,
> The Red Page Rhadamanthus I.
> The Master, too, of the Event
> Am I on this weird Continent:
> This phrase I took from—thanks herewith!—
> My little brother Meredith.
> I make or mar. My daring hand
> Explores the entrails of the land,
> And finds, beneath a greasy hat,
> An Austral Homer at Cow Flat.
> I seize him by his shaggy hair,
> And lift him high, and hold him there,
> And wave him like a Habakkuk;
> And yell to notify my luck.
> Should any dare at me to jeer
> And say "His swan's a goose, we fear,"
> I crown his head with laurel-wreath—
> And promptly fling it in their teeth.

VOICE FROM PROOF-SHEETS

A primrose by a river's brim
A splendid sunflower is to him.

VOICE FROM W.P.B.

But he himself—bear this in mind!—
Must be the first that flower to find.

SEVERAL VOICES FROM PROOF-SHEETS (*conclusively*)

His simple task is to be good
To members of the Brotherhood.

R.P. EDITOR (*with gay irony*)

A month goes by. I drop him hard,
And take up with a newer bard—
The Shakespeare of Dead Dingo Swamp.
The Cow Flat Homer has to tramp.
The adjectives I decked him with,
I take them back to use on Smith—
Or Jones, or whatsoever name
The Shakespeare of the Swamp may claim—
And, like a kite without a tail,
He flops into the hollow vale.

G. ESSEX EVANS

1863-1909

The Women of the West

They left the vine-wreathed cottage and the mansion on the
    hill,
The houses in the busy streets where life is never still,
The pleasures of the city, and the friends they cherished best:
For love they faced the wilderness—the Women of the West.

175

The roar, and rush, and fever of the city died away,
And the old-time joys and faces—they were gone for many a
day;
In their place the lurching coach-wheel, or the creaking
bullock-chains,
O'er the everlasting sameness of the never-ending plains.

In the slab-built, zinc-roofed homestead of some lately taken
run,
In the tent beside the bankment of a railway just begun,
In the huts on new selections, in the camps of man's unrest,
On the frontiers of the Nation, live the Women of the West.

The red sun robs their beauty and, in weariness and pain,
The slow years steal the nameless grace that never comes
again;
And there are hours men cannot soothe, and words men can-
not say—
The nearest woman's face may be a hundred miles away.

The wide bush holds the secrets of their longing and desires,
When the white stars in reverence light their holy altar fires,
And silence, like the touch of God, sinks deep into the
breast—
Perchance He hears and understands the Women of the
West.

For them no trumpet sounds the call, no poet plies his arts,
They only hear the beating of their gallant, loving hearts.
But they have sung with silent lives the song all songs
above—
The holiness of sacrifice, the dignity of love.

Well have we held our fathers' creed. No call has passed us
by.

We faced and fought the wilderness, we sent our sons to die.
And we have hearts to do and dare, and yet, o'er all the rest,
The hearts that made the Nation were the Women of the
    West.

SYDNEY JEPHCOTT

1864-1951

Thredbo River

Summer, like a dread disease,
Whelms the world in sultry shine;
From Hell's mouth the mocking breeze
Troubles all the swooning trees—
Heart o' mine! O, heart o' mine!—
'Mongst those mountains now to roam;
Cooling thy fever in the foam,
In the foam of Thredbo River,
Thredbo River pouring down to Jindabyne!

O, the weariness, the fever,
Burning, barren heart o' mine!
O, to lie, my heart! alone;
Just a smooth, enduring stone
In the Thredbo's deepest pool,
Packed with plunging waters cool
Where light's shadowy arrows shine!
Cold and old grey boulders,
Shoulders leaned to shoulders,
Baffling back white waters eager
That their heavy breasts beleaguer—
Torrents white of Thredbo River—
Thredbo River roaring down to Jindabyne!

Sunset

The weary wind is slumbering on the wing:
Leaping from out meek twilight's purpling blue
Burns the proud star of eve as though it knew
Itself the big king jewel quivering
On the black turban of advancing night.
In the dim west the soldiers of the sun
Strike all their royal colours one by one,
Reluctantly surrender every height.

Marlowe

With Eastern banners flaunting in the breeze
Royal processions sounding fife and gong
And showering jewels on the jostling throng
March to the tramp of Marlowe's harmonies.

He drained life's brimming goblet to the lees:
He recked not that a peer superb and strong
Would tune great notes to his impassioned song
And top his cannonading lines with ease.

To the wild clash of cymbals we behold
The tragic ending of his youthful life:
The revelry of kisses bought with gold,
The jest and jealous rival and the strife,
A harlot weeping o'er a corpse scarce cold,
A scullion fleeing with a bloody knife.

178

1865-1897

The Crazy World

The world did say to me,
"My bread thou shalt not eat,
I have no place for thee
In house nor field nor street.

"I have on land nor sea
For thee nor home nor bread,
I scarce can give to thee
A grave when thou art dead."

"O crazy World," said I,
"What is it thou canst give,
Which wanting, I must die,
Or having, I shall live?

"When thou thy all has spent,
And all thy harvests cease,
I still have nutriment
That groweth by decrease.

"Thy streets will pass away,
Thy towers of steel be rust,
Thy heights to plains decay,
Thyself be wandering dust;

"But I go ever on
From prime to endless prime,
I sit on Being's throne,
A lord o'er space and time.

"Then, crazy World," said I,
"What is it thou canst give,
Which wanting, I must die,
Or having, I shall live?"

1865-1923

Sea-grief

Along the serried coast the Southerly raves,
Grey birds scream landward through the distance hoar,
And, swinging from the dim, confounded shore,
The everlasting boom of broken waves

Like muffled thunder rolls above the graves
Of all the wonder-lands and lives of yore,
Whose bones asunder bleach for evermore,
In sobbing chasms and under choking caves:

O breaking heart—whose only rest is rage,
White tossing arms, and lips that kiss and part
In lonely dreams of love's wild ecstasy,

Not the mean earth thy suffering can assuage
Nor highest heaven fulfil thy hungry heart,
O fair, full-bosomed, passionate weeping sea.

BERNARD O'DOWD

1866-1953

From *Young Democracy*

Hark! Young Democracy from sleep
  Our careless sentries raps:
A backwash from the Future's deep
  Our Evil's foreland laps.

Unknown, these Titans of our Night
  Their New Creation make:
Unseen, they toil and love and fight
  That glamoured Man may wake.

Knights-errant of the human race,
  The Quixotes of to-day,
For man as man they claim a place,
  Prepare the tedious way.

They seek no dim-eyed mob's applause,
  Deem base the titled name,
And spurn, for glory of their Cause,
  The tawdry nymphs of Fame.

No masks of ignorance or sin
  Hide from them you or me:
We're Man—no colour shames our skin,
  No race or caste have we.

The prognathous Neanderthal,
  To them, conceals the Bruce;
They see Dan Aesop in the thrall;
  From swagmen Christ deduce.

    .   .   .   .   .   .

Outcast from social gaieties;
  Denied life's lilied grace;
They mount their hidden Calvaries
  To save the human race.

The bowers of Art a few may know;
  A few wait highly placed:
Most bear the hods of common woe,
  And some you call disgraced.

But whether in the mob or school,
  In church or poverty,
They teach and live the Golden Rule
  Of Young Democracy:

P

That culture, joy and goodliness
  Be th' equal right of all:
That Greed no more shall those oppress
  Who by the wayside fall:

That each shall share what all men sow:
  That colour, caste 's a lie:
That man is God, however low—
  Is man, however high.

The Cow

This is a rune I ravelled in the still,
Arrogant stare of an Australian cow—
"These prankt intruders of the hornless brow,
Puffed up with strange illusions of their skill
To fence, to milk, to fatten and to kill,
Once worshipped me with temple, rite and vow,
Crowned me with stars, and bade rapt millions bow
Before what abject guess they called my will!

"To-day, this flunkey of my midden, Man,
Throws child-oblations in my milking byre,
Stifles in slums to spare me lordly fields,
Flatters with spotless consorts my desire,
And for a pail of cream his birth-right yields,
As once in Egypt, Hellas, Ind, Iran!"

From *The Bush*

As many, Mother, are your moods and forms
As all the sons who love you. Here, you mow
Careering grounds for every brood of storms
The wild sea-mares to desert stallions throw;
Anon, up through a sea of sand you glance

With green ephemeral exuberance,
And then quick seeds dive deep to years of slumber
From hot-hoofed drought's precipitate return:
There, league on league, the snow's cold fingers number
The shrinking nerves of supple-jack and fern.

To other eyes and ears you are a great
Pillared cathedral tremulously green,
An odorous and hospitable gate
To genial mystery, the happy screen
Of truants or of lovers' rambling there
'Neath sun-shot boughs o'er miles of maidenhair.
Wee rubies dot the leaflets of the cherries,
The wooing wagtails hop from log to bough,
The bronzewing comes from Queensland for the berries,
The bell-bird by the creek is calling now.

And you can ride, an Eastern queen, they say,
By living creatures sumptuously borne,
With all barbaric equipages gay,
Beneath the torrid blue of Capricorn.
That native lotus is the very womb
That was the Hindoo goddess' earthly tomb.
The gang-gang screams o'er cactus wildernesses,
Palm trees are there, and swampy widths of rice,
Unguents and odours ooze from green recesses,
The jungles blaze with birds of Paradise.

But I, in city exile, hear you sing
Of saplinged hill and box-tree dotted plain,
Or silver-grass that prays the North Wind's wing
Convey its sigh to the loitering rain:
And Spring is half distraught with wintry gusts,
Summer the daily spoil of tropic lusts
The sun and she too fiercely shared together

Lingering thro' voluptuous Hindoo woods,
But o'er my windless, soft autumnal weather
The peace that passes understanding broods.

When, now, they say "The Bush!" I see the top
Delicate amber leaflings of the gum
Flutter, or flocks of screaming greenleeks drop
Silent, where in the shining morning hum
The gleaning bees for honey-scented hours
'Mid labyrinthine leaves and white gum flowers.
Cantering midnight hoofs are nearing, nearing,
The straining bullocks flick the harpy flies,
The "hatter" weeds his melancholy clearing,
The distant cow-bell tinkles o'er the rise.

You are the brooding comrade of our way,
Whispering rumour of a new Unknown,
Moulding us white ideals to obey,
Steeping whate'er we learn in lore your own,
And freshening with unpolluted light
The squalid city's day and pallid night,
Till we become ourselves distinct, Australian,
(Your native lightning charging blood and nerve)
Stripped to the soul of borrowed garments, alien
To that approaching Shape of God you serve.

Brooding, brooding, your whispers murmur plain
That searching for the clue to mystery
In grottos of decrepitude is vain,
That never shall the eye of prophet see
In crooked Trade's tumultuous streets the plan
Of templed cities adequate to man.
Brooding, brooding, you make us Brahmins waiting
(While uninspired pass on the hurtling years)
Faithful to dreams your spirit is creating,
Till Great Australia, born of you, appears.

For Great Australia is not yet: She waits
(Where o'er the Bush prophetic auras play)
The passing of these temporary States,
Flaunting their tawdry flags of far decay.
Her aureole above the alien mists
Beacons our filial eyes to mountain trysts:
'Mid homely trees with all ideals fruited,
She shelters us till Trade's Simoon goes by,
And slakes our thirst from cisterns unpolluted
For ages cold in brooding deeps of sky.

We love our brothers, and to heal their woe
Pluck simples from the known old gardens still:
We love our kindred over seas, and grow
Their symbols tenderly o'er plain and hill:
We feel their blood rebounding in our hearts,
And speak as they would speak our daily parts:
But under all we know, we know that only
A virgin womb unsoiled by ancient fear
Can Saviours bear. So, we, your Brahmins, lonely,
Deaf to the barren tumult, wait your Year.

.   .   .   .   .   .

Where is Australia, singer, do you know?
These sordid farms and joyless factories,
Mephitic mines and lanes of pallid woe?
Those ugly towns and cities such as these
With incense sick to all unworthy power,
And all old sin in full malignant flower?
No! to her bourn her children still are faring:
She is a Temple that we are to build:
For her the ages have been long preparing:
She is a prophecy to be fulfilled!

185

All that we love in olden lands and lore
Was signal of her coming long ago!
Bacon foresaw her, Campanella, More,
And Plato's eyes were with her star aglow!
Who toiled for Truth, whate'er their countries were,
Who fought for Liberty, they yearned for her!
No corsair's gathering ground, or tryst for schemers,
No chapman Carthage to a huckster Tyre,
She is the Eldorado of old dreamers,
The Sleeping Beauty of the world's desire!

She is the scroll on which we are to write
Mythologies our own and epics new:
She is the port of our propitious flight
From Ur idolatrous and Pharaoh's crew.
She is our own, unstained, if worthy we,
By dream, or god, or star we would not see:
Her crystal beams all but the eagle dazzle;
Her wind-wide ways none but the strong-winged sail:
She is Eutopia, she is Hy-Brasil,
The watchers on the tower of morning hail!

Yet she shall be as we, the Potter, mould:
Altar or tomb, as we aspire, despair:
What wine we bring shall she, the chalice, hold:
What word we write shall she, the script, declare:
Bandage our eyes, she shall be Memphis, Spain:
Barter our souls, she shall be Tyre again:
And if we pour on her the red oblation
All o'er the world shall Asshur's buzzards throng:
Love-lit, her Chaos shall become Creation:
And dewed with dream, her silence flower in song.

Australia

Last sea-thing dredged by sailor Time from Space,
Are you a drift Sargasso, where the West
In halcyon calm rebuilds her fatal nest?
Or Delos of a coming Sun-God's race?
Are you for Light, and trimmed, with oil in place,
Or but a Will o' Wisp on marshy quest?
A new demesne for Mammon to infest?
Or lurks millennial Eden 'neath your face?

The cenotaphs of species dead elsewhere
That in your limits leap and swim and fly,
Or trail uncanny harp-strings from your trees,
Mix omens with the auguries that dare
To plant the Cross upon your forehead sky,
A virgin helpmate Ocean at your knees.

From *Alma Venus*

Door of existence, beacon of our haze,
Horn of beautitude, clue to the maze,
Pole for the magnet, chalice of the Quest,
Ark of the wilderness, star of the West,
Moon of our dream-tide's pallid solitudes,
Builder of homes and harmonist of feuds,
Crowned with the stars and throned upon the night,
Mother of dolour dearer than delight,
Storm in the lily's virginal repose,
Flame of the amethyst, breath of the rose,
First foam and fairest from the far Deep flung,
Ancient of Days, perpetually young!

.   .   .   .   .   .

Though sun and earth shall duly pass away,
Though all the gods shall ripen and decay,

It is Their Will Who bade the world exist:
And woe to him or her who doth not list
The sole clear mandate from the Otherwhere
Flushed through the Universe—Beget or bear!"
Love we or dread we may not all ignore
The single beacon on the circling shore
Where Being laps upon the caverned steep
Wherefrom we drifted and whereto we creep.
Beacon! although You lead us but to gloom!
A guiding star, it may be, to the tomb!
Comet flung from the Void through trackless Light!
Yet is Your rosy flame in ion, mite,
And great pathetic man, the only trace
Of something more than chance in Time and Space,
That purpose dimly threads the crazy web,
That tides of anguish ultimately ebb,
That green hope signals underground a Nile,
That faith is wiser than an ostrich wile,
That there is something in us will elude
The withering fingers of vicissitude,
And man's ripe earth by a guttering sun betrayed
Will not in cold and useless ruin fade.

LOUIS LAVATER

1867-1953

Mopoke

Mopoke! . . . Mopoke! . . .
Mysterious bird,
What loneliness
In thy one word!

Mopoke! . . . Mopoke! . . .
The vague profound
Of forest night
Is in the sound.

The shifting hollows
Are clogged with dark;
My eyes can find
No standing mark,
Save in the distance—
Oh, so far—
A hand of sky
Holds a sleepy star.

Night in the forest
Is solemn and strange,
And home is somewhere
Over the range. . . .
How far have I come,
How far must I go,
Ere my window shines
Like a star below?

Mopoke! . . . Mopoke! . . .
'Tis nearer now;
I strain my eyes
To an unseen bough
And . . . though I listen
Nothing is heard,
Rustle of leaf
Nor rustle of bird;
But a fleeting darkness
Near? . . . or far? . . .
Blots for a moment
My sleepy star.

Faithless

There's not a tear that brims thine eye unshed
But clouds my vision wheresoe'er I go,
There's not a weary hour that bows thy head

But mine is weighted with a kindred woe;
There's not a burning thought that sears thy brain,
There's not a poniard pang that stabs thee through,
There's no remembrance trails a lingering pain
But I, the faithless, I must share it too.
O heart that breaks for treasons not thine own,
O eyes that weep, that may be weeping now
Unheard, unheeded, ah! but not alone—
O loved one, lost and longed for, where art thou?

I seek thee daily in the crowded street,
Praying to God that we may never meet!

RODERIC QUINN

1867-1949

The Camp Within the West

O did you see a troop go by
Way-weary and oppressed,
Dead kisses on the drooping lip
And a dead heart in the breast?

Yea, I have seen them one by one
Way-weary and oppressed;
And when I asked them, "Whither speed?"
They answered, "To the West!"

And were they pale as pale could be,
Death-pale, with haunted eyes?
And did you see the hot white dust
Range round their feet and rise?

O, they were pale as pale could be;
And pale as an embered leaf
The hot white dust had risen, but
They laid it with their grief.

190

Did no one say "The way is long,"
And crave a little rest?
O no; they said "The night is nigh,
Our camp is in the West!"

And did pain pierce their feet, as though
The way with thorns were set,
And were they visited by strange
Dark angels of regret?

O, yea; and some were mute as death,
Though, shot by many a dart,
With them the salt of inward tears
Went stinging through the heart.

And how are these wayfarers called,
And whither do they wend?
The Weary-Hearted—and their road
At sunset hath an end.

Shed tears for them . . . *Nay, nay, no tears!*
They yearn for endless rest;
Perhaps large stars will burn above
Their camp within the West.

The Fisher

All night a noise of leaping fish
Went round the bay,
And up and down the shallow sands
Sang waters at their play.

The mangroves drooped on salty creeks,
And through the dark,
Making a pale patch in the deep,
Gleamed, as it swam, a shark.

In streaks and twists of sudden fire
Among the reeds
The bream went by, and where they passed
The bubbles shone like beads.

All night the full deep drinking-song
Of nature stirred,
And nought beside, save leaping fish
And some forlorn night-bird.

No lost wind wandered down the hills
To tell of wide
Wild waterways; on velvet moved
The silky, sucking tide.

Deep down there sloped in shadowy mass
A giant hill;
And midway, mirrored in the tide,
The stars burned large and still.

The fisher, dreaming on the rocks,
Heard Nature say
Strange secret things that none may hear
Upon the beaten way,

And whisperings and wonder stirred,
And hopes and fears,
And sadness touched his heart, and filled
His eyes with star-stained tears:

And so, thrilled through with joy and love
And sweet distress,
He stood entranced, enchained by her
Full-breasted loveliness.

Emus

My annals have it so:
A thing my mother saw,
Nigh eighty years ago,
With happiness and awe.

Along a level hill—
A clearing in wild space.
And night's last tardy chill
Yet damp on morning's face.

Sight never to forget:
Solemn against the sky
In stately silhouette
Ten emus walking by.

One after one they went
In line, and without haste:
On their unknown intent,
Ten emus grandly paced.

She, used to hedged-in fields
Watched them go filing past
Into the great Bush Wilds
Silent and vast.

Sudden that hour she knew
That this far place was good,
This mighty land and new
For the soul's hardihood.

For hearts that love the strange,
That carry wonder;
The Bush, the hills, the range,
And the dark flats under.

Lovers

To be unloved brings sweet relief:
The strong adoring eyes
Play the eternal thief
With the soul's fit disguise.

He will not sleep, and let be drawn
The screen of thy soul's ark;
They keep, those lidless eyes,
Thy sanctuary stark.

God, when he made each separate
Unfashioned his own act,
Giving the lover eyes,
So his love's soul be sacked.

To be unloved gives sweet relief;
The one integrity
Of soul is to be lone,
Inviolate, and free.

Lichen

Parasite lichen
Lies grey on the years;
Lily buries herself
When winter appears.

Bright rose burns away,
Leaving lichen alone—
Fellow of frost,
Suckling of stone.

I am for lily,
I am for rose—
Delicate beauty
Trembles and goes.

Lion

There was no ceremony
When the last god died,
No dramatic moment
When a new Faith slew;
But slow, undeified,
The once feared and cherished,
Outworn, forgotten,
Lion Life never knew
When the last god perished.

What next shall he lose
In his large going?
Leaves flung from his flanks
In terrible unknowing!

Communal

Seers have no monopoly:
Nor may the white saints
Gather God to themselves
By their praisings and plaints.

For a moment, Moses,
For an instant, Paul;
Glimpses, tones, and touches
Come to each and all.

I had my strange hour,
Superior to the mists,
And gained sufficient power
For ten evangelists.

Flesh

I have seen a gum-tree,
Scarred by the blaze
Of the pioneer axe,
Mend after long days;
Lip to lip shut
Of the separate bark,
Till the gape of the wound
Was a vanishing mark.

I have seen in the hunt
The pulse of rent flesh;
Seen the fingers of Time
Unite it afresh.
I have heard a man's cry
As the teeth of the mill
Bit marrow and bone—
To hurt, not to kill.

Oh, strong is the flesh
To cure and defend:
'Tis but the stopt heart
That Time cannot mend.

Cubes

Nina's cross: her alphabet
Flung upon the floor.
Hoity toity! in a pet,
Wanting something more.

You have there the whole of it,
Little Goldilocks,
All the wisdom and the wit,
On those pretty blocks.

All the science and the verse,
Eastern, European;
Rearrange, transpose, disperse:
There's the Bodleian!

Inspiration

There's half a god in many a man,
And Life is there to say—
To give to his capacity
The option of a day.

Two beings to an enterprise—
Oneself, and oneself's god—
One to use little heart and head,
And one to give the nod.

There's half a god in many a man,
If he would only heed,
And listen for the Other Voice,
Obey the hidden lead.

And when the Hour is at his side,
Let him quiescent stand,
The Wonder flooding at his heart,
The apple in his hand.

DAVID McKEE WRIGHT

1869-1928

From *Dark Rosaleen*:

I

On a shining silver morning long ago
God made Ireland and you,
While His garden angels taught the green to grow,
Walking softly in the tears of His dew.

Ω

They had seven fine crocks of yellow seed,
Seven slips of the Heaven-bushes tall,
And seven holy bees for honey-mead,
But you, Heart, never there at all.

Then God felt up with fingers white
In the blue where the great blooms are,
And He plucked from the branches of the light
His youngest and best-loved star.

He set it, with the wonder of His hand,
In the brown mould crying in the dew
Till it grew to a blossom in the land,
And, Heart, but the face of it was you.

God made Ireland for love,
With a green dress trailing on the sea,
And one star less up above,
But the Dark Rosaleen for me.

IX

My Love is the voice of a song
Out of green leaves,
Blown in the dusk along,
Over hedges and sheaves,
Down to a quiet place
Below the hill
Where the darkening waters' face
Is very still.

My love is a light and a sign;
For all through the heavy night,
When never a star will shine,
Her hand is white,

Leading me, leading me
Over the misty hollow
And hill to the sea . . . .
Heart, let me follow!

My Love is the grace of God.
With bare feet will I walk
To her over the black sod
And the bruised flower on its stalk;
For she has the pity of years,
And my heart goes clean,
Washed with her holy tears,
Of dark things seen.

My Love is a white girl
With lips like a June rose;
And under a brown curl
I whisper what no one knows.
For, oh, woman of mine,
'Tis all the world I would miss
If daylight and night-shine
Were not in your kiss.

Danny's Wooing

'Twas the spring in the air
And a laughter that ran
Under Murna's black hair
To the heart of a man;
With the sloe-bush in leaf
And the wet clover green—
Och, April, you thief,
Is it love that you mean?

'Twas her mother's white goat
On the side of the hill,
And the rain on my coat
With the sun laughing still,
And the thought of her eyes—
Sure, my heart is a gift,
In the black of surprise,
When her eyelashes lift!

'Twas the word that I spoke
With the wind blowing clear,
And the small sob that broke
In my throat full of fear—
"Och, Danny," she said,
"There's the white cream to set
And the pigs to be fed,
And you're plaguing me yet."

Would she slip past the door?
Och, her tongue was too wise;
But I listened far more
To the look in her eyes—
"Sure, stay and be kist;"
But she turned by the wall
With a fine-lady twist
Of her neck and her shawl.

'Twas the spring in the air
And a laughter that ran
With the toss of her hair
To the heart of a man—
"Och, Murna, come out,
Girl of dreams, and be kist"—
But she hit me a clout
With the white of her fist.

Would she slip past the door?
Sure, her mouth was too red,
With the cheek of me sore,
And those eyes in her head.
Troth, I kist her too well—
Twenty times at the least . . . .
"Now, Danny, we'll tell
A small word to the priest."

MARIE E. J. PITT

1869-1948

A Gallop of Fire

When the north wind moans thro' the blind creek courses
And revels with harsh, hot sand,
I loose the horses, the wild, red horses,
I loose the horses, the mad, red horses,
And terror is on the land.

With prophetic murmur the hills are humming,
The forest-kings bend and blow;
With hoofs of brass on the baked earth drumming
O brave red horses, they hear us coming,
And the legions of Death lean low.

O'er the wooded height, and the sandy hollow
Where the boles to the axe have rung,
Tho' they fly the foeman as flies the swallow,
The fierce red horses, my horses, follow
With flanks to the faint earth flung.

Or with frenzied hieroglyphs, fear embossing
Night's sable horizon bars,
Thro' tangled mazes of death-darts crossing,
I swing my leaders and watch them tossing
Their red manes against the stars.

201

But when south winds sob in the drowned creek courses
And whisper to hard wet sand,
I hold the horses, the spent red horses,
I hold the horses, the tired red horses,
And silence is on the land.

Yea, the south wind sobs 'mong the drowned creek courses
For sorrows no man shall bind—
Ah, God! for the horses, the black plumed horses,
Dear God! for the horses, Death's own pale horses,
That raced in the tracks behind.

CHRISTOPHER BRENNAN

1870-1932

From *Towards the Source*:

Let Us Go Down, the Long Dead Night Is Done

Let us go down, the long dead night is done,
the dolorous incantation has been wrought;
soul, let us go, the saving word is won,
down from the tower of our hermetic thought.

See—for the wonder glimmers in the gates,
eager to burst the soundless bars and grace
the wistful earth, that still in blindness waits,
perfect with suffering for her Lord's embrace.

The spaces of the waters of the dawn
are spiritual with our transfigured gaze;
the intenser heights of morning, far withdrawn,
expect our dream to shine along their ways.

But speak the word! and o'er the adoring whole
straight from the marge of the perfected hours
sudden, large music through the vast, shall roll
a sea of light foaming with seedless flowers;

202

lilies that form on some ethereal wave,
still generate of the most ancient blue,
burst roses, rootless, knowing not the grave
nor yet the charnel thought by which they grew.

So we shall move at last, untortured powers,
and in white silence hear, as souls unborn,
our hymn given back by the eternal hours
singing together in the eternal morn.

I Saw My Life as Whitest Flame

I saw my life as whitest flame
light-leaping in a crystal sky,
and virgin colour where it came
pass'd to its heart, in love to die.

It wrapped the world in tender harm
rose-flower'd with one ecstatic pang:
God walk'd amid the hush'd alarm,
and all the trembling region rang

music, whose silver veils dispart
around the carven silences
Memnonian in the hidden heart—
now blithe, effulgurant majesties.

From *The Twilight of Disquietude*:
The Years That Go to Make Me Man

The years that go to make me man
this day are told a score and six
that should have set me magian
o'er my half-souls that struggle and mix.

But wisdom still remains a star
just hung within my aching ken,
and common prudence dwells afar
among contented homes of men.

In wide revolt and ruin tost
against whatever is or seems
my futile heart still wanders lost
in the same vast and impotent dreams.

On either hand life hurries by
its common joy, its common mirth;
I reach vague hands of sympathy,
a ghost upon this common earth.

My Heart Was Wandering in the Sands

My heart was wandering in the sands,
a restless thing, a scorn apart;
Love set his fire in my hands,
I clasp'd the flame unto my heart.

Surely, I said, my heart shall turn
one fierce delight of pointed flame;
and in that holocaust shall burn
its old unrest and scorn and shame;

surely my heart the heavens at last
shall storm with fiery orisons,
and know, enthroned in the vast,
the fervid peace of molten suns.

The flame that feeds upon my heart
fades or flares, by wild winds controll'd;
my heart still walks a thing apart,
my heart is restless as of old.

From *The Quest of Silence*:

Fire in the Heavens, and Fire along the Hills

Fire in the heavens, and fire along the hills,
and fire made solid in the flinty stone,
thick-mass'd or scatter'd pebble, fire that fills
the breathless hour that lives in fire alone.

This valley, long ago the patient bed
of floods that carv'd its antient amplitude,
in stillness of the Egyptian crypt outspread,
endures to drown in noon-day's tyrant mood.

Behind the veil of burning silence bound,
vast life's innumerous busy littleness
is hush'd in vague-conjectured blur of sound
that dulls the brain with slumbrous weight, unless
some dazzling puncture let the stridence throng
in the cicada's torture-point of song.

From *Lilith*:

The Anguish'd Doubt Broods over Eden (viii)

The anguish'd doubt broods over Eden; night
hangs her rent banners thro' the viewless height;
trophies and glories whence a trouble streams
of lamentable valour in old dreams:
out of its blank the watcher's soul is stirr'd
to take unto itself some olden word:

Adam to Lilith

O thou that achest, pulse o' the unwed vast,
now in the distant centre of my brain
dizzily narrow'd, now beyond the last
calm circle widening of the starry plain,

where, on the scatter'd edge of my surmise,
the twilit dreams fail off and rule is spent
vainly on vagrant bands the gulfs invite
to break away to the dark: they, backward sent,
tho' dumb, with dire infection in their eyes,
startle the central seat:—O pulse of night,
passing the hard throb of sun-smitten blood
when the noon-world is fused in fire and blent
with my then unattained hero-mood;
what will with me the imperious instinct
that hounds the gulfs together on that place
vanishing utterly out of mortal trace,
the citadel where I would seem distinct—
if not thou ween'st a vanity, my deep
unlighted still, the which thy refluent sweep
intolerably dilates, a tide that draws
with lunatic desire, distraught and fond,
to some dark moon of vastness, hung beyond
our little limits of familiar cause,
as tho' the tense and tortured voids should dash
ruining amorously together, a clash
portentous with some rose of thinnest flame,
secret, exhaled in the annull'd abyss,
that, with this soul, passes in that fell kiss
and to the soft-sprung flush all sanctity
surrenders, centring in the blossom'd Name,
as the dark wings of silence lovingly
hover above the adventurous song that fares
forth to the void and finds no lip that shares
its rapture, just the great wings spreading wide.

Lilith on the Fate of Man

Last, since a pinch of dust may quench the eyes
that took the azure curve of stainless skies

and still the fiercest heart, he seeks to whelm
infinite yearning with a little realm,
beating together with ungentle hands,
enslaved, the trembling spawn of generous lands,
whom he shall force, a busy swarm, to raise,
last bulwarks of his whelming discontent,
heaven-threatening Babels, iron Ninevehs
square-thought with rigid will, a monument
of stony rage in high defiant stones
eternized with blasphemous intent,
and carve the mountain-cone to hide his bones,
a wonder to blank tribes of shrunken days:
but in that cave before his upstart gates
where elder night endures unshaken, waits
that foe of settled peace, the smiling sphinx,
or foul Echidna's mass'd insidious links,
reminding him that all is vanities;
and when, at last, o'er his nine roods he lies,
stretch'd in the sarcophage whereover grief
makes way before one huge gust of relief,
not the wing-blast of his vain shade shall drive
his wizen'd captives from their dungeon-hive,
and make a solitude about his bed;
nor the chill thought petrific his low head
exudes in rays of darkness, that beyond
this perturb'd sphere congeal, an orb of dread:
I, Lilith, on his tomb immensely throned,
with viewless face and viewless vans outspread;
in the wide waste of his unhallow'd work,
calm coils of fear, my serpent-brood shall lurk;
and I shall muse above the little dust
that was the flesh that held my world in trust.

Interlude: *The Casement*

The window is wide and lo! beyond its bars
dim fields of fading stars
and cavern tracts, whence the great store of tears
that Beauty all the years
hath wept in wanderings of the eyeless dark,
remembering the long cark
whereunder we, her care, are silent bow'd,
invades with numbing shroud
this dwindling realm of listless avatars.
Dim fields of fading stars,
and shall yet ye with amaranth rapture burn
and maiden grace return
sprung soft and sudden on the fainting night,
rose passioning to white;
or must our task remain and hopeless art
that sickeneth the heart
from yon dull embers to evoke the ghost
of the first garden lost,
sad necromancers we? Then let the blast,
that waked you ancient, cast
into the deeps your useless lagging dearth,
O blazon'd shame of Earth,
who then might hail the last oblivion,
knowing you doomward blown
before the advance of night's relentless cars,
dim fields of fading stars!

From *The Wanderer*:

How Old Is My Heart

How old is my heart, how old, how old is my heart,
and did I ever go forth with song when the morn was new?
I seem to have trod on many ways: I seem to have left

I know not how many homes; and to leave each
was still to leave a portion of mine own heart,
of my old heart whose life I had spent to make that home
and all I had was regret, and a memory.
So I sit and muse in this wayside harbour and wait
till I hear the gathering cry of the ancient winds and again
I must up and out and leave the embers of the hearth
to crumble silently into white ash and dust,
and see the road stretch bare and pale before me: again
my garment and my home shall be the enveloping winds
and my heart be fill'd wholly with their old pitiless cry.

I Cry to You as I Pass Your Windows

I cry to you as I pass your windows in the dusk . . . .
Ye have built you unmysterious homes and ways in the wood
where of old ye went with sudden eyes to the right and left;
and your going was now made safe and your staying com-
    forted,
for the forest edge itself, holding old savagery
in unsearch'd glooms, was your houses' friendly barrier.
And now that the year goes winterward, ye thought to hide
behind your gleaming panes, and where the hearth sings
    merrily
make cheer with meat and wine, and sleep in the long night,
and the uncared wastes might be a crying unhappiness.
But I, who have come from the outer night, I say to you
the winds are up and terribly will they shake the dry wood:
the woods shall awake, hearing them, shall awake to be toss'd
    and riven,
and make a cry and a parting in your sleep all night
as the wither'd leaves go whirling all night along all ways.
And when ye come forth at dawn, uncomforted by sleep,
ye shall stand at amaze, beholding all the ways overhidden
with worthless drift of the dead and all your broken world:

and ye shall not know whence the winds have come, nor shall
    ye know
whither the yesterdays have fled, or if they were.

Come Out, Come Out, Ye Souls That Serve

Come out, come out, ye souls that serve, why will ye die?
or will ye sit and stifle in your prison-homes
dreaming of some master that holds the winds in leash
and the waves of darkness yonder in the gaunt hollow of
    night?
nay, there is none that rules: all is a strife of the winds
and the night shall billow in storm full oft ere all be done.
For this is the hard doom that is laid on all of you,
to be that whereof ye dream, dreaming against your will.
But first ye must travel the many ways, and your close-wrapt
    souls
must be blown thro' with the rain that comes from the home-
    less dark:
for until ye have had care of the wastes there shall be no
    truce
for them nor you, nor home, but ever the ancient feud;
and the soul of man must house the cry of the darkling waves
as he follows the ridge above the waters shuddering towards
    night,
and the rains and the winds that roam anhunger'd for some
    heart's warmth.
Go: tho' ye find it bitter, yet must ye be bare
to the wind and the sea and the night and the wail of birds
    in the sky;
go: tho' the going be hard and the goal blinded with rain
yet the staying is a death that is never soften'd with sleep.

O Desolate Eves

O desolate eves along the way, how oft,
despite your bitterness, was I warm at heart!
not with the glow of remember'd hearths, but warm
with the solitary unquenchable fire that burns
a flameless heat deep in his heart who has come
where the formless winds plunge and exult for aye
among the naked spaces of the world,
far past the circle of the ruddy hearths
and all their memories. Desperate eves,
when the wind-bitten hills turn'd violet
along their rims, and the earth huddled her heat
within her niggard bosom, and the dead stones
lay battle-strewn before the iron wind
that, blowing from the chill west, made all its way
a loneliness to yield its triumph room;
yet in that wind a clamour of trumpets rang,
old trumpets, resolute, stark, undauntable,
singing to battle against the eternal foe,
the wronger of this world, and all his powers
in some last fight, foredoom'd disastrous,
upon the final ridges of the world:
a war-worn note, stern fire in the stricken eve,
and fire thro' all my ancient heart, that sprang
towards that last hope of a glory won in defeat,
whence, knowing not sure if such high grace befall
at the end, yet I draw courage to front the way.

The Land I Came Thro' Last

The land I came thro' last was dumb with night,
a limbo of defeated glory, a ghost:
for wreck of constellations flicker'd perishing
scarce sustain'd in the mortuary air,

and on the ground and out of livid pools
wreck of old swords and crowns glimmer'd at whiles;
I seem'd at home in some old dream of kingship:
now it is clear grey day and the road is plain,
I am the wanderer of many years
who cannot tell if ever he was king
or if ever kingdoms were: I know I am
the wanderer of the ways of all the worlds,
to whom the sunshine and the rain are one
and one to stay or hasten, because he knows
no ending of the way, no home, no goal,
and phantom night and the grey day alike
withhold the heart where all my dreams and days
might faint in soft fire and delicious death:
and saying this to myself as a simple thing
I feel a peace fall in the heart of the winds
and a clear dusk settle, somewhere, far in me.

From *Pauca Mea*:

I Said, This Misery Must End

I said, This misery must end:
Shall I, that am a man and know
that sky and wind are yet my friend,
sit huddled under any blow?
so speaking left the dismal room
and stept into the mother-night
all fill'd with sacred quickening gloom
where the few stars burn'd low and bright,
and darkling on my darkling hill
heard thro' the beaches' sullen boom
heroic note of living will
rung trumpet-clear against the fight;
so stood and heard, and rais'd my eyes

erect, that they might drink of space,
and took the night upon my face,
till time and trouble fell away
and all my soul sprang up to feel
as one among the stars that reel
in rhyme on their rejoicing way,
breaking the elder dark, nor stay
but speed beyond each trammelling gyre,
till time and sorrow fall away
and night be wither'd up, and fire
consume the sickness of desire.

R

V

THE EARLY TWENTIETH CENTURY

J. LE GAY BRERETON

1871-1933

Buffalo Creek

A timid child with heart oppressed
  By images of sin,
I slunk into the bush for rest,
  And found my fairy kin.

The fire I carried kept me warm:
  The friendly air was chill.
The laggards of the lowing storm
  Trailed gloom along the hill.

I watched the crawling monsters melt
  And saw their shadows wane
As on my satin skin I felt
  The fingers of the rain.

The sunlight was a golden beer,
  I drank a magic draught;
The sky was clear and, void of fear,
  I stood erect and laughed.

And sudden laughter, idly free,
  About me trilled and rang,
And love was shed from every tree,
  And little bushes sang.

The bay of conscience' bloody hound
  That tears the world apart
Has never drowned the silent sound
  Within my happy heart.

1872-1942

Song Be Delicate

Let your song be delicate.
The skies declare
No war—the eyes of lovers
Wake everywhere.

Let your voice be delicate.
How faint a thing
Is Love, little Love crying
Under the Spring.

Let your song be delicate.
The flowers can hear:
Too well they know the tremble
Of the hollow year.

Let your voice be delicate.
The bees are home:
All their day's love is sunken
Safe in the comb.

Let your song be delicate.
Sing no loud hymn:
Death is abroad . . . oh, the black season!
The deep—the dim!

Love's Coming

Quietly as rosebuds
Talk to the thin air,
Love came so lightly
I knew not he was there.

Quietly as lovers
Creep at the middle moon,
Softly as players tremble
In the tears of a tune;

Quietly as lilies
Their faint vows declare
Came the shy pilgrim:
I knew not he was there.

Quietly as tears fall
On a wild sin,
Softly as griefs call
In a violin;

Without hail or tempest,
Blue sword or flame,
Love came so lightly
I knew not that he came.

Beauty Imposes

Beauty imposes reverence in the Spring.
Grave as the urge within the honeybuds,
It wounds us as we sing.

Beauty is joy that stays not overlong.
Clad in the magic of sincerities,
It rides up in a song.

Beauty imposes chastenings on the heart,
Grave as the birds in last solemnities
Assembling to depart.

Break of Day

The stars are pale.
Old is the Night, his case is grievous,
His strength doth fail.

Through stilly hours
The dews have draped with Love's old lavishness
The drowsy flowers.

And Night shall die,
Already, lo! the Morn's first ecstasies
Across the sky.

An evil time is done.
Again, as someone lost in a quaint parable,
Comes up the Sun.

Strawberries in November

Have you heard of the quaint people,
Part of the berry clan?
They carry the shape and colour
Of the cooled heart of a man.

They see of the old sorrow
That all have seen before;
The Spring in her last folly
Is burned on the yellow floor.

Oh, these are the shy people,
The fierce light gives them pain;
They cry to the green mercy
And they drink of the white rain.

220

The red sun knows not pity,
It calls on the grass to die,
It spares not lake or river,
For it needs them in the sky.

They pray to the green heavens:
"Are we not timorous too?
And we send our hapless wishes
On the old roads in the blue."

They nestle close as lovers,
They will not live apart;
If you look at the crimson people
You look at the human heart.

The Orange Tree

The young girl stood beside me. I
Saw not what her young eyes could see:
—A light, she said, not of the sky
Lives somewhere in the Orange Tree.

—Is it, I said, of east or west?
The heartbeat of a luminous boy
Who with his faltering flute confessed
Only the edges of his joy?

Was he, I said, borne to the blue
In a mad escapade of Spring
Ere he could make a fond adieu
To his love in the blossoming?

—Listen! the young girl said. There calls
No voice, no music beats on me;
But it is almost sound: it falls
This evening on the Orange Tree.

—Does he, I said, so fear the Spring
Ere the white sap too far can climb?
See in the full gold evening
All happenings of the olden time?

Is he so goaded by the green?
Does the compulsion of the dew
Make him unknowable but keen
Asking with beauty of the blue?

—Listen! the young girl said. For all
Your hapless talk you fail to see
There is a light, a step, a call,
This evening on the Orange Tree.

—Is it, I said, a waste of love
Imperishably old in pain,
Moving as an affrighted dove
Under the sunlight or the rain?

Is it a fluttering heart that gave
Too willingly and was reviled?
Is it the stammering at a grave,
The last word of a little child?

—Silence! the young girl said. Oh, why,
Why will you talk to weary me?
Plague me no longer now, for I
Am listening like the Orange Tree.

To a School-girl

O most unconscious daisy!
Thou daybreak of a joy!
Whose eyes invade the impassioned man
In every wayside boy.

222

Can I, walled in by Autumn,
With buoyant things agree?
Speak all my heart to a daisy
If one should smile at me?

Out of the Summer fallen,
Can I of Summer sing?
Call that I love on the deep yellow
Between me and the Spring?

May

Shyly the silver-hatted mushrooms make
  Soft entrance through,
And undelivered lovers, half awake,
  Hear noises in the dew.

Yellow in all the earth and in the skies,
  The world would seem
Faint as a widow mourning with soft eyes
  And falling into dream.

Up the long hill I see the slow plough leave
  Furrows of brown;
Dim is the day and beautiful: I grieve
  To see the sun go down.

But there are suns a many for mine eyes
  Day after day:
Delightsome in grave greenery they rise,
  Red oranges in May.

'Tis the White Plum Tree

It is the white Plum Tree
Seven days fair
As a bride goes combing
Her joy of hair.

As a peacock dowered
With golden eyes
Ten paces over
The Orange lies.

It is the white Plum Tree
Her passion tells,
As a young maid rustling,
She so excels.

The birds run outward,
The birds are low,
Whispering in manna
The sweethearts go.

It is the white Plum Tree
Seven days fair
As a bride goes combing
Her joy of hair.

The Poor Can Feed the Birds

Ragged, unheeded, stooping, meanly shod,
The poor pass to the pond: not far away
The spires go up to God.

Shyly they come from the unpainted lane;
Coats have they made of old unhappiness
That keeps in every pain.

The rich have fear, perchance their God is dim;
'Tis with the hope of stored-up happiness
They build the spires to Him.

The rich go out in clattering pomp and dare
In the most holy places to insult
The deep Benevolence there.

But 'tis the poor who make the loving words.
Slowly they stoop; it is a Sacrament:
The poor can feed the birds.

Old, it is old, this scattering of the bread,
Deep as forgiveness, or the tears that go
Out somewhere to the dead.

The feast of love, the love that is the cure
For all indignities—it reigns, it calls,
It chains us to the pure.

Seldom they speak of God, He is too dim;
So without thought of after happiness
They feed the birds for Him.

The rich men walk not here on the green sod,
But they have builded towers, the timorous
That still go up to God.

Still will the poor go out with loving words;
In the long need, the need for happiness
The poor can feed the birds.

To a Blue Flower

I would be dismal with all the fine pearls of the crown of a
    king;
But I can talk plainly to you, you little blue flower of the
    Spring!

Here in the heart of September the world that I walk in is
    full
Of the hot happy sound of the shearing, the rude heavy scent
    of the wool.

Soon would I tire of all riches or honours or power that they
    fling;
But you are my own, of my own folk, you little blue flower
    of the Spring!

I was around by the cherries to-day; all the cherries are pale:
The world is a woman in velvet: the air is the colour of ale.

I would be dismal with all the fine pearls of the crown of a
    king;
But I can give love-talk to you, you little blue flower of the
    Spring!

The Crane is My Neighbour

The bird is my neighbour, a whimsical fellow and dim;
There is in the lake a nobility falling on him.

The bird is a noble, he turns to the sky for a theme,
And the ripples are thoughts coming out to the edge of a
    dream.

The bird is both ancient and excellent, sober and wise,
But he never could spend all the love that is sent for his eyes.

He bleats no instruction, he is not an arrogant drummer;
His gown is simplicity—blue as the smoke of the summer.

How patient he is as he puts out his wings for the blue!
His eyes are as old as the twilight, and calm as the dew.

The bird is my neighbour, he leaves not a claim for a sigh,
He moves as the guest of the sunlight—he roams in the sky.

The bird is a noble, he turns to the sky for a theme,
And the ripples are thoughts coming out to the edge of a
dream.

The Sundowner

I know not when this tiresome man
With his shrewd, sable billy-can
And his unwashed Democracy
His boomed-up Pilgrimage began.

Sometimes he wandered far outback
On a precarious Tucker Track;
Sometimes he lacked Necessities
No gentleman would like to lack.

Tall was the grass, I understand,
When the old Squatter ruled the land.
Why were the Conquerors kind to him?
Ah, the Wax Matches in his hand!

Where bullockies with oaths intense
Made of the dragged-up trees a fence,
Gambling with scorpions he rolled
His Swag, conspicuous, immense.

In the full splendour of his power
Rarely he touched one mile an hour,
Dawdling at sundown, History says,
For the Pint Pannikin of flour.

Seldom he worked; he was, I fear,
Unreasonably slow and dear;
Little he earned, and that he spent
Deliberately drinking Beer.

Cheerful, sorefooted child of chance,
Swiftly we knew him at a glance;
Boastful and self-compassionate,
Australia's Interstate Romance.

Shall he not live in Robust Rhyme,
Soliloquies and Odes Sublime?
Strictly between ourselves, he was
A rare old Humbug all the time.

In many a Book of Bushland dim
Mopokes shall give him greeting grim;
The old swans pottering in the reeds
Shall pass the time of day to him.

On many a page our Friend shall take
Small sticks his evening fire to make;
Shedding his waistcoat, he shall mix
On its smooth back his Johnny-cake.

'Mid the dry leaves and silvery bark
Often at nightfall will he park
Close to a homeless creek, and hear
The Bunyip paddling in the dark.

The Cool, Cool Country

All kings are hollow,
All queens are calm;
No hope or holy man,
Sequel or psalm.

Unholy wenches
Lie sweet and clean
In the cool, cool country
Below the green.

A lover's quietness
Fills up the day;
The eyes know not of
The lips' delay.

Malice of sunbeam or
Menace of moon
No more shall chasten us
With light or tune.

No shrill endeavour,
No gentle sin
Or blaze of honeycup
Can enter in.

No silken heavens
Delude the eye;
The drowsy centuries
Go feebly by.

Maids have no magic,
All feet are dumb;
Night has outwitted Love:
How shall he come?

The little brown wench
And the holy and lean
Are all good citizens
Under the green.

S

Love cannot sabre us,
Blood cannot flow;
'Tis the fine country
Open below.

ARTHUR H. ADAMS

1872-1936

The Australian

Once more this autumn-earth is ripe,
Parturient of another type.

While with the Past old nations merge
His foot is on the Future's verge.

They watch him, as they huddle, pent,
Striding a spacious continent,

Above the level desert's marge
Looming in his aloofness large.

No flower with fragile sweetness graced—
A lank weed wrestling with the waste;

Pallid of face and gaunt of limb,
The sweetness withered out of him;

Sombre, indomitable, wan,
The juices dried, the glad youth gone.

A little weary from his birth;
His laugh the spectre of a mirth,

Bitter beneath a bitter sky,
To Nature he has no reply.

Wanton, perhaps, and cruel. Yes,
Is not his sun more merciless?

So drab and neutral is his day,
He finds a splendour in the grey,

And from his life's monotony
He draws a dreary melody.

When earth so poor a banquet makes
His pleasures at a gulp he takes;

The feast is his to the last crumb:
Drink while he can . . . the drought will come.

His heart a sudden tropic flower,
He loves and loathes within an hour.

Yet you who by the pools abide,
Judge not the man who swerves aside;

He sees beyond your hazy fears;
He roads the desert of the years;

Rearing his cities in the sand,
He builds where even God has banned;

With green a continent he crowns,
And stars a wilderness with towns;

With paths the distances he snares;
His gyves of steel the great plain wears.

A child who takes a world for toy,
To build a nation or destroy,

His childish features frozen stern,
His manhood's task he has to learn—

From feeble tribes to federate
One white and peace-encompassed State.

But if there be no goal to reach?
The way lies open, dawns beseech!

Enough that he lay down his load
A little further on the road.

So, toward undreamt-of destinies
He slouches down the centuries.

R. H. LONG

1874-1948

The Skylark's Nest

Here Nature holds as in a hollowed hand,
For keen and loving eyes alone to see,
The larks and lyrics that are yet to be:
But ere this spartan nesting-place was planned,
A frugal builder with discretion scanned
'Neath sheltering cave and arborous scrub and tree
The mason's lore, the weaver's artistry,
Then scooped this simple hollow in the sand.

What truths foregather in this modest nest
That innocence shall yet reveal to Man,
Teaching that Beauty unadorned is blest,
And Art's true bulwark is the puritan;
For in those realms, that unto God belong,
From simplest nest may soar the sweetest song.

232

Poet and Peasant

The Poet's thoughts are of the skies.
The Peasant's of the ground:
The one sees life like incense rise,
The other, life's dull round:
Nor self-fulfilment shall be won
Till we infuse, O Brother,
More peasant in the soul of one,
More poet in the other.

HUGH McCRAE

1876-1958

Colombine

Exit the ribald clown
Enter like bubbling wine,
Lighter than thistledown,
Sweet little Colombine.

Whisht! and behold the game,
Long eyes and pointed chin
Paler than candleflame,
At her feet Harlequin.

Look how their shadows run,
Swift as she flies from him!—
Moths in the morning sun,
Out of a garden dim.

Faint through the fluttering
Fall of a flute divine,
Softly the 'cellos sing
'Colombine, Colombine.'

233

Softly the 'cellos sing:
'Colombine' . . .
'Colombine' . . .

Muse-haunted

He heard, and dreamed the night-wind on
The moon's gold horn was blowing,
The music of far Helicon
A-down Parnassus flowing.

And with that strange sad ecstasy
Of men who, slowly sailing,
Behold a mermaid in the sea,
Below their lantern-railing,
Spark like a star within the wave—
So he with yearning listened,
While high above his shadowy cave
The eye of Venus glistened.

.   .   .   .   .   .

The hawk entowered in the sky,
The lonely lord of heaven,
At daybreak saw him solitary;
And yet again at even.

I Blow My Pipes

I blow my pipes, the glad birds sing,
The fat young nymphs about me spring,
The sweaty centaur leaps the trees
And bites his dryad's splendid knees;
The sky, the water, and the earth
Repeat aloud our noisy mirth . . .
Anon, tight-bellied bacchanals,

With ivy from the vineyard walls,
Lead out and crown with shining glass
The wine's red baby on the grass.

.   .   .   .   .   .

I blow my pipes, the glad birds sing,
The fat young nymphs about me spring,
I am the lord,
I am the lord,
I am the lord of everything!

Ambuscade

Or the black centaurs, statuesquely still,
Whose moving eyes devour the snuffling mares,
And watch with baneful rage their nervous strides
Whip the dark river white, lest unawares
Some danger seize them. . . . Statuesquely still,
Behind the waving trellises of cane,
The centaurs feel their hearts (besieged with blood)
Stagger like anvils when the sled-blows rain
Shower on shower in persistent flood. . . .

Now Cornus, he, the oldest of the group,
With many wounds, strong arms, and clay-rolled hair,
Coughs for a signal to his dreadful troop,
And springs, wide-fingered, from the crackling lair.
Loudly the victims neigh, they thrash the stream,
They tear their foemen's beards with frothy teeth,
And fill the banks with sparkling spires of steam
That heavenward roll in one tumultuous wreath.

Within the branches of an ancient oak,
A Mother-Satyr, sleeping with her young,
Smit by a sudden stone, upbraids the stroke,
Then turns to see from whence it has been flung.

Scarce does she view the cursed Centaur-pack,
Than, standing clear, she blows a whistle shrill,
Which, like an echo, straight comes flying back
Louder and louder down the empty hill.

A roar of hooves, a lightning-view of eyes
Redder than fire, of long, straight whistling manes,
Stiff crests, and tails drawn out against the skies,
Of angry nostrils webbed with leaping veins,
The stallions come. . . .

Mad Marjory

King Paladin plunged on his moon-coloured mare
Athwart the deep shadows of Avalon wood,
And a heron, afloat on the indolent air,
Down dropped him a plume in his galloping-hood.

Mad Marjory watched from the forester's gate,
While tossing her baby with passionate glee:
"God save you!" she hailed him, "who, out of your state,
Unbended to father this darling in me.

"Let Hobble the miller throw dust on my name,
'Tis little I care about him or the rest;
My child is as much of the King's as the same
Who gobbles the milk o' the Queen's ain breast."

The Uncouth Knight

With his two-fist sword, enscintillant, he cut an apple down
To stop the clocking clamour of the daughter of the clown,
Who ploughed the frosty headland: and the princess looked
between
The windows of the hawthorn hedge that walled the road
with green.

"Run, Lady Kate, to yonder knight, and pray him clip for me
The fairest pippin o' them a' upon the pippin-tree."
And Lady Kate has gathered now her kirtle in her hand,
And thro' the steamy mallow's gone to do the Queen's command.

"Good e'en, good e'en, Sir Rusty Breast," she spake with bitter scorn,
"Cleave me an apple for the Queen, and thou'rt a knight true-born."
The knight, from his shankpillion high, leered down on Lady Kate,
Then sheathed his sword and screwed amain his helmet-feather straight.

"My little smutch-face lass," said he unto the ragged brat,
"How daur ye eat the gowden fruit a queen's eyes hunger at?"
Forthy he bended, and he took the ribstone at her mouth . . .
What tho' her bitter tears fell down like raindrops from the South.

He brake the apple in his palm: "I'll cut no more," quod he,
"Let half the beggar's fruit suffy to stay the Queen's bodie."
Then threw them twain upon the ground, and laughed with all his might . . . .
Was ever such, in this wide world, another uncouth knight?

Joan of Arc

. . . a Shepherdess, one June de Arque, who, putting on Man's apparel,
drove the English out of Paris into Normandy. She used to go on with
marvellous courage and resolution and

her word was *Hara Ha!*

but she was taken Prisoner, and the English had a fair revenge upon her,
for by an arrest of the Parliament of Rouen she was burnt for a witch.

—JAMES HOWELL. 3 March 1622.

INTRODUCTION

Always she loved the sound of bells . . . .
Old Baudrieau, the ringer, tells
How she would bring him skeins of wool,
Dyed in the grain, for leave to pull
His great grass rope that, groaning, swung
Against its iron cheek, the tongue
That told with honest hammer-stroke
The good Domremy village folk,
Threading their apple-shaded ways,
Duty to God and rightful praise.

Her sweet face winged with golden hair,
Foot in the loop, she woke the air:
"Voices of angels," André said,
Pole in hand at his draw-well head,
To whom the Duke of all Lorraine,
Slipping the coils of helmet chain,
Choked in his drink, "*Ma foi*, André,
Devils or angels! You shall pay . . . .
Else, like the dry combs cast away
Out of the hives on market-day
Over a heap of merd and straw,
Broken in back, with sunken jaw,
Look you to lie! . . . Just as I throw
This coarse cracked cup!"
                    "My Lord Duke . . . No!"

Joan of the Bells, the corn is inned . . .
Mothers and sons, their heads deep-chinned
In the rough clasp their fingers make,
Glory to God for Jesus' sake.

Joan of the Bells, high in your tower,
Who is he stands this lonely hour,

238

White on the beech-top, dimly seen,
Only the grave-yard in between?
Michael the Saint! Behold his spear
Plays at a star-point, sharp and clear,
And aureoled with rosy whorls,
His lion's fell of chestnut curls,
Under the cross-barred shield, forsooth,
Sinks to his baldrick's buckling tooth;
Lifting his hand . . . the moon, uprist,
Shines through his body's silver mist,
Headpiece and hauberk, lappet chain,
Glimmer like strings of jangled rain.

Flower of fire! He fades away . . .
The purple beech-leaves only stay.
Then, heavily, as though the ground
Edge of a woodsman's axe had found,
Through the shelled rind, its buried heart,
The great tree shakes, and bursts apart,
While a deep murmur weighed with sighs
Comes from the shadow . . . "Joan, arise!
Thy country, bruised and dragged to death,
Beseeches with her failing breath
The unrelenting stars for sign
Of succour to her battle-line . . . .

"Flachon and great de Bador, shot,
Poison the furrows where they rot,
Their brains pashed out by iron shoes
The English horsemen love to use;
Swords in the trough, and banners torn
Under the Rose of Albion's thorn,
Lily from lily. It is said
Liberty cometh with a maid.
When strength the strongest soldier fails

Full often innocence prevails . . .
Wherefore, through innocence, alone,
Thou art appointed leader, Joan . . . .
'Get thee to Chinon,' saith the Lord,
There shalt thou find prepared a sword
Lief to thy hand and sharp to smite
Bedford's shoulderly Suffolk quite
Clean to the marrow . . . God you speed!"
"Alas! and who am I, to lead—?
A girl—and green in years, to dress
Trained liegemen for the battle-press—?"
Maketh him answer, on her knees,
This little Joan, while, through the trees,
Saint Michael's voice rolls o'er the sward,
" 'Get thee to Chinon,' saith the Lord!"

Now speaks the thunder, long and loud,
Now cries the rain; and a great cloud
Wrings at her hands, as though, askance,
Over the fields of shattered France . . . .
Swift thrust the lightnings, in and in,
Like flame-stuck arrows aimed to win
The summer-nests that pack the spouts,
Eave-bursting, of a King's redoubts;
Till, suddenly, the beech-tree sways
Where from its middest springs a blaze
Of pure white fire, and—wondrous sight—
Chained to the trunk a phantom knight,
All maidenly, and small, and young,
With honey-coloured ringlets hung
Down to the dragon-scrolling greaves
Between the curled smoke-blackened leaves.

"Alas," saith Joan, "and must I die?
Wherefore to Chinon? Wherefore I"?

June Morning

The twisted apple, with rain and magian fire
Caught in its branches from the early dawn,
I, from my bed, through the fogged pane see, and desire
Of its sharp sweetness, something: green the lawn
And stiff with pointed spears of daffodils run wild;
The sluggard sun draws the drowned Daphne back to life—
And all the drowsy doves, brown sparrows, husband, wife,
Are stirring on the housetops—child to early child
Coo-eeing and calling; blind windows open eyes. . . .
And in the air the bitter fragrance floats
Of someone's gardener's pipe; I will arise
And in the stinging shower forget gold motes,
Thick pillows, blankets, books; travel the wholesome road
And give my body to the sun.

Evening

How tenderly the evening creeps between
The fading curtain of this apple-bough,
A ghost of rose and grey, mid foliage green
Jewelled with stripes of rain.

Ah, look where now,
Trembling, but joyous, like a challenged bride,
The moon, along a bed of daffodil,
Opens a cloud against her golden side . . .
As one expectant of her Lord's sweet will.

Song of the Rain

Night,
And the yellow pleasure of candlelight . . .
Old brown books and the kind fine face of the clock
Fogged in the veils of the fire; its cuddling tock.

241

The cat
Greening her eyes on the flame-litten mat;
Wickedly wakeful, she yawns at the rain
Bending the roses over the pane.
And a bird in my heart begins to sing
Over and over the same sweet thing.

'Safe in the house with my boyhood's love,
And our children asleep in the attic above.'

Enigma

I watch her fingers where they prance
Like little naked women, tango-mad,
Along the keys, a cup-shot dance—
Music, who'll say, more joyous or more sad?

A mystery . . . but not so strange
As she. Enigma is her pretty name;
And though she smiles, her veiled eyes range
Through tears of melancholy and shame.

She laughs and weeps. . . . Is it because
Only tonight she gave herself to me?
The new bud frightened to be glad . . .
The child's first vision of the insatiate sea.

The Mouse

All Christmas night upon the shelf;
Among the apples yellow-faced,
There played a pretty maiden mouse
Divinely slim and very chaste.

Who, when I held my candle up,
Did twink her little eyes at me . . .
So mad, so bright, so mischievous;
I thought of *you*, dear Dorothy!

Camden Magpie

(*To Zoë Crookston*)

Ho! Ho! The fine fellow
Topped on the willow—
Dipping his black and white
Into the yellow.

How mightn't Hokusai,
This summer morning,
Clap you in magical
Net without warning!—

Ink on his finger-nail,
Cleverly wiggled:
Dokoro—Tsukari!
—What thought you jiggled—

He'd have you, he'd hold you,
This Japanese wizard,
So fast by the feather,
So fast by the gizzard,

That it wouldn't be you
On the Bassingthwaighte fence,
Or in Adams's yard,
Not by any pretence.

And it wouldn't be you
Piratically sailing
To Thunderbolt's Rock
Across the high paling—

Only your atomy,
Soon out of focus, I
Watch—and then turn to
"Magpie"—signed Hokusai.

LOUIS ESSON

1879-1943

The Shearer's Wife

Before the glare o' dawn I rise
To milk the sleepy cows, an' shake
The droving dust from tired eyes,
Look round the rabbit traps, then bake
    The children's bread.
There 's hay to stook, an' beans to hoe,
An' ferns to cut i' th' scrub below;
Women must work, when men must go
    Shearing from shed to shed.

I patch an' darn, now evening comes,
An' tired I am with labour sore,
Tired o' the bush, the cows, the gums,
Tired, but must dree for long months more
    What no tongue tells.
The moon is lonely in the sky,
Lonely the bush, an' lonely I
Stare down the track no horse draws nigh
    An' start . . . at the cattle bells.

244

1879-

The Reaper

Under the dying sun
And the moon's frail shell,
The fields are clear as glass:
I love them well.

A horse's amber flanks
Shine in the grain.
The wheel of the reaper cleaves
A yellow lane.

The reaper is ruddy gold
Unearthly bright,
Driving an amber cloud,
Touched with its light.

They say the earth's a stone
Wrinkled and old,
Yet she has steeds of fire
And men of gold!

H. M. GREEN

1881-1962

The Cicada

Listen to the cicada's burning drone
    From tree to tree,
Grinding his brazen wheel; so Time grinds down
    My proud mortality.
But as the singer stands against his choir
And stands against the silence, so with me;
Focus of intense noon, the spirit is fire
And shall inform the flesh, though faint it be.
Deep was the fount, and if the cruse be clay,
Yet shall I burn bright through a long day.

T

From *Life's Testament:*

II

The brain, the blood, the busy thews
That quickened in the primal ooze
Support me yet; till ice shall grip
The heart of Earth, no strength they'll lose.

They take my thought, they laugh, they run—
Ere megatherial moons, begun;
And shall, till they shall drop within
The shattering whirlwinds of the sun.

In subtle and essential ways,
Rich with innumerable days,
To mould, to charge, to impel me still,
Each through my broadest being plays.

They surged to this hour, this transfuse—
The brain, the blood, the busy thews;
That act of mine the ultimate stars
Shall look on sprang in primal ooze.

VI

I worshipped, when my veins were fresh,
A glorious fabric of this flesh,
Where all her skill in living lines
And colour (that its form enshrines)
Nature had lavished; in that guess
She had gathered up all loveliness.
All beauty of flesh, and blood, and bone
I saw there: ay, by impulse known,
All the miracle, the power,
Of being had come there to flower.

246

Each part was perfect in the whole;
The body one was with the soul;
And heedful not, nor having art,
To see them in a several part,
I fell before the flesh, and knew
All spirit in terms of that flesh too.

But blood must wither like the rose:
'Tis wasting as the minute goes:
And flesh, whose shows were wonders high,
Looks piteous when it puts them by.
The shape I had so oft embraced
Was sealed up, and in earth was placed—
And yet not so; for hovering free
Some wraith of it remained with me,
Some subtle influence that brings
A new breath to all beauteous things,
Some sense that in my marrow stirs
To make things mute its ministers.
I fall before the spirit so,
And flesh in terms of spirit know—
The Holy Ghost, the truth that stands
When turned to dust are lips and hands.

VIII

This miracle in me I scan—
The whole circumference of Man;
I see all number, time, and space
Looking from my neighbour's face.

XI

All that I am to Earth belongs:
This Heaven does me violent wrongs.
My fight from fitful loins, my birth,

Are fashioned to the mode of Earth—
Deliberate things, not swiftly given
As some report it falls in Heaven.
This mind is slow to work, this will,
This hand to act them tardier still—
Not dowered with that immediate sense
Deemed in celestial excellence.
True Earth am I, of Earth I'm knit—
O, let me be at peace with it.

XIII

God, to get the clay that stayed me,
Rifled through remotest spheres;
God, to form the breath that bade me
Rise, to thew this heart, arrayed me
From the immense of His.

Portioned so in that profound
Essence, I must travail till
I fling me to its farthest bound—
Till universal clay be crowned
In Godhead by the will.

Through foul mutations I must fight
To larger labours, when I fall
Spur me with the godly spright,
And shout defiance when they smite
Me bleeding to the wall.

Growing thus to the Greater Me
In travail, I will hurl despair,
Fret too and tremor, out, and be,
Through battle climbed to battle, free
To grapple God up there.

XVII

A choir of spirits on a cloud
Lifted up their carol loud:

"They crawl on interdicted clay
Who take the rabble-trodden way;
Spirits of ethereal plume
Go in liberty and come.
"The wingèd mind that cuts with ease
The ultimate starred immensities,
As wide as they, will not be lost:
The traversing mind no check may thrust
Out of the broadest sun-begirt abodes,
There thinking in a thought of God's.

"That world of frontier undefined,
The field of azure-leaping mind,
Is less than we.
There Time shall be
Marshal to Eternity."

From *Love Redeemed*

XXXII

Love feeds, like Intellect, his lamp with truth;
In the clear truths he finds its flame is measured.
And is not flesh, there, verity? In sooth!
So Love not by this fantasy is pleasured
That slurs the fact in flesh. Its atmosphere,
Too rare and nebulous, no fusing shows;
Its manna too ambrosial is and sheer:
Love craves that union, earthly hunger knows.
O sage is Love—he seeks the living line,

The miracles in breathing flesh explores,
The riches in the depth of sense, divine,
The veiled things only eternal longing pours
    Light unobscured on—yes, his doubting done,
    With flesh the imminent two converts to one.

LXXXII

Who questions if the punctual sun unbars
Earth's pageant, and flings gold upon the east?
If the swift intersessions of high stars
Make beautiful the night, with magic dressed?
Who asks if grass attires this populous earth?
If leaves put forth their flourish upon trees?
If buds on waking sprays have comeliest birth?
And who, that scans, inquires the why of these?
Who questions, tell, man's breath or blood, that comes
We know not whence, yet is, and dates his day?
These, being, have truth beyond all mortal sums
Of much and less, and prompt nor yea or nay.
    A certitude sublime they have, above
    Belief and non-belief. So has our love.

LXXXVIII

As fire, unfound ere pole approaches pole,
Leaps into splendour as their forces twin,
So heavenly flame, when soul is drawn to soul,
To radiance breaks—illuming all within.
Perception then is summed: love only crowns it:
Spirit is kingly then; inspired is sense:
This piteous earth a god inhabits, gowns it—
Dowered with that new and charged intelligence.
Then eyes will plumb to what profound in eyes!

And lip, to lip betrothed, how sagely burn!
Lo, even these hands, grown intimate, devise
A subtler speech than tongues, so wanting, learn;
    Blood towers in hailing who hath made it strong;
    Yea, flesh itself is bursting into song!

DOROTHEA MACKELLAR

1885-

My Country

The love of field and coppice,
Of green and shaded lanes,
Of ordered woods and gardens
Is running in your veins;
Strong love of grey-blue distance,
Brown streams and soft, dim skies—
I know but cannot share it,
My love is otherwise.

I love a sunburnt country,
A land of sweeping plains,
Of ragged mountain ranges,
Of droughts and flooding rains.
I love her far horizons,
I love her jewel-sea,
Her beauty and her terror—
The wide brown land for me!

The stark white ring-barked forests,
All tragic to the moon,
The sapphire-misted mountains,
The hot gold hush of noon.
Green tangle of the brushes,
Where lithe lianas coil,
And orchids deck the tree-tops
And ferns the warm dark soil.

Core of my heart, my country!
Her pitiless blue sky,
When sick at heart, around us,
We see the cattle die—
But then the grey clouds gather,
And we can bless again
The drumming of an army,
The steady, soaking rain.

Core of my heart, my country!
Land of the Rainbow Gold,
For flood and fire and famine,
She pays us back threefold;
Over the thirsty paddocks,
Watch, after many days,
The filmy veil of greenness
That thickens as we gaze.

An opal-hearted country,
A wilful, lavish land—
All you who have not loved her,
You will not understand—
Though earth holds many splendours,
Wherever I may die,
I know to what brown country
My homing thoughts will fly.

Fancy Dress

("Last night the moon had a golden ring. . . .")

She smiled behind a lawny cloud,
   A Tudor lady in a ruff,
A chubby Holbein, douce and proud,
   Starchy, but genial enough.

252

Wide ring on ring of lawn and lace
Spread round her unimpressive face
Which yet was deeply memorable—
Lady, the Holbein type wears well!

Dusk in the Domain

Elf-light, owl-light,
Elfin-green sky;
Under the fig trees
Bats flit by;

Under the fig trees
Sprawl in a ring
Slim-limbed courtiers,
Brown Elf King.

Crowned with autumn's
Tawny gold,
Lizard-eyed, cricket-thighed,
Neither young nor old:

Like the fig-leaves'
Broad yellow wreath
Round each forehead—like
The waves beneath

Lipping the weed-hung
Low sea-wall—
Ageless, careless
Lords of all!

Grey rock-monsters
Out of the grass
Heaved, lie staring;
Moths drift past

On their business—
None have the elves,
Who hold high festival
By themselves.

.   .   .   .

So I saw them
Very plain,
Green-dusky Elfland,
Their Domain.

So I saw them
As I went through:
Seven slum children from
Wooloomooloo!

NETTIE PALMER

1885-

The Mother

In the sorrow and the terror of the nations,
In a world shaken through by lamentations,
     Shall I dare know happiness
     That I stitch a baby's dress?

So: for I shall be a mother with the mothers,
I shall know the mother's anguish like the others,
     Present joy must surely start
     For the life beneath my heart.

Gods and men, ye know a woman's glad unreason,
How she cannot bend and weep but in her season,
     Let my hours with rapture glow
     As the seams and stitches grow.

And I cannot hear the word of fire and slaughter;
Do men die? Then live, my child, my son, my daughter!
    Into realms of pain I bring
    You for joy's own offering.

VANCE PALMER

1885-1959

The Farmer Remembers the Somme

Will they never fade or pass!
The mud, and the misty figures endlessly coming
In file through the foul morass,
And the grey flood-water lipping the reeds and grass,
And the steel wings drumming.

The hills are bright in the sun:
There's nothing changed or marred in the well-known places;
When work for the day is done
There's talk, and quiet laughter, and gleams of fun
On the old folks' faces.

I have returned to these:
The farm, and the kindly Bush, and the young calves lowing;
But all that my mind sees
Is a quaking bog in a mist—stark, snapped trees,
And the dark Somme flowing.

FREDERICK T. MACARTNEY

1887-

Desert Claypan

This ultimate austerity
of desert land
once wore the rustling vestments of the sea,
but now the sand
is heaped or thinned
by useless shovelling of the alternate wind.

A mimic harvest flecks
dry distances with sheaves of spinifex,
and here at the edge of a cracked claypan
eroded roots
seem fingers of a thirst-crazed man
seeking the water it imputes.

No river, but the trace
as of dried tears on a worn face;
no upland forest to imply
a rain-responsive sky;
only a tree,
thin as a wandering aborigine,
defending, with its spears of shade
sharp from the light along the blade,
the integrity whereby its tense
endurance asks no recompense.

ZORA CROSS

1890-

From *Elegy on an Australian Schoolboy*

O brother in the restless rest of God!
To-day the bells should ring
Your birthday greetings where to grass and sod
The cosmos petals cling.
But we are children in the hands of men
Who use us for their game;
You never lived to know how sword and pen
Make but a few men's fame.

You have been spared the agonies that come
With doubts of the world's best,
The knowledge that the wisest oft are dumb,
Unheeded of the rest.

256

You are most rich who never learned the lie
Of mankind unto Man,
Who thought all souls kept faith serene and high
With life's most noble plan.

And yet I think God cannot dream decay
Of that we hold most dear . . . .
I, small, but looking greatly on the day,
Forget my woman fear.
I must not mourn for one who loved life well,
The sunshine and the dew,
Each merry tale his comrades had to tell,
And dear books, old and new.

I must not weep; for you would live again
And know the happy sun,
Race the white moon and carol with the rain
And down the play-tracks run.
Run then, and laugh and cry and clap your hands
As a blithe, wayward boy;
Swim, dive and gambol. . . . Ah, those other lands.
What may they give of joy?

My God! I may be dreaming in a sleep
Some thought of Yours this day.
Only I know the tide of Life is deep
About my young, full way.
O woman, lover, maker of Man's soul!—
His long-lost Paradise,
All that in Peace or War he dreamed his goal
Are his if she be wise.

Make of her breast a home of truth and peace,
A place of holy joy,
Till through her mother-sweetness nations cease
To ravish and destroy.

So may she give the everlasting life
Earth hungers for in vain—
Immortal mother and immortal wife
Who heals the whole world's pain.

JAMES DEVANEY

1890-

Song of the Captured Woman

I did not cry at all
Till I went down by the white edges of the lake.
I watched the wild swans rising from the lake
With sweet wild cries;
They went away, away to the south to my Murrawal River
    country,
And I to remain here in this place!
Ah, I could not follow the wild swans.

The women here are kind to the captured woman,
The lake men are straight and tall ones,
But their songs are strange to me, and their ways are not my
    ways.
The emu to the great brown plains,
The swamp-hen to her native reed-beds,
The eaglehawk to his own wide empty skies;
But I am a Murrawal River woman
And my country is down by the Murrawal River,
The talking Murrawal where my own people sit down.

I saw the wild black swans, wild and free,
Rise out of the reeds and go;
Now they are there, down on the shady Murrawal River, the
    bends I know,
And I to remain here in this place!

It was then I sat down and cried,
For I would be again with my own people,
My own poor laughing people down by the Murrawal River,
The singing Murrawal, the Voice-that-does-not-cease.

The Evening Gleam

The evening gleam of still waters
Can stay the feet that roam,
As if the soul in its long homelessness
Came suddenly home.

I know not still what beauty is.
I would cry the wise:
What verity is half discovered here
To too dim eyes?

Something of otherworldly kind,
More than the thing seen;
Something possessed a moment, other
Than light and form mean.

Beauty is simple and austere.
Is it all of sense and time?
The evening gleam of still waters
Mocks art of rhyme.

Mortality

The lone watch of the moon over mountains old.
Night that is never silent, and none to hark.
Down in the inky pool a fish leaps
With splash of silver light in the liquid dark.

I walk the unknown ways of a foreign land.
The close reeds whisper their secrecies,

259

And hidden water tunes—earth's oldest voice.
What alien waif is mind among mindless these?

Old, old, everything here is old.
Life the intruder but so briefly stays,
And man the dreamer—soon old changeless time
Will grass his ways.

Fold him, spade him away. Where are they now,
The high courage and love, the laboured store?
Down in the inky pool a fish leapt—
Life is no more.

DULCIE DEAMER

1890-

Artemis

I am type of singleness . . . .
Dazzling breasts that never bless
With their bared surrendering
Amorous strengths that man may bring
To their conquest. They are free
As two wild white mares may be—
Two young mares that scream and rear
Should a stallion trample near—
Fierce as panthers, fair as doves,
Spurning yoke and curb of loves . . .
Loins and thighs and knees of snow
Never stress of love may know.
As far mountain-snows that lie
In a pallid, holy sky,
By a fainting wanderer seen
From a midnight-dark ravine,
Spur his thirst and hurt his soul,
So I stand—the hopeless goal

Of the finite world's desire . . . .
All the flowers of noonday's fire
Fade before my sovereign white
(Hueless hue of death's delight).
Tallest lilies round my knees
In their pallor seem to freeze.
'Neath my huntress-sandalled feet
Bruised roses yield their sweet,
Like crushed hearts that redly wet
Love's bare feet upon them set.
Am I crueller than Love—
I, the god no prayer can move,
I, the buried fountain sealed,
I, the beauty unrevealed,
I, the vase of unlipped wine,
I, the never-entered shrine,
I, the smooth, unridden steed,
I, the untrodden mountain-mead
Thick with starry, virgin flowers
Where the footless cliff uptowers? . . .
Love's keen feet are bloody-red:
Round the fervent marriage-bed
Taloned roses, vine on vine,
Like fanged and lovely serpents twine—
A bed of tears and fever-drouth,
Striving limbs and sobbing mouth,
Famished flame and slain desire,
And the muted Orphic lyre . . . .
Have I offered bitter bread?—
Though your hungers are unfed,
Though my feet you still pursue
Over glimmering leagues of dew,
Wonder is the wood before you,
Beauty is the planet o'er you . . . .
Only to Endymion dead

U

Did I bow my long-tressed head—
Sealed his eye-lids with the kiss
Of inviolate Artemis.
I, th' immortal dream that flies
Ever from life-dazzled eyes;
I, the joy forever sought,
I, the quarry never caught
(Silver bird or pallid fawn
Fleeing through the dews of dawn)
I, the snow-white heart of heat
Where all colours fuse and meet,
I, the death wherein is life,
I, the unshaken core of strife—
When you grasp me, Hunter-soul,
God-like you have grasped the Whole!

LESBIA HARFORD

1891-1927

Beauty and Terror

Beauty does not walk through lovely days,
Beauty walks with horror in her hair;
Down long centuries of pleasant ways
Men have found the terrible most fair.

Youth is lovelier in death than life,
Beauty mightier in pain than joy,
Doubly splendid burn the fires of strife
Brighter than the brightness they destroy.

Revolution

She is not of the fireside,
My lovely love;
Nor books, nor even a cradle
She bends above.

262

No, she is bent with lashes,
Her flesh is torn;
From blackness into blackness
She walks forlorn.

But factories and prisons
Are far more fair
Than home or palace gardens
If she is there.

Day's End

Little girls—
You are gay,
Little factory girls
At the end of day.

There you stand
Huddled close
On the back of a tram,
Having taken your dose.

And you go
Through the grey
And the gold of the streets
At the close of the day.

Blind as moles:
You are crude,
You are sweet—little girls—
And amazingly rude.

But so fine
To be gay,
Gentle people are dull
At the end of the day.

Experience

I must be dreaming through the days
And see the world with childish eyes
If I'd go singing all my life,
And my songs be wise.

And in the kitchen or the house
Must wonder at the sights I see.
And I must hear the throb and hum
That moves to song in factory.

So much in life remains unsung,
And so much more than love is sweet;
I'd like a song of kitchenmaids
With steady fingers and swift feet.

And I could sing about the rest
That breaks upon a woman's day
When dinner's over and she lies
Upon her bed to dream and pray

Until the children come from school
And all her evening work begins;
There's more in life than tragic love
And all the storied, splendid sins.

He Had Served Eighty Masters

He had served eighty masters; they'd have said
He "worked for these employers" to earn bread.

And they, if they had heard him, would have sneered
To brand him inefficient whom they feared.

For to know eighty masters is to know
What sort of thing men who are masters grow.

This Way Only

O you dear trees, you have learned so much of beauty,
You must have studied this only the ages long!
Men have thought of God and laughter and duty
And of love. And of song.

But you, dear trees, from your birth to your hour of dying
Have cared for this way only of being wise.
Lovely, lovely, lovely the sapling sighing,
Lovely the dead tree lies.

KATHLEEN DALZIEL

1881-

He Could Have Found His Way

He could have found his way there with shut eyes;
Under the hawthorn's overhanging gloom,
He heard the fat bees fumbling through the bloom,
The starling's long, low whistle of surprise—
"Has he come home?"

So well he knew the pattern of a place
He never had set eyes on till this hour,
While the unseen beckoned, the unknown set the pace.
Blindly he went, as saints to heaven's grace
Or night-moths to a flower.

A light enveloped all things, not of day,
However it poured through polished leaves in sunny
Shafts of strange colour of greeny-gold bush honey
But shed from—what? How many lives away?
No clue now, to any!

Then something reached out arms and gathered him in.
Preoccupied bees still crept through the pale curds
Of bloom, the sweet conversation of the birds
Continued, as he felt that spell begin
To work, not needing words.

LEON GELLERT

1892-

Anzac Cove

There's a lonely stretch of hillocks:
There's a beach asleep and drear:
There's a battered broken fort beside the sea.
There are sunken, trampled graves;
And a little rotting pier:
And winding paths that wind unceasingly.

There's a torn and silent valley:
There's a tiny rivulet
With some blood upon the stones beside its mouth.
There are lines of buried bones:
There's an unpaid waiting debt:
There's a sound of gentle sobbing in the South.

January, 1916

In the Trench

Every night I sleep
And every night I dream
That I'm strolling with my sheep
By the old stream.

Every morn I wake,
And every morn I stand
And watch the shrapnel break
On the smashed land.

266

Some night I'll fall asleep
And will not wake at dawn.
I'll lie and feed my sheep
On a green Lawn.

These Men

Men moving in a trench, in the clear noon,
Whetting their steel within the crumbling earth;
Men, moving in a trench 'neath a new moon
That smiles with a slit mouth and has no mirth;
Men moving in a trench in the grey morn,
Lifting bodies on their clotted frames;
Men with narrow mouths thin-carved in scorn
That twist and fumble strangely at dead names.

These men know life—know death a little more,
These men see paths and ends, and see
Beyond some swinging open door
Into eternity.

The Jester in the Trench

"That just reminds me of a yarn," he said,
And everybody turned to hear his tale.
He had a thousand yarns inside his head.
They waited for him, ready with their mirth
And creeping smiles—then suddenly turned pale,
Grew still, and gazed upon the earth.
They heard no tale. No further word was said.
And with his untold fun,
Half leaning on his gun,
They left him—dead.

1900-

Budding Spring

(*To Elioth Gruner*)

Against the clear intensity of dawn
  The willow stands apart.
Ah, now the deepening skies have drawn
  The tree into their heart . . .

And in great lucid petals of desire
  The breaking light untwines
The curlèd heavens, save where ribbèd fire
  Runs through the laden vines.

And all the roads of earth, its dewy ways
  Lead only to the sun,
Upwards for ever . . . . Not in any days
  This journey shall be done.

1905-

Fine Clay

O white clay, O fine clay of the earth cold,
Him I fashion cunningly surely will be sweet.
Godlike am I moulding him in the god's mould,
Hands, lips, feet.

Him I fashion delicate surely is more dear
Than all the strength of Heaven, strength of night and day,
More than all the mirrored stars in pools still and clear,
Him that I am fashioning of fine white clay.

Him I fashion cunningly surely will be fair.
Oh the fine white clay that in the earth lies!
As the gods I fashion him, lips, hands, hair,
Hands, lips, eyes.

Ah, alas, I wonder now that Evening's shade
Like a purple shadow on earth's grass is spread,
Will the gods love him, made as they are made,
Hands, lips, head?

Ah, shall they, the flower-crowned gods, whose eyes are
    bright,
Take him as their play-thing to break in their play?
More is he than all the gods who watch day and night,
Him that I am fashioning of fine white clay.

MARY GILMORE

1865-1962

Eve-song

I span and Eve span
A thread to bind the heart of man;
But the heart of man was a wandering thing
That came and went with little to bring:
Nothing he minded what we made,
As here he loitered, and there he stayed.

I span and Eve span
A thread to bind the heart of man;
But the more we span the more we found
It wasn't his heart but ours we bound.
For children gathered about our knees:
The thread was a chain that stole our ease.
And one of us learned in our children's eyes
That more than man was love and prize.
But deep in the heart of one of us lay
A root of loss and hidden dismay.

He said he was strong. He had no strength
But that which comes of breadth and length.

He said he was fond. But his fondness proved
The flame of an hour when he was moved.
He said he was true. His truth was but
A door that winds could open and shut.

And yet, and yet, as he came back,
Wandering in from the outward track,
We held our arms, and gave him our breast,
As a pillowing place for his head to rest.
I span and Eve span,
A thread to bind the heart of man!

Never Admit the Pain

Never admit the pain,
  Bury it deep;
Only the weak complain,
  Complaint is cheap.

Cover thy wound, fold down
  Its curtained place;
Silence is still a crown,
  Courage a grace.

Nurse No Long Grief

Oh, could we weep,
And weeping bring relief!
But life asks more than tears
And falling leaf.

Though year by year
Tears fall and leaves are shed,
Spring bids new sap arise,
And blood run red.

Nurse no long grief,
Lest the heart flower no more;
Grief builds no barns; its plough
Rusts at the door.

The Baying Hounds

There was no hunted one
With whom I did not run,
There was no fainting heart
With which I had not part,
The baying hounds bayed me,
Though it was I was free.

Where'er the hard-prest ran,
Was it or beast or man,
As step by step they went
My breath with them was spent;
The very ant I bruised
My heart held interfused.

From *Swans at Night*

Within the night, above the dark,
I heard a host upon the air,
Upon the void they made no mark,
For all that they went sailing there.

And from that host there came a cry,
A note of calling strange and high;
I heard it blown against the sky,
Till naught there seemed but it and I.

A long and lonely wraith of sound,
It floated out in distance wide,
As though it knew another bound,
A space wherein it never died.

I heard the swans, I heard the swans,
I heard the swans that speed by night;
That ever, where the starlight wans,
Fly on unseen within the height.

I never knew how wide the dark,
I never knew the depth of space,
I never knew how frail a bark,
How small is man within his place,

Not till I heard the swans go by,
Not till I marked their haunting cry,
Not till, within the vague on high,
I watched them pass across the sky.

. . . . .

I never knew how vast the sky,
I never knew how small was I,
Until I heard, remote and high,
The distant swans' far floated cry.

Old Botany Bay

"I'm old
Botany Bay;
Stiff in the joints,
Little to say.

I am he
Who paved the way,
That you might walk
At your ease to-day;

I was the conscript
Sent to hell
To make in the desert
The living well;

I bore the heat,
I blazed the track—
Furrowed and bloody
Upon my back.

I split the rock;
I felled the tree:
The nation was—
Because of me!"

*Old Botany Bay
Taking the sun
From day to day . . .
Shame on the mouth
That would deny
The knotted hands
That set us high!*

The Shepherd

Old Sam Smith
Lived by himself so long,
He thought three people
A "turruble throng".

But he loved "Old Shep",
Who could open and shut
The hide-hinged door
Of his old bark hut;

And he loved the trees,
The sun and the sky,
And the sound of the wind,
Though he couldn't tell why.

But besides all these,
He loved, to the full,
The smell of the sheep,
And the greasy wool.

So they buried him out
(For at last he died)
Out, all alone,
On a bleak hill side,

And there's never a sound
But the bleat of the sheep,
As they nibble the mound
That marks his sleep.

The Myall in Prison

Lone, lone and lone I stand,
With none to hear my cry.
As the black feet of the night
Go walking down the sky.

The stars they seem but dust
Under those passing feet,
As they, for an instant's space,
Flicker and flame and fleet.

So, on my heart, my grief
Hangs with the weight of doom,
And the black feet of its night
Go walking through my room.

The Waradgery Tribe

Harried we were, and spent,
  Broken and falling,
Ere as the cranes we went,
  Crying and calling.

Summer shall see the bird
  Backward returning;
Never shall there be heard
  Those, who went yearning.

Emptied of us the land,
  Ghostly our going,
Fallen, like spears the hand
  Dropped in the throwing.

We are the lost who went
  Like the cranes, crying;
Hunted, lonely, and spent,
  Broken and dying.

The Song of the Woman-drawer

I am the woman-drawer,
  I am the cry;
I am the secret voice;
  I am the sigh;

I am that which is heard
　　Low in the dusk;
Birds by a note reply,
　　The flowers in musk;

I am that dolorous plaint,
　　Uttered where calls
A lone bird wand'ring by
　　Dim waterfalls;

I am the woman-drawer;
　　Pass me not by;
I am the secret voice,
　　Hear ye my cry;

I am that power which night
　　Looses abroad;
I am the root of life;
　　I am the chord.

From *The Disinherited*

IX

The sudden autumn winds, like hounds
That bell upon a scent,
Came bloring through the forest lanes,
To burst above the bent.

But I lay snug within my bed,
Although the bellied fly
Cracked like a shot-gun in the blast,
That caught it, hurrying by.

Storm is the root of man, or man
Were but a flower that drank
Its hour of sun and rain, and then
To dust forgotten sank.

Dust is the womb of peace . . . and yet,
Born of the dust, began
All love, all power, all hate; and law,
That, governing, made man.

As slowly fell the formless wind,
There came the rounded rain;
I thought how it, dimensioned, lived,
But no storm lives again.

Brooding I lay, and brooding heard
Force cry upon the wind;
Force that, unshaped, must die, because
By law undisciplined.

And I was like the wind, to life
I gave no gift of form,
To raise, by its compelling power,
My heritage of storm.

The Pear-tree

"What be you a-lookin' at, Emily Ann?
Starin' with your eyes all set?"
"I been seein' a ghost, Amanda,
And I be a-seein' it yet."

"Where was it you seen it, Emily Ann?"
"It was hung on the big pear-tree.
I seen the ghost, Amanda,
And the ghost, it said it was me.

"Put your hand on my heart, Amanda,
Feel of the life of it there,
For the ghost was hung on the pear-tree
It had my eyes and my hair."

The Tenancy

I shall go as my father went,
A thousand plans in his mind,
With something still held unspent,
When death let fall the blind.

I shall go as my mother went,
The ink still wet on the line;
I shall pay no rust as rent
For the house that is mine.

Nationality

I have grown past hate and bitterness,
I see the world as one:
Yet, though I can no longer hate,
My son is still my son.

All men at God's round table sit
And all men must be fed;
But this loaf in my hand,
This loaf is my son's bread.

INDEX OF AUTHORS

*With Biographical and Bibliographical Notes**

ADAMS, Arthur Henry, 1872-1936, was born at Lawrence, New Zealand, and was educated at Otago University. He worked as a journalist in New Zealand, London and Sydney and was editor of the *Bulletin's* Red Page from 1906 to 1909. He was the author of some successful plays and novels, also *Maoriland and Other Verses* (1899), *London Streets* (1906), and *Collected Verses* (1913).

pp.—230-232

ALLEN, Leslie Holdsworthy, 1879-   , was born at Maryborough, Victoria, and educated at the University of Sydney and University of Leipzig (where he took his Ph.D.). He became professor of English at the Royal Military College, Duntroon, and lecturer in English and Classics at Canberra University College. He was appointed Chairman of the Commonwealth Literature Censorship Appeal Board. Publications: *Gods and Wood-Things* (1913); *Phaedra and Other Poems* (1921); *Araby and Other Poems* (1924); *Patria* (1941).

p.—245

BAYLDON, Arthur Albert Dawson, 1865-1958, was born at Leeds, England, and came to Australia in 1889. He was a professional swimmer and athlete. Publications: *Poems* (1897); *The Eagles* (1921); *Collected Poems* (1932); *Apollo in Australia and Bush Verses* (1944).

p.—178

BAYLEBRIDGE, William, 1883-1942, was born in Brisbane as Charles William Blocksidge, the son of a real estate agent, but

---

* Select bibliographies include verse only.

adopted the name of Baylebridge. He was educated at Brisbane Grammar School; travelled in Europe and the Middle East; and lived at Brisbane, and in the Blue Mountains near Sydney. He was of independent means, and dedicated his life to writing, publishing much work privately. *Moreton Miles* (1910); *The New Life* (1910); *Life's Testament* (1914); *Seven Tales* (1916); *A Wreath* (1916); *Selected Poems* (1919); *Love Redeemed* (1934); *Sextains* (1939); *This Vital Flesh* (1939). A Memorial Edition of *Collected Works*, edited by P. R. Stephensen, is being issued in six volumes.

pp.—246-251

BOAKE, Barcroft Henry Thomas, 1866-1892, was born in Sydney and educated at Sydney Grammar School. He became a surveyor and boundary rider in New South Wales and Queensland. He suffered from melancholia and died by hanging himself with his stockwhip at Middle Harbour, Sydney. *Where the Dead Men Lie and Other Poems* (1897) was edited with a memoir by A. G. Stephens.

pp.—115-117

BRADY, Edwin James, 1869-1952, was born at Carcoar, New South Wales, and educated in the U.S.A. and at Sydney. He worked as a wharf clerk, farmer, and journalist, and edited Sydney and country newspapers. For many years he lived at Mallacoota, Victoria. Publications: *The Ways of Many Waters* (1899); *Bells and Hobbles* (1911); *The House of the Winds* (1919); *Wardens of the Seas* (1933).

pp.—134-140

BRENNAN, Christopher John, 1870-1932, was born in Sydney and educated at St Ignatius College and Sydney University. He won a travelling scholarship to Berlin and returned to Sydney in 1894, where he became a librarian at the Sydney Public Library. Afterwards he was lecturer in French and German and Associate Professor of German and Comparative Literature at Sydney University. He was expelled in 1925 after his wife brought a suit for judicial separation, and lived for some years in tragic destitution, helped by friends and a literary pension. He died of cancer in Lewisham Hospital. Publications: *XVIII Poems* (1897); *XXI Poems* (1897); *Poems, 1913* (1914); *A Chant of Doom and Other Verses* (1918); *Twenty-Three Poems* (1938); *The Burden of Tyre* (1953); *The Verse of Christopher Brennan* (1960); also a verse drama *A Mask* (with J. Le Gay Brereton) (1913), and *The Prose of Christopher Brennan* (1962).

pp.—202-213

BRERETON, John Le Gay, 1871-1933, was born in Sydney and educated at Sydney Grammar School and the University of Sydney. He became Fisher Librarian, then Professor of English at the University of Sydney. He was an Elizabethan scholar and an authority on Marlowe. Besides plays and essays, he wrote: *The Song of Brotherhood* (1896); *Sea and Sky* (1908); *The Burning Marl* (1919); *Swags Up!* (1928).

p.—217

CAMBRIDGE, Ada, 1844-1926, was born at Norfolk, England, and married the Rev. G. F. Cross, an Anglican clergyman. They lived in country towns and at Williamston, Victoria, from 1870 to 1909. She was the successful author of over twenty novels, many expressing her unorthodox and radical views on marriage and society, and two volumes of hymns; also *The Manor House and Other Poems* (1875); *Unspoken Thoughts* (1887); *The Hand in the Dark* (1913).

pp.—82-84

"COCKATOO JACK" is given by Stewart and Keesing in *Old Bush Songs* as the reputed author, details unknown, of the folk ballad "The Numerella Shore", representing the free selector as a cattle duffer in the Monaro ("Maneroo") district of New South Wales after Sir John Robertson's Land Act of 1861. The correct name is Eumarella, not Numerella.

pp.—24-26

CROSS, Zora Bernice May, 1890-   , was born at Brisbane and educated at Ipswich Girls' Grammar School and the Teachers' Training College, Sydney. She became a teacher, an actress, then journalist and freelance writer. She wrote literary criticism, fiction, and children's verse; also, *Songs of Love and Life* (1917); *The Lilt of Life* (1918); and *Elegy on an Australian Schoolboy*, commemorating a younger brother killed in the first world war (1921).

pp.—256-258

CUTHBERTSON, James Lister, 1851-1910, was born at Glasgow, Scotland, and educated at the University of Oxford. He arrived in Melbourne in 1874, and became a teacher at Geelong Grammar School. *Barwon Ballads* (1893); *Barwon Ballads and School Verses* (1912).

pp.—96-97

DALEY, Victor James William Patrick, 1858-1905, was born at Navan, Ireland, and educated at the Christian Brothers', Devonport, England. Having worked as a railway employee, he arrived in Australia in 1878 and became a freelance journalist and writer in Melbourne and Sydney. He died at Waitara, Sydney, of tuberculosis. He was the author of radical and socialist verses under the nom-de-plume of "Creeve Roe". Publications: *At Dawn and Dusk* (1898); *Wine and Roses*, edited with memoir by Bertram Stevens (1911); *Creeve Roe*, edited by Muir Holborn and Marjorie Pizer (1947).

pp.—167-175

DALZIEL, Kathleen, née Walker, 1881-   , was born in Durban, South Africa. She came to Australia at the age of seven. The family lived in the bush and she had no education except from her mother's teaching. For over forty years she contributed verse to the *Bulletin*. *Known and Not Held* was published in 1941.

pp.—265-266

DEAMER, Dulcie, 1890-   , was born at Christchurch, New Zealand. She married Albert Goldie and travelled abroad as an

282

actress. She became a freelance writer and journalist in Sydney, and has written short stories, historical novels, and plays; also, *Messalina* (1932); *The Silver Branch* (1948).

pp.—260-262

DENNIS, Clarence Michael James, 1876-1938, was born at Auburn, South Australia and educated at Christian Brothers' College, Adelaide. A journalist and freelance writer in Melbourne, Dennis is best known for *The Sentimental Bloke* which, besides its many editions in book form, has been performed as a stage play, silent film, sound film, and musical comedy. *Backblock Ballads* (1913); *The Songs of a Sentimental Bloke*, illustrated by Hal Gye (1915); *The Moods of Ginger Mick* (1915); *Doreen* (1917); *The Glugs of Gosh* (1917); *Jim of the Hills* (1919); *A Book for Kids* (1921); *Rose of Spadgers, The Singing Garden* (1935); *Selected Verse*, edited by Alec H. Chisholm, (1950); etc.

pp.—145-149

DEVANEY, James Martin, 1890-   , was born at Bendigo, Victoria, and educated at St Joseph's Marist Brothers' College, Sydney. He became a teacher, tutor, and freelance writer, especially on natural history and aboriginal lore, mainly in Queensland. He has written historical novels, tales of the aborigines, and a biography of Shaw Neilson, whom he and his wife looked after in Brisbane in 1941. *Fabian* (1923); *Earth Kindred* (1931); *Where the Wind Goes* (1939); *Poems* (1950).

pp.—258-260

DONAHUE, Jack, 1808(?)-1830, was born in Ireland, and was transported for life in 1824, probably as a political prisoner. He was convicted of highway robbery and sentenced to death in 1828, but escaped to become the most notorious of early bushrangers in New South Wales. He operated in the Hawkesbury-Nepean district with Underwood, Walmsley, and Webber, and was shot dead in an engagement with the Mounted Police in the Bringelly scrub in September 1830. He is credited with the authorship of the "Brave Donahue" ballad by Thomas Walker's *Felonry of*

New South Wales. He became the folk hero of a cycle of Donahue ballads, one of which may have been the original version of
"The Wild Colonial Boy"; details in John Meredith's mono-
graph *The Wild Colonial Boy*.

pp.—19-20

DURACK, Mary (Mrs H. C. Miller), 1913-   , was born in
Adelaide and educated at the Loreto Convent, Perth, Western
Australia. She lived on North-west stations in Western Australia
and worked as a journalist in Perth. Her saga of her pioneering
ancestors, *Kings in Grass Castles*, was published in 1959. She has
also written novels and, with her sister Elizabeth, books on the
aborigines.

pp.—161-163

DYSON, Edward George, 1865-1931, was born near Ballarat,
Victoria. He became a miner, a worker in a Melbourne factory,
journalist, and freelance writer. He was most notable as a
short-story writer, and also wrote novels. *Rhymes from the Mines*
(1896); *"Hello Soldier!"* (1919).

pp.—113-114

ESSON, Thomas Louis Buvelot, 1879-1943, was born in Edinburgh and came to Australia as a boy. He became assistant at
the Melbourne Public Library, a freelance journalist and critic.
He is chiefly remembered for his plays. His books of verse are
Bells and Bees (1910); *Red Gums and Other Verses* (1912).

p.—244

EVANS, George Essex, 1863-1909, was born in London, and
arrived in Queensland in 1881. He was a farmer, teacher, public
servant, and publicist for the Queensland Government Tourist
Bureau. He died at Toowoomba, where a monument was erected
to him. Publications: *The Repentance of Magdalene Despar*
(1891); *The Secret Key* (1906); *Collected Verse* (1928).

pp.—175-177

FOOTT, Mary Hannay, née Black, 1846-1918, was born in Glasgow and came to Australia in 1853. She married T. W. Foott, manager of a station on the Paroo River, Queensland, in 1874. She was afterwards literary editor of the *Queenslander*, and died at Bundaberg. Her books of verse are *Where the Pelican Builds* (1885); and *Morna Lee* (1890).

pp.—84-85

FORSTER, William, 1818-1882, was born at Madras, India, and came to Australia as a boy. He became a squatter, and a politician serving as minister in various Cabinets of the New South Wales Parliament from 1842 to 1882 and as Premier in 1859. He wrote as a journalist, satirist, and dramatist; notably the verse plays *The Weirwolf* (1876); *The Brothers* (1877); and *Midas* (1884); also political satires in the *Atlas* magazine.

pp.—50-53

FULLERTON, Mary Elizabeth ("E"), 1868-1946, was born and educated in North Gippsland, Victoria. She left Australia for England in 1921. She was a novelist, journalist, lexicographer, and descriptive writer. Her early poetry was published under her own name; her later work, written in England, was published, through her friend and champion Miles Franklin, under the pseudonym of "E". *Moods and Melodies* (1908); *The Breaking Furrow* (1921); *Moles Do So Little with Their Privacy* (1942); *The Wonder and the Apple* (1946).

pp.—193-197

GAY, William, 1865-1897, was born at Renfrewshire, Scotland, and educated at Glasgow University. He emigrated for health reasons to New Zealand in 1885, and came to Melbourne in 1888, where he taught at Scotch College. He died of tuberculosis at Bendigo. He was the author of a prose essay on Walt Whitman; also, *Sonnets and Other Verses* (1894); *Sonnets* (1896); *Christ on Olympus* (1896); *Complete Poetical Works* (1911).

p.—179

GELLERT, Leon Maxwell, 1892-   , was born at Adelaide and educated at Adelaide High School and University. He served in the first A.I.F. and was at the landing at Gallipoli. As a journalist he became editor of *Art in Australia* and *Home* magazine, and was literary editor of the *Sydney Morning Herald*. His books of verse are: *Songs of a Campaign* (1917); *The Isle of San: a Phantasy* (1919); *Desperate Measures* (1928).

pp.—266-267

GERARD, Edwin ("TROOPER GERARDY") 1891-   , was born in South Australia and educated in Western Australia. He served with the Light Horse in Palestine in the first world war. *The Road to Palestine* (1918); *Australian Light Horse Ballads and Rhymes* (1919).

pp.—153-155

GIBSON, George Herbert ("IRONBARK"), 1846-1921, was born at Plymouth, England. Qualified as a solicitor, he arrived in New Zealand in 1869, then moved to New South Wales. After experience on the land, he joined the New South Wales Department of Lands, and as inspector travelled widely through the States. He was a contributor to the *Bulletin* as "Ironbark", and published *Southerly Busters* (1878); *Ironbark Chips and Stockwhip Cracks* (1893); *Ironbark Splinters from the Australian Bush* (1912).

pp.—93-96

GILMORE, Mary Jean, née Cameron, 1865-1962, was born near Goulburn, New South Wales, of Scottish descent. After working as a schoolteacher, she joined William Lane's New Australia colony in Paraguay and married her fellow colonist William Alexander Gilmore in 1897. She returned to Australia in 1902 and edited the Woman's Page of the Sydney *Worker* for twenty-three years. She was created a Dame of the Order of the British Empire in 1936 for services to Australian literature. She was a supporter of the Australian Labour movement, and a champion of many causes. When she died at Sydney, she was given a State funeral by the Commonwealth Government and the State of New

South Wales. Besides essays and such books of reminiscences as *Old Days: Old Ways*, she published *Marri'd and Other Verses* (1910); *The Passionate Heart* (1918); *The Tilted Cart* (1925); *The Wild Swan* (1930); *The Rue Tree* (1931); *Under the Wilgas* (1932); *Battlefields* (1939); *The Disinherited* (1941); *Selected Verse* (1948); *Fourteen Men* (1954).

pp.—269-278

GOODGE, William T., 1862-1909, was born in London. He came to Australia in his youth and worked as a jackeroo in western New South Wales. He contributed to the Orange *Leader* and eventually became its editor. In Sydney from 1902 until his death he was a prolific freelance journalist. *Hits! Skits! and Jingles!* was published in 1899.

pp.—97-98

GORDON, Adam Lindsay, 1833-1870, was born in the Azores Islands, the son of a retired Indian Army officer. He was educated at Cheltenham College and Woolwich Military Academy and came to Adelaide in 1853. He was a mounted policeman, a horse-trainer, a member of the South Australian Parliament 1865-6, a keeper of livery stables and a brilliant steeplechase rider. His burden of debts, combined with head injuries from riding falls and an inherited melancholia, led him to shoot himself at Brighton, Victoria. *The Feud* (1864); *Ashtaroth* (1867); *Sea Spray and Smoke Drift* (1867); *Bush Ballads and Galloping Rhymes* (1870).

pp.—60-66

GORDON, James William ("JIM GRAHAME"), 1874-1949, was born at Creswick, Victoria. He became known as a freelance writer and bush balladist. He was a mate of Henry Lawson when they humped their blueys from Bourke to Hungerford in 1892. His books of verse are: *Call of the Bush* (1940); *Home Leave and Departing* (1944); *Under Wide Skies: Collected Verse* (1947).

pp.—140-142

GREEN, Henry Mackenzie, 1881-1962, was born in Sydney and educated at the University of Sydney, graduating in Arts and Law. He was Librarian at the Fisher Library at the University from 1921 to 1946. He is chiefly known for his monumental *History of Australian Literature* (1961). His poems were published in *The Happy Valley* (1925); and *The Book of Beauty* (1929).

p.—245

HARFORD, Lesbia Venner, née Keogh, 1891-1927, was born at Brighton, Victoria, and educated at the University of Melbourne. Graduating in Arts and Law, she became a social worker, women's organizer, and worker in a clothing factory. *The Poems of Lesbia Harford* (1941), a posthumous volume, was edited by Nettie Palmer.

pp.—262-265

HARNEY, William Edward, 1895-1963, was born at Charters Towers, Queensland; served in the A.I.F. in the first world war; and was drover, cattleman, trader, trepanger, patrol officer, Protector of Aborigines under the Native Affairs branch of the Northern Territory, and Ranger of the Ayres Rock National Park. A famous raconteur, he became a popular radio and television personality on the A.B.C. and B.B.C. The author of autobiographical and descriptive books featuring aboriginal life and lore, he also published *Songs of the Songmen: Aboriginal Myths Retold (with A. P. Elkin)* (1949).

pp.—156-157

HARPUR, Charles, 1813-1868, was born at Windsor, New South Wales, where his Irish convict father was a schoolmaster and parish clerk. The poet worked as a clerk in the post office, Sydney, then became a farmer in the Hunter River district, and afterwards a schoolteacher at Jerry's Plains. He married Mary Doyle, the "Rosa" of his sonnets, in 1850. He was Gold Commissioner at Araluen, on the South Coast, from 1859 to 1866; then farmed at Eurobodalla. *Thoughts: A Series of Sonnets* (1845);

The Bushrangers: a Play and Other Poems (1853); *The Tower of the Dream* (1865); *Poems* (posthumous) (1883); *Selected Poems* (1944); *Rosa: Love Sonnets to Mary Doyle* (1948). A biography, *Charles Harpur: An Australian,* was published by J. Normington-Rawling in 1962.

pp.—53-59

HARRINGTON, Edward Phillip, 1896-   , was born at Shepparton, Victoria, and educated at the State school, Wanalta. He served with the 4th Light Horse in Palestine in the first world war. Publications: *Songs of War and Peace* (1920); *Boundary Bend and Other Ballads* (1936); *The Kerrigan Boys* (1944); *The Swagless Swaggie*: selected verse (1957).

pp.—157-161

HARTIGAN, Very Rev. Mgr Patrick Joseph ("JOHN O'BRIEN"), 1879-1952, was born at Yass, New South Wales, and educated at St Patrick's College, Goulburn, and Manly. He was parish priest at Narrandera, New South Wales; then Inspector of Catholic Schools at Goulburn; and Chaplain at the Convent of the Sisters of the Sacred Heart, Rose Bay, Sydney. He published his best known book, *Around the Boree Log,* in 1921.

pp.—149-153

JEPHCOTT, Sydney Wheeler, 1864-1951, was born at Colac-Colac, Victoria. He lived on the land in the Corryong district, New South Wales, near Mt Kosciusko, where he had a famous plantation of trees from many countries. He wrote: *The Secrets Of the South* (1892), and *Penetralia* (1912).

p.—177

KENDALL, Henry, 1839-1882, was born at Kirmington, in the Ulladulla district on the South Coast of New South Wales. After the family moved to the Clarence River district, North Coast, he became a cabin boy on a whaling brig. Subsequently he worked as a shop assistant; as a lawyer's clerk; as a public servant in Sydney 1857-69; and as a struggling freelance writer in

Melbourne, 1869-70, and Sydney, 1871-3. He was befriended by the Fagan family near Gosford, and became storekeeper for the Fagans at Camden Haven, North Coast, 1875-80; then Inspector of State Forests, Cundletown, on the Manning River, 1881-2. He died of consumption in Sydney, and was buried in Waverley Cemetery. He published *Poems and Songs* (1862); *Leaves from Australian Forests* (1869); *Songs from the Mountains* (1880); *Orara* (1881); etc.; and *Selected Poems* was published in 1957.

pp.—71-81

LAVATER, Louis, 1867-1953, was born at Melbourne and educated at the University of Melbourne. He became a musical composer, critic, teacher, and examiner; and was the compiler of an anthology of Australasian sonnets. His books of verse are: *Blue Days and Grey Days* (1915); *A Lover's Ephemeris* (1917); *This Green Mortality* (1922).

pp.—188-190

LAWSON, Henry, 1867-1922, was born on the Grenfell gold-diggings, his father being Nils Larsen, a Norwegian master-mariner, who turned digger, carpenter, contractor, and settler. His mother was Louisa Albury, later a leading feminist and editor of a women's magazine. He was educated at the Eurunderee Public School. Afflicted with deafness at the age of nine, he worked on the family selection and at casual bush jobs, and was a coachpainter's apprentice in Sydney. In 1891 he worked as a journalist on the staff of the *Boomerang*, Brisbane. With help from the *Bulletin* he went to Bourke in 1892 and tramped to Hungerford and back. In 1894 he was a telegraph linesman in New Zealand; then a freelance writer in Perth, Sydney, and London, with an interval as a teacher in New Zealand. Except for a period as a publicist at Leeton in 1916-17 and a brief holiday at Mallacoota with E. J. Brady in 1910, he lived from 1902 in Sydney. He is recognized as the greatest Australian short-story writer. His publications include: *Short Stories in Prose and Verse* (1894); *In the Days When the World Was Wide* (1896);

Verses, Popular and Humorous (1900); *When I was King* (1905); *The Skyline Rider* (1910); *My Army, Oh, My Army!* (1915); with collections and selections, including *Poetical Works* (1956).

pp.—117-125

LAWSON, William, 1876-1957, was born in England. He became a journalist and freelance writer in New Zealand and Australia, living mostly in Sydney. He wrote historical and romantic novels, historical and descriptive books; also *The Red West Road* (1903); *The Three Kings* (1914); *Bush Verses* (1914); *Bill the Whaler* (1944).

pp.—142-145

LINDSAY, Jack, 1900-   , was born in Melbourne, the elder son of Norman Lindsay. He was educated at the University of Queensland and became a freelance writer in Sydney and London, the prolific author of many books, including verse dramas, historical novels, literary criticism, translations of the classics, autobiography, etc.; edited *Vision*, a Sydney literary magazine, also anthologies, and texts of English authors. His books of verse are *Fauns and Ladies* (1923); *The Passionate Neatherd* (1926); *Second Front* (1944).

p.—268

LONG, Richard Hoopell, 1874-1948, was born in England. He arrived in Australia in 1879, and lived in Melbourne. He was a socialist and pacifist. Published *Verses* (1917).

pp.—232-233

LOWE, Robert, Viscount Sherbrooke, 1811-1892, was born in Nottinghamshire, England; educated at Winchester and the University of Oxford. He came to Sydney in 1842, practised law and became a prominent member of the N.S.W. Legislative Council (1843-50), known as a brilliant orator on education, land reform, transportation, and constitutional matters. He edited the important newspaper *Atlas*, to which he contributed political satires. Lowe returned to England in 1850 to become Chancellor of the Exchequer and Home Secretary. *Poems of a Life* (1885).

pp.—48-50

MACARTNEY, Frederick Thomas Bennett, 1887-   , was born and educated in Melbourne. He worked as a clerk, a reporter and freelance journalist, and was Clerk of the Courts, Sheriff and Public Trustee at Darwin. Afterwards, living in Melbourne, he was a lecturer on Australian literature, and edited the revised edition of E. Morris Miller's bibliography *Australian Literature* (1956). He is the author of literary criticism, short-stories, and a biography of "Furnley Maurice" (Frank Wilmot); his volumes of verse include *Poems* (1920); *Preferences* (1941); *Gaily the Troubadour* (1946); *Tripod for Homeward Incense* (1947); *Selected Poems* (1961).

pp.—255-256

McCRAE, George Gordon, 1833-1927, was born in Scotland and came to Melbourne in 1841. He was Deputy Registrar-General in Victoria, and a leading member of Melbourne literary circles, the friend of Kendall, Adam Lindsay Gordon, and Marcus Clarke, with associations described by Hugh McCrae in *My Father and My Father's Friends* (1935). He wrote novels, stories, travel sketches and light verses in newspapers and magazines; illustrated books; and his books of verse are: *The Story of Balladeadro* (1867); *Mamba, the Bright-Eyed: An Aboriginal Reminiscence* (1867); *The Man in the Iron Mask* (1873); *The Fleet and Convoy* (1915).

pp.—59-60

McCRAE, Hugh Raymond, 1876-1958, was born in Melbourne and educated at Hawthorn Grammar School. He was articled to an architect, but became a freelance writer and artist, an actor in America and Australia, lecturer, dramatic critic, and magazine editor. He lived near Camden, New South Wales, and in Sydney, where he died. He was awarded the O.B.E. for services to Australian literature in 1953. His writings include short-stories, reminiscences, and an imaginary biography in eighteenth century style, reprinted in *Story-Book Only* (1948). He edited *Georgina's Journal*, his grandmother's diary; and was both author and illustrator of *The Ship of Heaven* (1951), an operetta fantasy in verse, performed with music by Alfred Hill in Sydney in 1933. Other publications are: *Satyrs and Sunlight* (1909); *Colombine* (1920); *Idyllia* (1922); *Satyrs and Sunlight* (Fanfrolico Press) (1928); *The Mimshi Maiden* (1938); *Poems* (1939); *Forests of Pan* (1944); *Voice of the Forest* (1945); *The Best Poems of Hugh McCrae*, edited by R. G. Howarth (1961).

pp.—233-244

MACKELLAR, Isobel Marion Dorothea, 1885-   , was born in Sydney, daughter of Sir Charles Mackellar. She is the author of a novel and, with Ruth Bedford, two children's novels. Also, *The Closed Door* (1911); *The Witch Maid* (1914); *Dreamharbour* (1923); *Fancy Dress* (1926); *My Country and Other Poems* (1945).

pp.—251-254

NEILSON, John Shaw, 1872-1942, was born at Penola, South Australia, of Scottish ancestry. His father, John Neilson, a farmer and bush worker, wrote verses which won prizes. Shaw Neilson's education was very scanty, confined to fifteen months at Penola State school and twelve months at Minimay, in the south-west Wimmera, Victoria, when the family moved there in 1881. At fourteen he helped his father on selections and in casual labour at Nhill and Sea Lake in the Victorian mallee, till they were driven off the land by adversity in 1916. Neilson then worked as a casual labourer, fruit-picking, potato-digging, clearing scrub, doing heavy pick and shovel navvying on drains and in quarries until 1928, when friends got him an office job as messenger with the Country Roads Board in Melbourne. About 1906 his eyesight became defective, he could not read or write, and had to get members of his family or working mates to write down his poems. He owed much to A. G. Stephens, who acted as his constant critic, literary agent, publisher, and champion. *Old Granny Sullivan* (1916); *Heart of Spring* (1919); *Ballad and Lyrical Poems* (1923); *New Poems* (1927); *Collected Poems* (1934); *Beauty Imposes* (1938); *Unpublished Poems of Shaw Neilson,* edited by James Devaney (1947).

pp.—218-230

"O'BRIEN, JOHN"—see HARTIGAN, Very Rev. Mgr Patrick Joseph.

O'DOWD, Bernard Patrick, 1866-1953, was born at Beaufort, Victoria. His father was a policeman, later a farmer. O'Dowd was educated at State schools, the School of Mines and Grenville College, Ballarat, and the University of Melbourne. He was Assistant Librarian in the Supreme Court Library, Melbourne, 1887-1913; First Assistant State Parliamentary Draftsman, 1913-31; Parliamentary Draftsman, 1931-35. He was the editor of legal works; lecturer, secularist, radical, a founder of the *Tocsin* paper. A leading literary figure in Melbourne, he stated his poetic credo in *Poetry Militant*: An Australian Plea for the Poetry of Purpose. Publications in verse are: *Dawnward?* (1903); *The Silent Land* (1906); *Dominions of the Boundary* (1907); *The Seven Deadly Sins* (1909); *Poems* (1910); *The Bush* (1912); *Alma Venus!* (1921); *Selected Poems* (1928); *Poems*: collected edition (1941).

pp.—180-188

OGILVIE, William Henry, 1869-1963, was born at Kelso, Scotland; he came to Australia in 1889, and returned to Scotland in 1901. In Australia he was a drover, horse-breaker, and bush worker. He was the author of many books of verse including *Fair Girls and Gray Horses* (1898 and 1958); *Hearts of Gold* (1903); *The Australian* (1916); *From Sunset to Dawn* (1946); *Saddle for a Throne* (1952).

pp.—125-134

O'REILLY, Dowell Philip, 1865-1923, was born in Sydney and educated at Sydney Grammar School. He became a schoolteacher, then member of the New South Wales Parliament 1894-98, afterwards an officer in the Federal Taxation Department, Sydney. He was the father of the novelist Eleanor Dark and the friend of Brennan and Brereton. He was a short-story writer. His character and style are shown in *Dowell O'Reilly from His Letters*, edited by his wife (1927). His poetry is contained in *Australian Poems* (1884); *The Prose and Verse of Dowell O'Reilly* (1924).

p.—180

PALMER, Nettie, née Janet Gertrude Higgins, 1885- , was born in Bendigo, Victoria, and educated at the Presbyterian Ladies' College and the University of Melbourne. She married Vance Palmer in 1914. She is the author of critical works on Australian literature and Henry Handel Richardson, essays, a biography of Henry Bournes Higgins, and an autobiography (*Fourteen Years*, 1948). Her books of verse are *The South Wind* (1914); and *Shadowy Paths* (1915).

pp.—254-255

PALMER, Edward Vance, 1885-1959, was born at Bundaberg, Queensland, and educated at Ipswich Grammar School. He became a freelance writer and journalist in Brisbane, London and Melbourne; travelled in Europe, Russia, and Asia, and served in the A.I.F. in France in the first world war. He was a member (1942-47) and chairman (1947-53) of the Commonwealth Literary Fund Advisory Board; and, with his wife Nettie, was an eminent figure in Australian cultural development. His main reputation is as a novelist, short-story writer and critic, but he was also a dramatist, biographer, social interpreter, literary historian, and editor. Publications in verse: *The Forerunners* (1915); *The Camp* (1920).

p.—255

PATERSON, Andrew Barton, 1864-1941, was born at Narrambla, near Orange, New South Wales, and educated at Sydney Grammar School. Qualifying as a solicitor in Sydney, he became a war correspondent in South Africa, the Philippines, and China and during the first world war, when he was also an ambulance driver and remount officer in the A.I.F. Afterwards he was a journalist and editor of Sydney papers and a grazier on the Upper Murrumbidgee. He collected and edited the first substantial collection of folk ballads with *Old Bush Songs* (1905). He wrote station novels, short-stories, a treatise on land reform, and reminiscences. His own books of verse are: *The Man from Snowy River* (1898); *Rio Grande's Last Race* (1902); *Saltbush Bill, J.P.* (1917); *Collected Verse* (1921); *The Animals Noah Forgot* (1933).

pp.—41-42; 98-109

PITT, Marie Elizabeth Josephine, née McKeown, 1869-1948, was born in Gippsland, Victoria, and spent her life in farming and mining districts in Victoria and Tasmania, and in Melbourne, where she died. She was a feminist and was associated with the Labour movement and social reform. Her books include *The Horses of the Hills* (1911); *Poems* (1922); *Selected Poems* (1944).

pp.—201-202

QUINN, Roderic Joseph, 1867-1949, was born in Sydney and educated at Catholic schools. He studied law, and then taught school, before becoming a freelance writer and journalist. He wrote a novel and some short-stories but was best known for his poetry: *The Hidden Tide* (1899); *The Circling Hearths* (1901); *Poems* (1920).

pp.—190-192

SHAW, Winifred Maitland (Mrs R. M. Taplin), 1905-   , was born at Maitland, New South Wales. She was a country school-girl of fourteen when her first book was published. She later lived in Singapore and was interned in Changi prison camp during the Pacific war. She has since lived in London. *The Aspen Tree* (1920); *The Yellow Cloak* (1922); *Babylon*, illustrated by Hugh McCrae (1924).

pp.—268-269

SOUTER, Charles Henry, 1864-1944, was born in Aberdeen, Scotland and came to Sydney in 1879. He returned to Aberdeen to graduate in medicine, and, coming back to Australia, practised in a bush hospital, as a ship's surgeon, and as doctor in South Australia among the farmers of the mallee district. *Irish Lords* (1912); *To Many Ladies and Others* (1917); *The Mallee Fire* (1923); *The Lonely Rose* (1935).

pp.—109-113

SPENCER, Thomas Edward, 1845-1910, was born in London. After a visit to Australia as a youth of eighteen, he settled in Sydney in 1875 as a builder and contractor. He was the author of a novel and short-stories, many figuring the humorous character of Mrs Bridget McSweeney. His books of ballads are: *How McDougal Topped the Score* (1906); *Budgeree Ballads* (1908); *Why Doherty Died* (1910).

pp.—89-92

STEPHENS, James Brunton, 1835-1902, was born near Edinburgh, Scotland, and educated at Edinburgh University. After being a travelling tutor in Europe and a teacher in Scotland, he came to Brisbane in 1866 and taught as tutor on a cattle station and in State schools. Entering the public service, he became Under Secretary. He was an eminent man of letters in Brisbane. The author of a comic opera and a novel, he also published *Convict Once* (1871); *The Godolphin Arabian* (1873); *Poetical Works* (1902); *My Chinee Cook and Other Humorous Verse* (1902).

pp.—66-70

THATCHER, Charles Robert, 1831-1882(?), was born at Bristol, England. A flute player in theatre orchestras in London, he emigrated to the Victorian gold-diggings in 1853 and was a popular professional entertainer at Bendigo and other Victorian goldfields, singing songs of his own composition and parodies of music-hall songs with local allusions. His songs are preserved in *Thatcher's Colonial Songster* (1857) and *Thatcher's Colonial Minstrel* (1864). See *Goldrush Songster*, by Hugh Anderson (1958).

pp.—20-21

WENTWORTH, William Charles, 1790-1872, was born in Norfolk Island, the son of D'Arcy Wentworth, surgeon, and his de facto wife Catherine Crowley, a convict girl. He was educated at Bexhill, England, and the University of Cambridge where he submitted in 1823, when aged 32, his poem for the Chancellor's gold medal on the set subject, "Australasia". It was placed second after W. M. Praed's entry. Earlier, in 1813, he had crossed the Blue Mountains with Blaxland and Lawson. He was a barrister in Sydney; a radical leader in the fight for self-government, and a dominating figure in the N.S.W. Legislative Council. His change to conservative policies incurred criticism from liberals and radicals, including Charles Harpur. He was the "virtual founder" of Sydney University. *Australasia* was published in 1823 and reprinted in 1873.

pp.—45-48

WRIGHT, David McKee, 1869-1928, was born in Ireland and educated in London. He emigrated with his family to New Zealand in 1887, and there became a goldminer, a Congregational minister and a journalist. He came to Sydney in 1910 and became editor of the *Bulletin's* Red Page. He was the author of four books of verse in New Zealand; and, in Australia, *An Irish Heart* (1918).

pp.—197-201

INDEX OF TITLES

	Page
Adam to Lilith	205
After Johnson's Dance	110
All That I Am to Earth Belongs	247
Alma Venus	187
Ambuscade	235
Andy's Gone with Cattle	119
Anguished Doubt Broods over Eden, The	205
Anzac Cove	266
Artemis	260
Ascetic, The	171
As Fire, Unfound Ere Pole Approaches Pole	250
Australia (Bernard O'Dowd)	187
Australia (W. C. Wentworth)	45
Australian, The	230
Australia's on the Wallaby	38
Ballad of Queensland ("Sam Holt"), A	95
Ballad of the Drover	117
Banks of the Condamine, The	32
Baying Hounds, The	271
Beauty and Terror	262
Beauty Imposes	219
Bell-birds	73
Beyond Kerguelen	76
Bill the Whaler	142
Botany Bay	4
Brain, the Blood, the Busy Thews, The	246
Brave Donahue	19
Break of Day	220
Broken-down Digger, The	22
Broken-down Squatter, The	23
Budding Spring	268
Buffalo Creek	217
Bullocky Bill	30
Bush, The	182
Bush Christening, A	105

Page

Bushman's Song, A 106
Bushrangers, The 157

Camden Magpie 243
Camp Within the West, The 190
Cicada, The 245
Choir of Spirits on a Cloud, A 249
Clancy of the Overflow 108
Cleaning Up 113
Click Go the Shears, Boys 31
Coachman's Yarn, The 137
Cockies of Bungaree 26
Colombine 233
Come Out, Come Out, Ye Souls That Serve 210
Communal 195
Convict's Lament on the Death of Captain Logan, A 5
Cool, Cool Country, The 228
Cow, The 182
Crane is My Neighbour, The 226
Crazy World, The 179
Creek of the Four Graves, The 55
Cubes 196

Daley's Dorg Wattle 97
Danny's Wooing 199
Dark Rosaleen (*Extracts from*) 197
Day's End 263
Death of Ben Hall, The 131
Dedication, A 64
Desert Claypan 255
Devil and the Governor, The 50
Disinherited, The 276
Dominion of Australia, The 66
Dreams 169
Dusk in the Domain 253
Dying Stockman, The 29

Elegy on an Australian Schoolboy 256
Emus 193
Enigma 242

Page

Evening	241
Evening Gleam, The	259
Eve-song	269
Experience	264
Faith (Ada Cambridge)	82
Faith (Victor J. Daley)	171
Faithless	189
Fancy Dress	252
Farmer Remembers the Somme, The	255
Fine Clay	268
Fire in the Heavens, and Fire along the Hills	205
Fisher, The	191
Flash Jack from Gundagai	37
Flesh	196
From the Gulf	125
Gallop of Fire, A	201
God, to Get the Clay That Stayed Me	248
Golden Gullies of the Palmer, The	22
He Could Have Found His Way	265
He Had Served Eighty Masters	264
How McDougall Topped the Score	89
How Old Is My Heart	208
How the Fire Queen Crossed the Swamp	128
I Blow My Pipes	234
I Cry to You as I Pass Your Windows	209
I Said, This Misery Must End	212
I Saw My Life as Whitest Flame	203
I Worshipped, When My Veins Were Fresh	246
In a Wine Cellar	167
In the Trench	266
Inspiration	197
Interlude: The Casement	208
Irish Lords	111
Jester in the Trench, The	267
Jim Jones	3

x

Page

Jim the Splitter   80
Joan of Arc   237
June Morning   241

Land I Came thro' Last, The   211
Last of His Tribe, The   79
Let Us Go Down, the Long Dead Night is Done   202
Lichen   194
Life's Testament (*Extracts from*)   246
Lilith (*Extracts from*)   205
Lilith on the Fate of Man   206
Lion   195
Lofty Lane   153
Look Out Below!   20
Lost and Given Over   134
Love Feeds, Like Intellect, His Lamp with Truth   249
Love Redeemed (*Extracts from*)   249
Love Sonnets, VIII   57
Love's Coming   218
Lovers   194

Mad Marjory   236
Mamba the Bright-eyed   59
Man from Ironbark, The   102
Man from Snowy River, The   98
Marlowe   178
May   223
Me and My Dog   39
Midsummer Noon in the Australian Forest, A   53
Mopoke   188
Morgan   159
Mortality   259
Mother, The   254
Mouse, The   242
Muse-haunted   234
My Country   251
My Heart Was Wandering in the Sands   204
My Love Is the Voice of a Song   198
My Mate Bill   93
My Old Black Billy   160

	Page
My Other Chinee Cook	68
Myall in Prison, The	274
Narcissus and Some Tadpoles	173
Nationality	278
Never Admit the Pain	270
Night	171
Numerella Shore, The	24
Nurse No Long Grief	270
O Desolate Eves	211
Old Bark Hut, The	14
Old Botany Bay	272
Old Bullock Dray, The	9
Old John Bax	112
Old Keg of Rum, The	12
On a Shining Silver Morning	197
On Australian Hills	82
On the Road to Gundagai	34
Orange Tree, The	221
Orara	71
Overlander, The	27
Pauca Mea (*Extract from*)	212
Pear-tree, The	277
Play, The	145
Poet and Peasant	233
Poor Can Feed the Birds, The	224
Quest of Silence, The (*Extract from*)	205
Racing Eight, A	96
Ramble-eer, The	40
Reaper, The	245
Red Jack	161
Revolution	262
Rhyme of Joyous Garde, The	65
Said Hanrahan	149
Sea-grief	180

Page

Sentimental Bloke, The (*Extract from*) 145
September in Australia 75
Settler's Lament, The 7
Shearer's Song, The 35
Shearer's Wife, The 244
Shepherd, The 273
Sick Stockrider, The 60
Skylark's Nest, The 232
Sliprails and the Spur, The 124
Song Be Delicate 218
Song of the Captured Woman 258
Song of the Rain 241
Song of the Woman-drawer, The 275
Songs of the Squatters No. 1 48
Strawberries in November 220
Sundowner, The 227
Sunset 178
Swans at Night 271

Talbragar 120
Tamerlane 169
Tangmalangaloo 152
Teams, The 122
Temple of Infamy, The 57
Tenancy, The 278
These Men 267
This Miracle in Me I Scan 247
This Way Only 265
Thredbo River 177
'Tis the White Plum Tree 223
To a Blue Flower 225
To a School-girl 222
Towards the Source (*Extracts from*) 202
Tower of the Dream, The 56
Twilight of Disquietude, The (*Extracts from*) 203

Uncouth Knight, The 236

Waltzing Matilda 41
Wanderer, The (*Extracts from*) 208

	Page
Waradgery Tribe, The	275
Waterwitch, The	6
West of Alice	156
Whalan of Waitin' a While	140
What the Red-haired Bo'sun Said	109
Where the Dead Men Lie	115
Where the Pelican Builds	84
Who Questions If the Punctual Sun Unbars	250
Wild Colonial Boy, The	18
Women of the West, The	175
Words	54
Years That Go to Make Me Man, The	203
Young Democracy	180

INDEX OF FIRST LINES

I. *Folk Songs and Ballads*

A life that is free as the bandits' of old	19
A neat little packet from Hobart set sail	6
A strapping young stockman lay dying	29
A young man left his native shores	20
All you on emigration bent	7
As I came down Talbingo Hill	30
Come all you jolly travellers that's out of work, just mind	26
Come, Stumpy, old man, we must shift while we can	23
Farewell to Old England for ever	4
Hurrah for the Lachlan	35
I am a native of the land of Erin	5
I've shore at Burrabogie, and I've shore at Toganmain	37
I've worked on the Nine-Mile, likewise on the River	22
Me and my dog	39
My name is old Jack Palmer	12
O, listen for a moment lads, and hear me tell my tale—	3
Oh, hark the dogs are barking, love	32
Oh, my name is Bob the Swagman, before you all I stand	14
Oh! the shearing is all over	9
Oh, we started down from Roto when the sheds had all cut out	34
Once a jolly swagman camped by a billabong	41
Our fathers came to search for gold	38
Out on the board the old shearer stands	31
The earth rolls on through empty space, its journey's never done	40
Then roll the swag and blanket up	22
There's a nice green little gully on the Numerella shore	24
There's a trade you all know well	27
'Tis of a wild Colonial boy, Jack Doolan was his name	18

Page

II. *The Colonial Age*

A settler in the olden times went forth — 55
And is the great cause lost beyond recall? — 82

By channels of coolness the echoes are calling — 73
But hark! What hubbub now is this that comes — 57

Down in the south, by the waste without sail on it — 76

Fair as the night, when all the astral fires — 57

Grey Winter hath gone, like a wearisome guest — 75

He crouches, and buries his face on his knees — 79
Hold hard, Ned! Lift me down once more, and lay me in
  the shade — 60

In New South Wales, as I plainly see — 50

Land of my birth! though now, alas! no more — 45

Not a sound disturbs the air — 53

Oh, to be there to-night! — 82

She is not yet; but he whose ear — 66

The bard who is singing of Wollombi Jim — 80
The Commissioner bet me a pony—I won — 48
The day had fled, the moon arose — 59
The horses were ready, the rails were down — 84
The strong sob of the chafing stream — 71
They are rhymes rudely strung with intent less — 64

We were glad together in gladsome meads — 65
Words are deeds. The words we hear — 54

Yes, I got another Johnny; but he was to Number One — 68
Yes, wonderful are dreams: and I have known — 56

Page

III. *Bush Ballads and Popular Verse*

A cloud of dust on the long, white road — 122
A mermaid's not a human thing — 134
A peaceful spot is Piper's Flat. The folk that live around— — 89
Across the stony ridges — 117
After Johnson's dance — 110

Ben Hall was out on the Lachlan side — 131
Buckle the spur and belt again — 153

Four horsemen rode out from the heart of the range — 157

Give me the salt spray in my face — 109

I had written him a letter which I had, for want of better — 108
I have humped my bluey in all the States — 160
I'm travellin' down the Castlereagh, and I'm a station-hand — 106
It was the man from Ironbark who struck the Sydney town — 102

Jack Denver died on Talbragar when Christmas Eve began — 120

Long life to old Whalan of Waitin' a While — 140

Oh! don't you remember black Alice, Sam Holt — 95
Old Bill the Whaler said to me — 142
On the outer Barcoo where the churches are few — 105
Our Andy's gone with cattle now— — 119
Out on the wastes of the Never Never — 115

She rises clear to memory's eye — 161
Store cattle from Nelanjie! The mob goes feeding past — 125

That's his saddle across the tie-beam, an' them's his spurs up there — 93
The bishop sat in lordly state and purple cap sublime — 152
The clover-burr was two feet high, and the billabongs were full — 111
The colours of the setting sun — 124
The flood was down in the Wilga swamps, three feet over the mud — 128

Page

There was movement at the station, for word had passed
around   98
This a tale that the coachman told   137

We are travelling west of Alice Springs, and Sam is at the
wheel   156
"We'll all be rooned," said Hanrahan   149
"Wot's in a name?" she sez . . . An' then she sighs   145
When Morgan crossed the Murray to Peechelba and doom   159
When Old John Bax drove the mail to Coonabarabran   112
When the horse has been unharnessed and we've flushed
the old machine   113
Who knows it not, who loves it not   96

"You can talk about yer sheep dorgs," said the man from
Allan's Creek   97

IV. *Poets of the Nineties*

All night a noise of leaping fish   191
Along the serried coast the Southerly raves   180
As many, Mother, are your moods and forms   182

Come out, come out, ye souls that serve, why will ye die?   210

Door of existence, beacon of our haze   187

Faith shuts her eyes   171
Fire in the heavens, and fire along the hills   205

Hark! Young Democracy from sleep   180
How old is my heart, how old, how old is my heart   208

I cry to you as I pass your windows in the dusk   209
I have been dreaming all a summer day   169
I have seen a gum-tree   196
I said, this misery must end   212
I saw my life as whitest flame   203

Last sea-thing dredged by sailor Time from Space   187
Last, since a pinch of dust may quench the eyes   206

Page

Let us go down, the long dead night is done 202
Lo, upon the carpet, where 169

Mopoke! . . . Mopoke! . . . 188
My annals have it so 193
My heart was wandering in the sands 204
My love is the voice of a song 198

Nina's cross: her alphabet 196

O desolate eves along the way, how oft 211
O did you see a troop go by 190
O thou that achest, pulse o' the unwed vast 205
On a shining silver morning long ago 197

Parasite lichen 194

See how it flashes 167
Seers have no monopoly 195
Summer, like a dread disease 177
Suns, planets, stars, in glorious array 171

Then anguished doubt broods over Eden; night 205
The critic of the days of yore 174
The land I came thro' last was dumb with night 211
The narrow, thorny path he trod 171
The weary wind is slumbering on the wing 178
The window is wide and lo! beyond its bars 208
The world did say to me 179
The years that go to make me man 203
There was no ceremony 195
There's half a god in many a man 197
There's not a tear that brims thine eye unshed 189
They left the vine-wreathed cottage and the mansion on
    the hill 175
This is a rune I ravelled in the still 182
To be unloved brings sweet relief 194
'Twas the spring in the air 199

When the north wind moans thro' the blind creek courses 201
With Eastern banners flaunting in the breeze 178

Page

V. *The Early Twentieth Century*

A choir of spirits on a cloud	249
A timid child with heart oppressed	217
Against the clear intensity of dawn	268
All Christmas night upon the shelf	242
All kings are hollow	228
All that I am to Earth belongs	247
Always she loved the sound of bells	238
As fire, unfound ere pole approaches pole	250
Beauty does not walk through lovely days	262
Beauty imposes reverence in the Spring	219
Before the glare o' dawn I rise	244
Elf-light, owl-light	253
Every night I sleep	266
Exit the ribald clown	233
God, to get the clay that stayed me	248
Harried we were, and spent	275
Have you heard of the quaint people	220
He could have found his way there with shut eyes	265
He had served eighty masters; they'd have said	264
He heard, and dreamed the night-wind on	234
Here Nature holds as in a hollowed hand	232
Ho! Ho! The fine fellow	243
How tenderly the evening creeps between	241
I am the woman-drawer	275
I am type of singleness	260
I blow my pipes, the glad birds sing	234
I did not cry at all	258
I have grown past hate and bitterness	278
I know not when this tiresome man	227
I must be dreaming through the days	264
I shall go as my father went	278
I span and Eve span	269
I watch her fingers where they prance	242
I worshipped, when my veins were fresh	246

Page

I would be dismal with all the fine pearls of the crown of
  a king 225
"I'm old" 272
In the sorrow and the terror of the nations 254
It is the white Plum Tree 223

King Paladin plunged on his moon-coloured mare 236

Let your song be delicate 218
Listen to the cicada's burning drone 245
Little girls 263
Lone, lone and lone I stand 274
Love feeds, like Intellect, his lamp with truth 249

Men moving in a trench, in the clear morn 267

Never admit the pain 270
Night 241

O brother in the restless rest of God! 256
O most unconscious daisy! 222
O white clay, O fine clay of the earth cold 268
O you dear trees, you have learned so much of beauty 265
Oh, could we weep 270
Old Sam Smith 273
Once more this autumn-earth is ripe 230
Or the black centaurs, statuesquely still 235

Quietly as rosebuds 218

Ragged, unheeded, stooping, meanly shod 224

She is not of the fireside 262
She smiled behind a lawny cloud 252
Shyly the silver-hatted mushrooms make 223

"That just reminds me of a yarn," he said 267
The bird is my neighbour, a whimsical fellow and dim 226
The brain, the blood, the busy thews 246
The evening gleam of still waters 259

Page

The lone watch of the moon over mountains old   259
The love of field and coppice   251
The Poet's thoughts are of the skies   233
The stars are pale   220
The sudden autumn winds, like hounds   276
The twisted apple with rain and magian fire   241
The young girl stood beside me. I   221
There's a lovely stretch of hillocks   266
There was no hunted one   271
This miracle in me I scan   247
This ultimate austerity   255

Under the dying sun   245

"What be you a-lookin' at, Emily Ann?   277
Who questions if the punctual sun unbars   250
Will they never fade or pass!   255
With his two-fist sword, enscintillant, he cut an apple down   236
Within the night, above the dark   271